YOUR OWN PERSONAL TRAINER

John Shepherd

A & C Black London

First published 2004 by
A & C Black Publishers Ltd
37 Soho Square, London W1D 3QZ
www.acblack.com

ISBN 0 7136 6677 3

A CIP catalogue record for this book is available from the British Library.

Typeset in Apollo and Frutiger

Note: Whilst every effort has been made to ensure that the content of this book is technically accurate and as sound as possible, neither the author nor the publishers can accept responsibility for any injury or loss sustained as a result of use of this material.

Cover design by James Watson
Inside text design by Brian Stanley
Cover images © Corbis
Photography © Ultrafit/Grant Pritchard;
with the exception of p.6 © Ultrafit/Nigel Farrow

A & C Black uses paper produced with elemental chlorine-free pulp, harvested from managed sustainable forests.

Printed and bound in Singapore by Tien Wah Press Pte

CONTENTS

ACKNOWLEDGEMENTS

This book is dedicated to my mother and father Joyce and Stanley Shepherd.

Over my years as a sports fan, physical education student, athlete, gym instructor, coach, leisure centre manager and health, fitness and sports journalist, I have had the pleasure of meeting many people who have informed and taught me much about fitness training. Specifically, I would like to thanks Charles Mays (publisher and editor in chief of Ultra-FIT Magazine) who a number of years ago thought that I might make a good writer. Mark McKeon (Ultra-FIT consulting editor) and Andrew Hamilton (fellow Ultra-FIT contributor), both of who provided valuable comment and motivation in the writing of this book. I also want to acknowledge the help given to me by my friends and personal trainers Jai Garcia and John Monroe, who took time out from their busy schedules to advise, listen and comment on what 'makes a good fitness book'.

In terms of getting this project together Charlotte Croft, Sonia Wilson and Hannah McEwen at A & C Black must be thanked, as must designer Brian Stanley who has produced such a great 'look' for the book. Very special thanks go to photographer Grant Pritchard, who now believes that the photo-shoot was more tiring than rowing 2000 m flat out. Thanks also to models and personal trainers Amanda Hargreaves, Amanda MacLean, Joey Bull, David McGill and Steve Obe for their endurance.

Special thanks to my partner Glenn and brother David for supporting me on this project and our children, Jason, David, Rae, Kwame, Ashan and Danya for some fun fitness!

Photographed at David Lloyd Health and Fitness Club, Maidenhead.

Thanks to Puma, Asics and Body Care/Support Marketing for supplying kit.

INTRODUCTION

This book is aimed at everyone who wants to enhance their quality of life through improved fitness, and develop what we at *Ultra-FIT* magazine call a 'fitness lifestyle'.

Ultra-FIT is the UK and Australia's number one fitness lifestyle magazine. We've been bringing the best fitness knowledge, stories and trends to tens of thousands of men and women since our first issue back in 1989.

You should not be put off by our title, as this book (like *Ultra-FIT* magazine) is aimed at anyone wanting to improve their level of fitness – you don't have to be 'ultra-fit'. Whether you're just thinking about joining a gym, have recently become a new member, or are in your tenth year of working out you'll discover all the information in the following chapters that will enable you to understand fully the physical, mental and social processes involved in getting and staying fit.

Using the straightforward explanations and sample programmes provided in this book, you'll find it easy to understand and apply fitness concepts and knowledge to your personal fitness quest. Each chapter addresses a common fitness issue, like fat burning or cardiovascular training, and provides you with all the information you'll need to be able to understand, devise, develop, progress, fuel, stick to and *enjoy* your training. In short, this book will enable you to develop your own fitness lifestyle.

Fitness training should be enjoyable but, like anyone else who has worked out regularly, I know that at times it's not. We'd all rather put our feet up and watch TV some days, than pound away on the treadmill, eyes glued to the LCD display. With this book, however, I hope to make these occasions more of a rarity, and the goal of your own fitness lifestyle one that is eminently achievable. Of course, you need to take a realistic approach to this: working out is not always about perfectly formed physiques, 'treadmill smiles' and a great feeling after every training session. Often, the quest for fitness is a difficult one – more long haul than overnight journey. I acknowledge this and have provided you with valuable insights into how to last the fitness lifestyle course, by making working out an integral part of your life. We've all got a host of responsibilities and pressures, and sometimes there just doesn't seem to be enough time for anything else. But when you appreciate just what being fit can do for you, you'll be all the more motivated to find that time. There are just so many positive reasons for you to get in shape.

Joining a gym can be a daunting step. You might worry that it will be full of beautiful people who know their aerobic from their anaerobic training methods, and who work out to training programmes that keep them in peak condition. My experience though is that, while people are increasingly knowledgeable, they often don't know how to work out optimally and effectively. Training concepts often remain a mystery to them, and that's one of the areas this book aims to address.

The fitness industry often hypes itself up, offering wonder-workouts, wonder-machines and wonder-diets. Its desire to market itself in an attempt to entice new customers can confuse and over-complicate the basic premise of fitness. In this book I want to unravel its mysteries, simplify them and provide you with real, proven-to-work fitness knowledge that will offer you the best opportunity to attain your fitness goals.

This book, like *Ultra-FIT* magazine, will be your personal trainer, on call day and night to answer all your fitness questions.

John Shepherd

1 Why you should turn on your fitness lifestyle

As you read this book you'll learn more and more about how to improve your fitness. I'll provide you with the best techniques and strategies to get you running further and faster, developing stronger muscles, burning more fat and developing the body you want. But before you begin this journey, here are some really convincing reasons for adopting a fitness lifestyle.

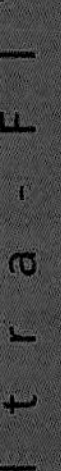

BREATHE LIFE INTO YOURSELF WITH CV WORKOUTS

Cardiovascular (CV) training can add years to our lives. The intensity* at which this type of activity is performed can also make a difference. In a Harvard study, burning 400 calories through high-intensity CV workouts reduced mortality more significantly than expending the same number of calories at a slower pace. It also seems that, to a point, the more exercise you perform the longer you can expect to live. The Harvard study went as far as to theorise that for every hour of exercise, an extra two hours could be added to your life. As scientists believe the human body is designed to survive for 110 years this may well be worth considering. As a result, I'd advise you to take up any free life membership offers your gym may run!

* See Chapter 4 for a full explanation of CV training intensities.

Fitness gains have no age barrier

Don't think you're too old to train. Here's some encouraging information. Our bodies respond to fitness training at any age. Individuals with an average age of 90.2 were put through a three-times-a-week eight-week weight-training programme. Their leg strength improved by a massive 174 per cent, and some of the participants were even able to throw away their walking aids.

Between the ages of 30 and 60 the human body need not deteriorate significantly provided that you exercise and maintain a healthy diet.

MAINTAIN STRENGTH, BURN FAT AND INCREASE YOUR METABOLIC RATE

We lose about 30 per cent of our muscular strength between the ages of 30 and 70 – that's if we don't do anything about it. This is the result of a decline in muscle mass and a drop-off in our body's production of growth hormone. Regular resistance training (weight training and body weight exercises) can maintain and even increase strength and muscle mass as we grow older, which can boost our metabolic rate (regular CV exercise can also do this). Metabolic rate has a very significant effect on whether our bodies gain or lose weight. If you can maintain or even increase it as you age, you will be a much more efficient calorie-burning machine and much less likely to develop unwanted body fat.

TRAINING TIP
Weight train and develop lean weight (muscle). Muscle burns up to three times as many calories as any other body part. The leaner you are, the more calories you'll burn, even with your feet up in front of the TV.

A regular exercise programme can significantly slow down the ageing process and better equip you for your older years.

BOOST YOUR HEART

Heart and lung function can be significantly improved by regular CV training, irrespective of age. Middle-aged men and women who participated in regular CV training over a 10-year period displayed virtually no age-related decline in their CV ability. Had they remained sedentary they could have experienced a 10–15 per cent drop-off in CV ability for every decade that passed after the age of 30 and, perhaps more significantly, would have had a less efficient and potentially more disease-prone heart.

Exercise fact: remain flexible

As we age, we experience a decline in our flexibility. Our 'range of movement' around our joints can decline by as much as 30 per cent by our seventh decade if we do nothing about it. Regular flexibility training can prevent this deterioration.

Exercise fact: remain speedy and agile

Ageing slows us down. You can expect a one per cent drop-off in your sprinting speed for every year after the age of 30, but the good news is that regular agility and speed work can significantly challenge this process.

Yoga and Pilates are great ways to maintain flexibility and strength (see Chapter 9).

ADVICE FOR THE OLDER PERSON

Daphne Belt

Daphne Belt took up the sport of triathlon at the age of 50. Since then, she has won numerous national and international titles. Here are some of her thoughts on the matter.

'If you are starting exercise later in life, you have to take it a little easier, perhaps not quite with the enthusiasm that young people go at things. You have to listen to your body. It might have been a long time since you really used your muscles and you should be careful not to overdo things at first. So do take a little more care of yourself, progress slowly, but don't wrap yourself up in cotton wool.'

Exercise can extend your life

Regular exercise can add years to your life. As soon as you sign up and commit to a fitness lifestyle the potential for longevity begins.

America's Harvard University carried out one of the largest ever surveys of the effects of exercise on longevity. It studied the lives of 17,000 men over a 22–26 year period and discovered that regular exercise, which involved burning 2000 calories (Kcal)* per week, increased their life span by two years.

* You can burn 2000 Kcal by performing approximately 4 × 1 hours of medium-intensity cardiovascular activity a week; see page 56 and 159 for exercise options and their calorie-burning potential.

CASE STUDY
Fit for life: Mavis Surridge

Indoor rowing is a sport that anyone of any age can do. Competitions are largely organised by and through Concept2, one of the world's leading manufacturers of rowing machines. The fitness benefits – improved CV fitness and strength – are the same whether you are 18 or 81. Mavis Surridge is 71 and a British and former world record holder in the 70-plus lightweight age group for the 2000 m race distance. Her best time is 9 minutes 22.6 seconds. But perhaps of greater importance than her rowing achievements is Mavis' lifelong commitment to exercise, which has significantly improved her quality of life. As she explains, 'I really feel the fitness benefits, I notice a difference with my breathing. I don't get out of puff, nor do I get any aches and pains.'

Mavis has always been active; she used to (and still does) play racquet sports. In her twenties and thirties she would regularly cycle 110–160 km. She still rides her racing bike to this day, three times a week.

Mavis incorporates weight training into her weekly workouts, which adds muscular strength to her high-CV fitness. This cross-training constitutes the ideal health and fitness combination.

Mavis exemplifies all the reasons why you should adopt a fitness lifestyle. As she says, 'I feel that I exhibit all the positive benefits of exercise. I am roughly the same shape as I've always been and am full of energy.'

See page 207 for Concept2 contact details.

EXERCISE AS THE BEST MEDICINE

Adopting a fitness lifestyle can increase resistance to numerous diseases.

Cancer

Cancer is second only to heart disease as the leading cause of death in many countries. It is caused by out-of-control cell duplication in a part of the body, which creates a block to the supply of nutrients and space needed for normal healthy cells to flourish. Stress, environmental factors, age, smoking and poor nutrition have all been identified as causes of cancer.

Prevention

Exercise can significantly reduce your chances of contracting cancer. Here's some positive reading:

- A daily workout can cut the chances of contracting breast cancer in older women by 20 per cent.
- A study of 2100 females aged between 20 and 69, who exercised for six hours a week showed that

they were 27 per cent less likely to develop ovarian cancer.

- Research from Taiwan indicated that men who exercised regularly had an 83 per cent lower chance of developing bowel cancer in comparison to sedentary men.

Cure

Numerous studies have also indicated exercise's role in the treatment of various cancers. Research carried out by the University of Alberta, Canada, which analysed 12 other studies, acknowledged this and noted that, with exercise, cancer patients experienced fewer bouts of diarrhoea, less pain and less fatigue, and also benefited from enhanced mood, reduced nausea and increased energy.

Three 20-minute CV workouts a week will significantly reduce your chances of contracting heart disease.

Coronary heart disease (CHD)

CHD is the number one killer in the UK. One in three people are at risk from suffering a heart attack because they are not taking sufficient exercise. Yet, three 20-minute CV workouts a week could drastically cut this risk. There are numerous reasons why this hour could add years to your life – exercise provides a release from stress and anxiety, improves body composition by reducing body fat and improves the efficiency of your heart.

Obesity

Obesity has reached epidemic proportions worldwide. At the turn of the twenty-first century, 20 per cent of people in the UK were classified as obese (see page 166 for a further explanation). It is estimated that this figure will rise to 25 per cent by 2010. Just as worrying is research which indicates that one in five of the country's under-fives are also overweight. Stroke, hypertension, kidney disease, diabetes, osteoarthritis, menstrual irregularities, heart problems, breast cancer and hypertension are just some of the medical conditions that can be attributed to being overweight. Adopting a fitness lifestyle will keep your body within acceptable body fat and weight limits, and will significantly improve your chances of living a disease-free life.

TRAINING TIP

Don't let exercise and your hectic schedule stress you out too. You should train seriously but not to the extent that it takes over your life. The fitness lifestyle must be a fun one.

Diabetes

Exercise can significantly reduce the development of diabetes in adulthood, it does this by normalising blood glucose levels and evening out our energy levels. One study indicated that men who exercise are 42 per cent less likely to develop diabetes than those who don't.

See how David Bloom used exercise to beat diabetes and a brain tumour, in the case study on page 11.

Arthritis

Up to eight million people in the UK suffer from arthritis. Exercise again provides a potential cure and treatment as it can reduce pain by strengthening and mobilising joints.

Always consult your doctor or physiotherapist before embarking on an exercise programme if you do suffer from arthritis.

Osteoporosis

Osteoporosis means 'a thinning of the bones'. It makes us more prone to broken bones as we age. It normally affects women but can also affect men. Resistance training and other load-bearing forms of exercise, like running, will bolster our bones against osteoporosis. These alter the bones' metabolic functioning and increase their density and mineral content.

Stress and depression

Stress, like obesity, is reaching epidemic proportions, but just a few hours a week spent exercising can significantly reduce its effects. Working out will bolster self-esteem and replace the negative feelings and hormonal responses associated with stress – anxiety and depression – with positive ones.

LOOK BETTER AND FEEL SEXIER

We are often concerned about the way we look. Maintaining a regular fitness and healthy eating routine will make us look and feel younger. We'll remain attractive and have a better sex life.

TRAINING TIP

Remind yourself why exercise will improve your health and increase your chances of living a longer, more fulfilling life. This should make it a great deal easier for you to adopt a fitness lifestyle. Don't think that you have to train like an Olympian to reap the benefits, as a relatively moderate amount of regular exercise will have a significant effect: two to three workouts a week that mix CV exercise and resistance training is all that is needed.

Personal reflections

I was an international long jumper in my younger days, and have always enjoyed training for speed and agility. At the age of 40 I returned to masters athletic competition (this is for men and women over the age of 35 and is organised in categories according to age). In my first year I ran 7.5 seconds for the 60 m, which was only three-tenths of a second behind my previous best, which I set as a 23 year old. This goes to show that with the right training (and motivation) speed need not decline as significantly as might be thought. And, just as crucially, that age-related decline in physical ability can be challenged significantly.

If you're over 35, and would like to get involved in athletics at masters level, contact your local athletics club or the British Masters Athletic Federation at www.bvaf.org.uk. If you're younger, visit the UK Athletics website at www.ukathletics.net or, again, contact your local athletics club.

CASE STUDY

David Bloom

Be encouraged by David Bloom's story of how exercise helped him regain his health after a brain tumour and helped him cope with diabetes.

'I started an exercise programme to improve my strength following radiotherapy for a brain tumour, and the onset of diabetes. I was really weak and had lost my balance so much that I had to hold on to the treadmill bars when I started running to prevent myself falling. Prior to the illness I had played a fair amount of tennis but was overweight and really unfit so the illness came on top of an already bad base.

'Having a personal trainer to set and monitor my programmes was marvellous. My trainer is very patient and knows just how far to push me, even if I have been stiff on occasions. He also helped me to exercise regularly when I was too lazy to do so. Now, I only see him once a week and do the rest myself. I even find that I miss my exercise if I don't do it regularly.

'The single most important benefit of my exercise regime has been the control of my blood sugar, which is a well-known benefit to diabetics. Being a doctor, I knew this, but to see the glucose level fall and stay down for days after my workout is very gratifying. Furthermore, I have regained my strength and balance, and feel incredibly well.

'I am 59 years old and a management consultant in life sciences. This involves a lot of running around and travel that used to wear me out. I now have a lot more energy. My tennis has also improved and I find myself moving around the court faster and feel nearly as good as I did 10 years ago! My partner has been very supportive and, apart from nagging me to do more stomach exercises, has helped me to train.'

David Bloom's weekly workouts

- Two gym sessions
- Two or three games of tennis (including one lesson)
- One long walk
- Occasional swimming

Typical gym session

- Treadmill (uphill walking)
- Weights*
    - Lat pull-down
    - Bench press
    - Squats
    - Shoulder press
- Rowing (between 500 and 1000 m)

* See Chapter 5 for descriptions of these and other exercises.

POLAR

2

How fit are you?

Testing your fitness and training your body type

Rather like asking someone how intelligent they are, asking someone how fit they are can result in some pretty ambiguous and sometimes over-confident answers. When I was a gym instructor I used to take weight training induction classes. After a preliminary introduction, I would usually warm people up with a lap's jog around an athletics track (that's 400m, about a quarter of a mile), however I soon found out that nearly half of the groups I took could not manage the distance and yet all on being asked whether they were able to complete the lap had said 'yes' – they believed that they were 'fit'. As a sports centre manager many years later, a duty manager was taking a CV fitness test and was asked if he was fit. He replied that, in all honesty, he wasn't. However, when tested, he displayed a very high level of CV fitness. Asked why this was, he realised that he had neglected to inform us that he cycled about 20 km every day, to and from work, and had done so for the last six years! He didn't realise that this was 'training'. Being fit means different things to different people. In this chapter I will provide you with some simple fitness tests that you can do for yourself, so you will know how fit you are. I will also tell you how to train for your 'body type'.

WORKING OUT HOW FIT YOU ARE

Are you new to exercise, an intermediate or an advanced trainer?

I will make reference throughout this book to 'those who are new to exercise' or at an 'intermediate' or 'advanced' level. There are numerous workout options, programmes and training tips, and references designed for and linked to these levels of fitness. So how do you know what level you are at? Table 2.1 offers a guide, using visits to the gym and type of training as criteria.

Table 2.1

What is your fitness level?

FITNESS EXPERIENCE	YOU HAVE:
New to exercise	little or virtually no gym experience, or have just returned to training after a long lay-off (two years plus)
Intermediate	been training regularly for at least nine months to a year for both improved CV and resistance training fitness (three to four sessions a week)
Advanced	a long and continuous association with fitness training (CV and resistance) lasting more than 18 months (three to four sessions a week).

TRAINING TIP

Everyone is new to exercise if they have not previously trained with a particular exercise, exercise method or system. In these situations always underestimate what you think you can achieve

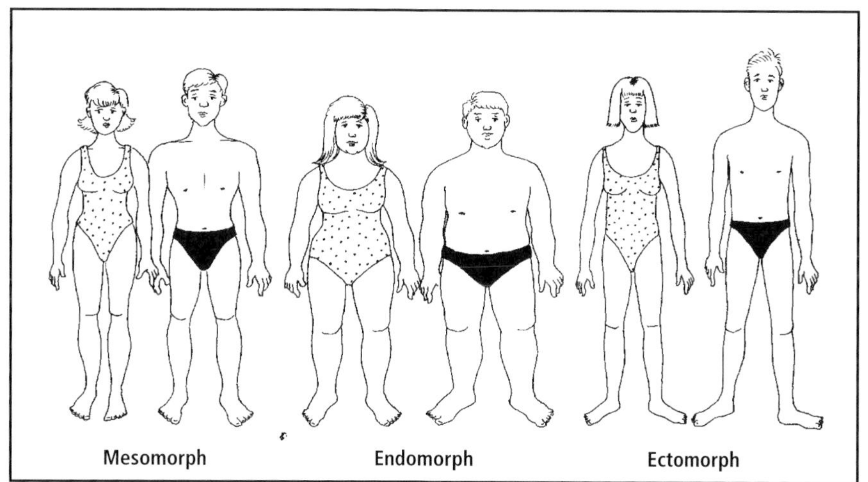

BODY TYPES

The way our bodies respond to training is heavily influenced by our genetic make-up. Next time you go to your local gym take a good look around at the people working out. Chances are you'll see all shapes and sizes. You may envy the 'gym bunnies' with their cellulite-free legs, flat stomachs and toned arms, or marvel at the 'gym gods', with their perfect pecs, triangular torsos, six packs and tight bums. Perhaps you will aspire to look like them, but months of training may pass without achieving the results you desire. The explanation could be that you are doing the wrong training (hopefully you won't be after reading this book), but it's more than possible that your inability to attain your goals is based on the fact that you are training in the wrong way for your body type.

Making a fitness comeback?
Research indicates that those returning to exercise, provided that they previously trained regularly, will find it easier and quicker to regain fitness than those with little or no training experience.

It's all in the genes. Or is it?

The unfortunate reality of 'gym world' is that gym bunnies and gym gods often possess physiques that are simply the result of them being blessed with the right genes. Put simply, some people are better able to gain muscle than others, just as others are better equipped to run or row effortlessly for hours. There are limitations to what each of us embarking on a fitness programme will be able to achieve. You need to be aware of these so that you don't set yourself unrealistic body image goals or training targets. The good news is that with the right training you will be able to maximise the fitness returns for your body and seriously challenge your genetic predisposition.

What body type are you?

Although scientists have devised numerous body type classifications, they are derived from three basic 'types'. In not quite politically correct terms these can be described as 'fat', 'skinny' and 'athletic', or somewhat more correctly as 'endomorphic', 'ectomorphic' and 'mesomorphic'. It should be stressed that these three body types are broad-brush-stroke pictures of individual shapes and not specific blueprints. In reality, most of us will be an amalgamation of all three types. Crucially, no one body type should be regarded as being superior to another, each has its own advantages and disadvantages when it comes to developing fitness (see Table 2.2).

How will your body respond to training?

Study the information provided in Table 2.2 and reference it to your own body type and training goals. This will enable you to construct a highly relevant training programme.

Table 2.2
Body types

BODY TYPE	POSITIVE TRAINING RESPONSES AND RECOMMENDATIONS
Mesomorphic Usually tall with broad shoulders, narrow waist, broad hips, upright posture and good muscular definition. **Metabolism:** Fairly fast.	Mesomorphs respond well to most types of CV and resistance training. They can sustain low body fat levels. They can perform both minor and major muscle group exercises very effectively. They can vary their energy balance (calorie consumption versus energy expenditure) in relation to whether they need to gain or lose weight. They tend to be able to be quite free with their food choices. **Good fitness class options:** ■ all.
Ectomorphic Small bone structure, often look 'fragile'. Very lean and slim. **Metabolism:** Fast.	Ectomorphs find it easy to lose weight and keep it off. They often respond well to CV training, because their low body weight makes them ideally suited to it. For fitness training purposes, three CV sessions a week are ideal – more than that and they could achieve potentially unhealthy body fat levels. Using resistance training to gain muscle will prove difficult. Much of their success will depend on diet. They will have to ensure optimum protein and carbohydrate consumption and take in more calories than they would normally need to maintain their body weight to build muscle. They should emphasise quality over quantity while training, and allow plenty of time for muscles to recover after workouts. When weight training, they should use major muscle group exercises. They should consider supplementing with creatine when looking to increase muscle size (see page 189). They should avoid circuit training and exercise bike classes, and other very high calorie-burning workouts if seeking increased muscle size. **Good fitness class options:** ■ weights based classes, if seeking an increase in muscle ■ bike, rowing or treadmill group classes if after CV fitness – but no more than two to three times a week.
Endomorphic Large bone structure, but perhaps with shorter limbs. Wide frame. Less muscle definition, less even distribution of fat. **Metabolism:** Slower.	Endomorphs respond well to power and resistance training due to their natural strength. They can develop large muscles and can ultimately burn fat well due to muscles' ability to increase metabolic rate. They will get the best results from more moderate-intensity CV training using weight-bearing equipment and exercise options like running and power walking. They should base their training around cross-training that combines weights and CV training in their workout plan. For optimum body shaping and weight loss, they should ensure a positive energy balance and expend more calories than they consume. **Good fitness class option:** ■ low-impact aerobics, weights-based classes, beginners' rowing and cycling classes and water-based workouts.

TRAINING DISADVANTAGES

Mesomorphs can become over-trained, and may suffer from over-training syndrome (OTS; see page 146), so they need to work out to a balanced training programme incorporating 'easy' and rest days.
They can put on weight quickly when they stop training.
Their training needs to be progressive and constantly changing to prevent stagnation – the result of their ability to respond more quickly than the other two body types to a training stimulus.

Ectomorphs find it difficult to put on muscle.
They can be injury prone, due to their less robust body type.
They can achieve unhealthily low body fat levels.

Endomorphs find it harder to lose weight and can carry too much body fat (their bodies also have more fat cells, which can increase their likelihood to put weight on.
They can sustain injuries if they do too much weight-bearing exercise too soon in their training programme, especially if they are overweight. In this instance cycling and cross-training machines would make good exercise options as they are load-bearing.

TRAINING TIP

Don't be afraid of fitness tests. The results will enable you, your personal trainer or gym instructor to programme your future workouts optimally. Don't become too preoccupied with how you rank against others; concern yourself with how you rank against yourself and what you need to do to improve your fitness.

Personal reflections

When I first took part in the sport of indoor rowing as an assignment for Ultra-FIT magazine, I thought all my years of long jump training would make rowing the required 2 km distance in a respectable time relatively easy. I fell straight into the 'I'm fit, so I can do anything' trap. My first race attempt in training after about a week of specific rowing workouts (please don't try this) left me in a heap, and what should have been an even-paced effort turned into an interval training (stop/start) workout. So, be warned, having a high level of fitness in one sport or fitness activity can give you an advantage, but in no way does it mean you will be fit to do everything well.

ARE YOU FIT AND HEALTHY ENOUGH TO START AN EXERCISE PROGRAMME?

As part of your gym induction or fitness test you should be asked about your health and medical history. Your gym instructor or personal trainer may use a Physical Activity Readiness Questionnaire (called PAR-Q for short) to do this. The PAR-Q should throw up any health or previous illness issues that might affect your ability to exercise safely. These could range from a bad back, to low or high blood pressure, to diabetes. It's possible that you could be asked to consult your doctor before starting your exercise programme; if this does happen, you should not feel disappointed as your health and safety is crucial. In most cases you will be given the all-clear to exercise; the positives far outweigh the negatives and, on your return to the gym, you'll be able to provide your fitness professional with highly valuable information that will enable them to construct the most effective training programme for you.

TRAINING TIP

Fitness tests are specific, just as fitness is. A test could measure something that you have not been training for, so keep this in mind to avoid potential disappointment. As an example, if you are a weight trainer you won't expect to score highly on a CV test.

FITNESS TESTS

I've selected a number of tests that cover virtually all the vital aspects of fitness. You should be able to carry out many of these yourself. They are the same as, or very similar to, the ones that would feature in the tests offered at a gym or by a personal trainer.

I recommend that your first fitness test is taken under the expert guidance of a suitably qualified fitness professional and then, once you gain in fitness and confidence and have been training to a specific set of fitness goals for a period of three months or more, that you perform your own tests. Obviously, if you don't feel entirely happy about doing this, you should by all means book yourself another test at your gym or with your personal trainer.

Important note

Some of the following tests (such as the maximum heart rate test) should not be performed by those new to exercise. These are marked accordingly.

If you are in any way unsure about your health or are over 35 please consult your doctor.

Cardiovascular (CV) tests

There are many ways to test your CV fitness. Some require specialist equipment like a VO2MAX or lactate threshold test (see pages 59–61). But there are also many simple tests that you can do that will provide you with a great indication of your CV ability. As well as the 'standard' tests, I'll show you how to develop your own specific ones using your preferred item of CV kit.

Basic CV fitness: three-minute step test

Equipment required

A step approximately 20–25 cm high.

How to do the test

Step up and down on the step. Use the commands 'up, two, three, four', repeated every four seconds, to achieve the right pace.

Stepping technique:

- up – step up with your right leg
- two – follow through to step on the step with your left leg
- three – step down with your right leg
- four – step down with your left leg.

Repeat with your left leg leading and continue in alternating lead leg style for three minutes.

On completion of the test sit down immediately and after 10 seconds record your heart beat over one minute by taking your pulse, then use Table 2.3 to get an indication of your CV fitness.

Table 2.3

Three-minute step test: fitness level indicator

	Men (bpm)*	Women (bpm)*
Poor	107 and over	115 and over
Fair	93–106	101–114
Average	84–92	91–100
Good	69–83	74–90
Excellent	68 and under	73 and under

* bpm = beats per minute

TRAINING TIP

Once your maximum heart rate has been established you will be able to get the most out of your CV training by working out within specific heart rate zones.

Constructing your own CV tests

With practice and the fitness knowledge derived from this book, you'll be able to construct your own CV tests. This is particularly useful if you are training for a specific fitness goal, like a 2 km row or a 5 km run, when a test like the step test would have little specific relevance. Some examples are given in Table 2.4.

Table 2.4

How to develop your own CV tests

TEST	WHAT TO DO	TEST EXAMPLE	SUITABLE FOR
CV power: one effort	Record the distance you can cover on a piece of CV kit, e.g. rower for a specific time or distance.	5000 m row 1500 m cycle 20 minutes' stepping	Intermediate and advanced trainers, who have gained an idea of their capabilities and 'understanding' of pace and time judgement, on a piece of CV kit they use regularly.
CV power: multiple efforts (intervals)	Similar to the above test, but record the distance you travel over each of a number of intervals of effort, while taking a controlled recovery between each.	3 × 3 minutes' rowing with 3 minutes' recovery between each effort.	Advanced trainers, with the same proviso as above.
Sub-maximal CV power	Record how far you can go on a piece of CV kit at a designated heart rate level or RPE.* * RPE is rate of self-perceived exertion, a self-regulated way of pacing your training (see page 52); for an understanding of heart rate zones, turn to page 55.	Row for 15 minutes at an RPE of 5/6.	All levels – because you work 'within yourself' by selecting an RPE or heart rate zone with which you are comfortable.

Personal reflections

When I first trained for indoor rowing I had no idea of pace judgement or what type of distance or time would make for a useful test, apart from performing the actual 2 km race distance.

After a period of about three months I began to use 10-minute periods for a number of 'personal' tests to measure my training progress. My 'test one' simply involved rowing as far as I could in 10 minutes; this length of time allowed me to row in excess of race distance.

My 'test two' required a more even distribution of effort as I performed 2 × 10-minute rows with 6 minutes' easy rowing in between.

The initial test gave me a great indication of what I would be capable of over the 2 km race distance flat out, while test two did the same, but also provided me with an indication of how my general base of CV ability was developing. I knew that the better my combined performances over a pair of 10-minute efforts, the better my base CV was becoming.

Maximum heart rate test (not suitable for those new to exercise)

Heart rate maximum (HRMax) varies with age, genetics and even the type of CV training you do. It's because of this that calculative methods of determining HRMax, like the '220 minus your age' formula (see page 51), although very useful, should be viewed only as a rough guide.

A maximum heart rate (HRMax) test will provide you with a true reading of your heart's capacity. It is important to realise that this will be specific to the piece of CV kit that you perform the test on – HRMax is usually higher on a treadmill or rowing machine than on an exercise bike or when swimming. The test requires a high degree of motivation and discomfort, and this is what makes it unsuitable for those new to exercise.

Equipment required

Preferably a heart rate monitor, although you can take your pulse (heart rate) manually (see page 53). It's also possible that the piece of CV kit you are using has a built-in heart rate monitor, ask your gym instructor.

How to do the test

Warm up with 10 to 15 minutes of easy cycling. Then cycle for a minute at a time, each time increasing your effort by 1 km per hour. Maintain a steady rate of pedalling, about 80 rpm, and continue until you cannot sustain the required pace. You'll probably find that the test lasts between 8 and 12 minutes. At the moment you stop, record your heart rate – you will have achieved your HRMax.

Do not take this test if you are tired or have been in a period of very intense training.

Resting heart rate (RHR) test

Equipment required

Heart rate monitor, although you can take your pulse manually.

How to do the test

Simply record your heart rate a couple of minutes after waking up in the morning. For best results, do this over five consecutive days and calculate your average score.

Regular training will improve the efficiency of your heart – the lower your RHR the fitter you have become.

Body fat tests

Many people dread discovering their body weight and body fat measurements and, paradoxically, become preoccupied with them. However, used sensibly, the following tests will assist your training progress and motivate you to further improvement.

Waist-to-hip ratio test

This simple test will provide an indication of whether your body is within acceptable body fat levels.

Equipment required

A tape measure and a calculator.

How to do the test

All you need to do is divide your waist measurement by your hip measurement in centimetres (or inches) and compare the reading to the figures given in the accompanying box.

Calculating waist-to-hip ratio

How to measure your hips and waist correctly

- Waist: measure at the point of maximum girth – above your hip bone.
- Hips: measure at the point of maximal buttock protrusion.

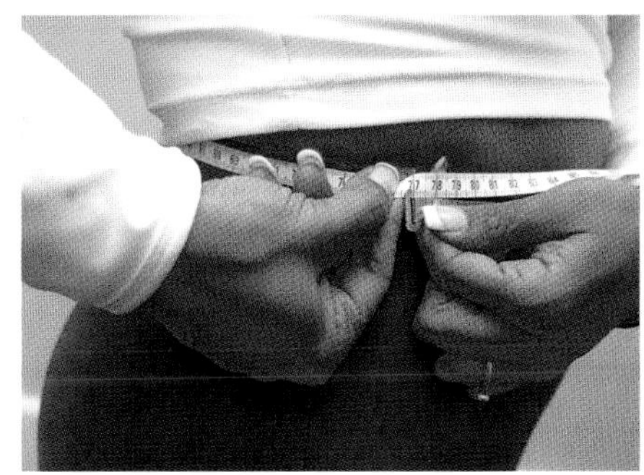

- Women: your ratio should be 0.8 or less.
- Men: your ratio should be 1.0 or less.

If the ratios are less than 0.65 and 0.75 respectively, you are very lean – perhaps too lean – and this could result in health problems. Consult your doctor.

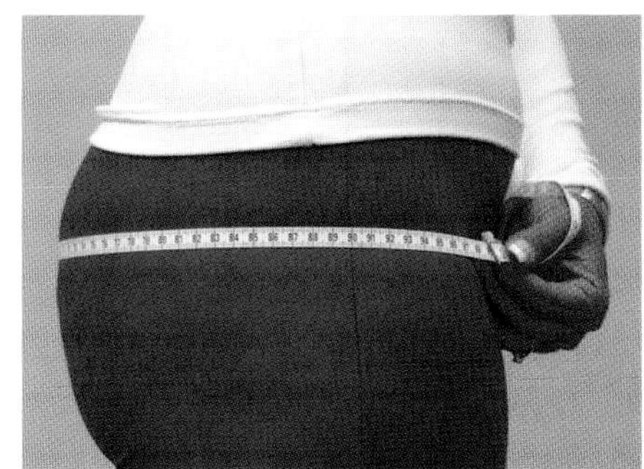

Body mass index (BMI) test

Like the waist-to-hip ratio test you also use a calculation to come up with a body mass index (BMI) score, which you can then reference to the figures provided in Table 2.5 to determine whether you are underweight or overweight. BMI is a good indicator of your health. It's a particularly useful test for the new to exercise and the intermediate trainer, but it can be less valuable for the advanced trainer or sportsperson due to the fact that the reference population used for the calculations is that for the 'average' person and not the highly trained – it's actually possible for someone who is very lean and muscled to achieve an 'overweight' BMI score.

Equipment required Calculator.

How to do the test

Divide your weight in kilograms by your height in metres squared and compare your result to the figures given in Table 2.5.

For example, if you weigh 75 kg and are 1.8 m tall, your BMI would be 75 ÷ (1.8 × 1.8 [=3.24]) = 23

Table 2.5

BMI reference scores

	BMI
Underweight	less than 20
Ideal weight	20–25
Overweight	26–30
Obese*	31–40
Grade 3 obesity	more than 40

* See page 166 for more information on obesity.

Sum of skinfolds test (using callipers)

If you wish to self-test using skinfold callipers you can do so using the following information. Readings are usually taken over three to seven body sites and added together to calculate a 'sum of skinfolds' score in mm. By periodically carrying out this test you will be able to ascertain the extent of your fat loss progress. You'll need to ask a partner to help you administer the test. Skinfold callipers are available from specialist fitness retailers.

How to do the test

Use callipers on selected skinfold measurement sites, as described in Table 2.6.

Table 2.6
Skinfold measurement sites

SITE	WHERE TO PLACE THE CALLIPERS
Suprailiac (just above the hip bone)	Pinch the skin to create a diagonal skinfold.
Triceps (back of upper arms)	Pinch vertically equidistant between the top of the elbow and the top of the shoulder.
Subscapular (lower outside back)	Pinch the skin so it achieves an approximate 120-degree angle to the floor.
Thigh	Pinch the skin vertically in the middle of the thigh, a third of the way down from the hip bone.
Abdominal	Pinch vertically in a position 2 cm to the right of the belly button.

If you take a calliper-based test at your gym, you can have your body fat percentage computed from the readings. The equations used are very complicated and are based on age and gender variables (that's why I have not provided them here).

FAT TEST INACCURACY

I have to stress that most fat testing methods presented are potentially inaccurate. Calliper readings are subject to: (1) the skill of the test performer – how good they are at placing the callipers in the right place; (2) the quality of the callipers; (3) the duration of calliper 'pinch' on the various skinfold measurement sites (this should be for no more than four seconds). Calliper and BIM machine readings can also be affected by your level of hydration and body temperature. BIM machines pass an imperceptible electrical current through your body to calculate your body fat percentage; unfortunately they can actually underestimate an overweight person's body fat by as much as 2–5 per cent.

Flexibility tests

Flexibility is a very specific and difficult fitness attribute to test.

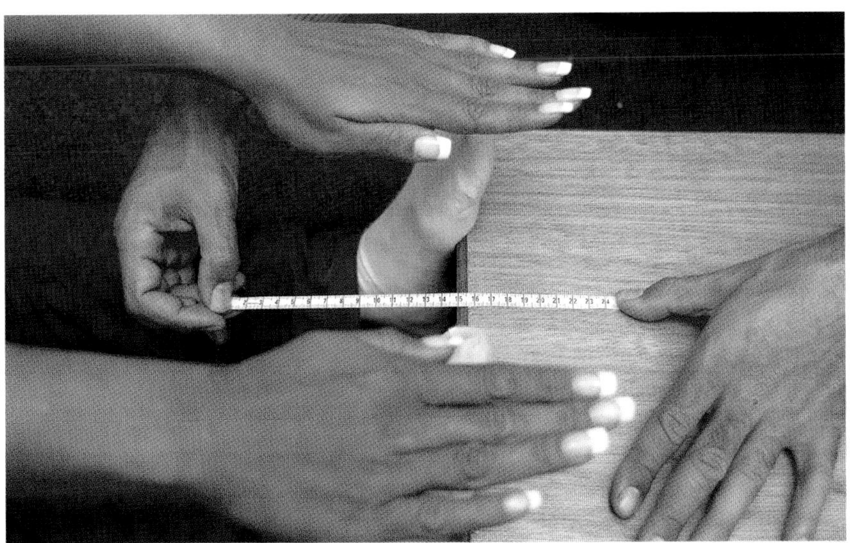

Equipment required

A tape measure or ruler and a small box approximately 40 cm square. Put the tape measure or ruler on top of the box, allowing 15 cm to protrude over the end towards you.

How to do the test

Sit on the floor, your legs fully extended, with your feet shoulder width apart against the box. Reach forwards with your arms fully extended and slide your hands along the ruler as far as you can. Hold for three seconds. Measure the distance that you reach, in front of or beyond your toes, and compare your score to the information given in Table 2.7. Don't bounce or bend your knees when taking the test, and make sure you are warmed up first (see Chapter 3).

Sit and reach test

The sit and reach test is the standard test of flexibility. It measures your lower back and hamstring flexibility, so it obviously tells you nothing about the range of movement of your other body parts.

Table 2.7
Sit and reach test scores (cm)

	Men	Women
Below average	less than 0	less than 2
Average	+2	+5
Excellent	more than 5	more than 8

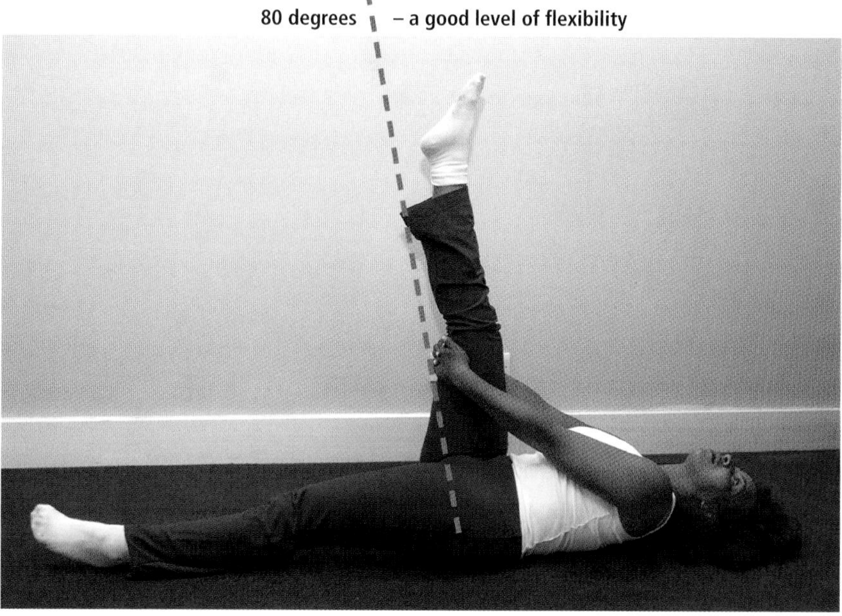

Others ways to test your flexibility

You can devise your own flexibility tests for other body parts that don't have comparative norms, and rely on your own judgement.

Lying hamstring test

Warm up and lie on your back with your left leg pressed firmly into the ground. Pull your right leg in towards your chest, by reaching forwards and taking hold of the back of the thigh. Next, straighten your right leg upwards. Remain relaxed. Don't lock out your knee joint when you extend it. Perform the stretch three times and make a note as to how far you were able to pull the leg back – just before vertical, vertical, beyond vertical – on your best attempt. Swap leg positions, repeat and record the leg position attained in the same way for your left leg.

In the photograph, you will see a line drawn at 80 degrees from the hip. If you can attain an 80-degree or greater stretch, your flexibility for this exercise is good to excellent. If it is less than 80 degrees then you should work on improving your range of movement.

Constructing other flexibility tests

With a little thought you will be able to devise similar tests for other body parts.

Muscular strength endurance tests

Most people will be familiar with sit-ups and press-ups, these body weight resistance exercises are often considered to be tests of strength but in reality they are tests of muscular strength endurance. Strength endurance refers to the body's ability to repeat a strength-orientated move repeatedly until fatigue eventually prevents any further progress.

Press-up test

The press-up provides a good test of upper body strength endurance. You could, of course, select your own body weight exercises and your own test protocols, such as how many repetitions of an exercise you could complete in a minute or continuously in one go. You could then use your own test to measure your specific strength endurance improvements.

How to do the test

Simply see how many press-ups you can do without stopping and reference your score to Table 2.8. If you are unable to complete full prone press-ups, you can perform a less intense version that requires you to balance and pivot from your knees. For a guide to correct press-up technique turn to page 111.

Table 2.8

Press Up Test – How do you compare?

SCORE AT AGE	20-29	30-39	40-49	50-59	60+
Men					
High	>45	>35	>30	>25	>20
Average	35-44	25-34	20-29	15-24	10-19
Below average	20-34	15-24	12-19	8-14	5-9
Low	<19	<14	<11	<7	<4
Women					
High	>34	>25	>20	>15	>5
Average	17-33	12-24	8-19	6-14	3-4
Below average	6-16	4-11	3-7	1-5	1-2
Low	<5	<3	<2	0	0

Adapted from Pollock, Wilmore and Fox, Health and Fitness through Physical Activity (1978)

Muscular strength tests

One of the most popular gym-based fitness tests measures strength with a 'grip dynameter'. Your score for both left and right hands can then be correlated to statistical norms. This test is safe to administer, but not very relevant when it comes to constructing an all-body-part weight-training programme.

What's needed is a much more specific test. For your weight training to be effective you need to develop the right type of strength for your fitness goals (see page 89). To do this you need to have an idea of how much you could lift in one go, on all the exercises you want to use in your training programme. This is what's known as your 'one repetition maximum' (1RM). Unfortunately it's not advisable for those new to exercise to go all out to discover their 1RM as they will not yet have developed the strength or level of weight-lifting proficiency to do this. However, there are calculative ways to discover a notional 1RM, through using much lighter weights (see page 77).

3

Warming up,

stretching and cooling down

Stretching is a vital component in any fitness regime. The trouble is that many of us don't pay enough attention to it. You might think that touching your toes a couple of times as part of your warm-up is enough to prepare you for your workout – it's not. In this chapter I'll tell you why stretching should not be ignored, and why warming up and cooling down are crucial for a safe and effective training regime.

Note that the terms stretching, mobility and flexibility are often used interchangeably – you could do a 'stretching' or 'flexibility' class at your local gym, or work on your 'mobility' at home.

WHY STRETCH?

To avoid injury

In the gym or before any sports activity, you should ensure that your muscles are thoroughly prepared for the activity that will follow. Stretching can play an important role in this preparatory process, although perhaps not as important a one as you may think. More on this later.

To stay flexible as we age

As we grow older, our ROM decreases as our connective tissue loses its elasticity. A regular flexibility and exercise routine will prevent this decline and can even increase ROM.

To improve posture and body image

A lack of attention to regular stretching can contribute to poor posture – too much time working at a computer can literally bend us over, while too much time spent in the weights room can result in bowed arms and tight leg and chest muscles. A regular stretching programme will straighten us out, elongate tight muscles and reduce tension.

To improve sports performance

All sports have different ROM requirements. A footballer does not require the same level of flexibility as a gymnast, and vice versa.

For more information on sports-specific training see Chapter 11.

TRAINING TIP

Wear kit that will maintain an elevated body temperature when you warm up and stretch, but make sure that it is loose enough to allow you to move freely.

Personal reflections

I've never been a great one to stretch, probably because I was not blessed with great flexibility in the first place. As a child I was unable to sit cross-legged in school assemblies due to my natural level of flexibility, or should I say inflexibility. As an athlete it took me a good year or so before I developed sufficient hamstring and lower back flexibility to touch my toes. But even as a mature trainer and someone who should know better, I'm still guilty of not stretching enough, particularly away from my sports training. To counter this, I'll occasionally do a yoga class in order to emphasise stretching for a period in my training. These workouts will re-elongate my muscles, help get rid of tension and reduce the lower back pain from which I occasionally suffer.

Can you be 'too' flexible?

Perhaps surprisingly, the answer is yes. If you develop too much flexibility you can actually weaken your joints, making them more prone to injury. You need to decide on the functional level of flexibility you need for your fitness, sports and everyday activity levels, and train to achieve and maintain these.

Example of a passive stretch

■ **Seated hamstring stretch:** for the lower back and hamstring muscles. Sit on the floor and bend forwards from your hips. Slide your hands down your shins until they cannot reach any further.

TRAINING TIP

Don't continue to stretch if you feel sharp pain in a muscle or joint.

HOW TO IMPROVE YOUR FLEXIBILITY

There are various ways to stretch. Some are more dynamic than others and some require assistance from a partner.

Always perform at least 5–10 minutes of gentle cardiovascular (CV) work before you stretch as this will prepare your muscles for stretching.

Passive stretching

During a passive stretch a muscle or group of muscles is gently eased into an elongated position. Holding the end position of a seated hamstring stretch is a good example of this. Gravity or external force, the latter provided by yourself, a partner, machine, belt or rope, applies the force to the stretch. To improve your flexibility with a passive stretch you need to repeat each stretch at least five times, attempting to move that little bit further with each attempt. Passive stretches should be held for 15–20 seconds.

Passive stretching is not very effective at overcoming the stretch/reflex mechanism (see box) and, in practice, tends to maintain rather than improve flexibility.

Range of movement and the stretch/reflex mechanism

We stretch to improve or at least maintain our range of movement (ROM). ROM can be around a joint, as in the case of the ankle, or around a series of joints, as in the case of the spine. When you perform a flexibility exercise you stretch your 'connective tissue'. This consists of our muscles, ligaments and tendons. In order to improve your ROM, you need to stretch beyond your previous limits – this involves bypassing the 'sticking point' that we all encounter when trying to stretch, which is technically known as the 'stretch/reflex mechanism'. It's actually designed to protect us against strains and pulls, by preventing a muscle from being extended beyond its normal safe ROM. Some stretching methods are better able to overcome this than others.

Active stretching

Active stretching can seem very similar to passive stretching at first because it also involves holding a stretch. But there is a big difference: an active stretch utilises a different form of muscular contraction. When we actively stretch we 'hold' a body part in a stretched position without the assistance of external force. Active stretches should be held for 10–15 seconds. Repeat each one five times on each side.

Like passive stretches, their active counterparts have difficulty overcoming the stretch/reflex mechanism. This is because the end of the stretch tends to reside at this very point, rather than beyond it. Active stretches do, however, have their own benefits in that they are more closely allied to the way movement is carried out in fitness, sports and everyday life. We will reach up to grab a lat pull-down bar (see page 89), or forwards to take hold of the oar of a rowing machine, or up to take a cup from a shelf. All these movements contain an element of an active stretch. That's why these stretches can be seen as more relevant for sports and fitness purposes than passive stretches.

Examples of active stretches

■ **Straight arm lift:** for shoulders. Take one arm up so that it is in alignment with your body and reaching straight up above you.

■ **Leg raise:** for hamstrings. Lie on your back and lift one leg up. Bend the other one and keep its foot flat on the floor. Pull the raised leg back until it cannot travel any further. Keep your back flat against the ground.

> **TRAINING TIP**
>
> **The goal of our flexibility training is the attainment of a range of movement that will enable us to perform our chosen fitness or sports activity technically correctly, with reduced injury risk.**

Examples of dynamic stretches

■ **Leg swings:** for hamstrings and hip flexors. Stand side on to a wall and support yourself against it with your nearest hand. Swing your inside leg (the one nearest the wall) forwards and backwards, without bending at the hips or letting your trunk cave in. Try to remain relaxed. Gradually progress the speed and length of the swings. Complete 10 times, change position and work the other leg.

Always control dynamic stetches

■ **Chest press**: for chest, shoulders and front upper arms. Stand with your feet shoulder width apart. Keep your head up. Lift your elbows up in front of your chest and touch your fingertips together, to form a sort of triangle, which should be parallel to the ground. To initiate the dynamic movement, push your arms and shoulders back and then swing your lower arms out behind you. Try to make the movement smooth and controlled. Complete 10 reps.

Dynamic stretches

A dynamic stretch involves swinging and or rotating body parts over an arc or through a plane of movement.

Despite seeming ideally suited to beating the stretch/reflex mechanism, dynamic stretching, like active and passive stretching, can also fall short. In fact, this type of stretch, more than the other two methods, actually invokes the response from the mechanism in the way that it was designed to protect us against pulls and strains. Dynamic stretching can, however, be a very good warm-up option for anyone involved in sports like football, sprinting and the martial arts. These rely on equally dynamic muscular contractions to generate power and movement, thus this type of stretching can actually help train and develop this requirement.

Dynamic stretches: safety tips

Dynamic stretching can cause injury. If the stretch/reflex mechanism were foolproof then we would never pull or strain our muscles. ROM control can easily be lost when stretching in this way, so you must approach this method with respect.

Those new to exercise should avoid dynamic stretches.

Women, stretching and pregnancy

Pregnant women are more flexible due to the presence of the hormone relaxin in their bodies. It is crucial that they do not stretch beyond their previous non-pregnancy ROM as damage to their joints could result. Previous levels of flexibility will return after childbirth.

HOW TO IMPROVE YOUR FLEXIBILITY continued

PNF stretches

Proprioceptive neuromuscular facilitation (PNF) stretching is one of the best ways to improve your ROM. Of all the types of stretching mentioned so far it can best overcome the stretch/reflex mechanism. Although it is possible to perform PNF stretches on your own, perhaps with the aid of a towel or band, you will get better results if you work with a partner. PNF stretching works on the basis of two directional force increasing the potential for our muscles to stretch beyond their normal ROM. This method turns off the stretch/reflex mechanism. Consider the following examples to see how.

Examples of PNF stretches

■ **PNF hamstring stretch.** Lie on your back on the floor. Relax, arms by your sides, and get your partner to lift one leg up and back towards your head. Maintain a slight bend at the knee joint in this leg. Keep your other leg flat against the ground. Your partner should push the leg being stretched back to the point where the stretch/reflex mechanism kicks in. Hold this position for 15–20 seconds, then push back against your partner through the heel of the leg being stretched – they must obviously be braced and ready to offer resistance (see picture). Next comes the key element in the PNF stretch's ability to overcome the stretch/reflex mechanism: you need to relax and then let your partner attempt to push your leg further back. You should find that it will move beyond its previous position due to the de-activation of the stretch/reflex mechanism. Hold for a further 10–15 seconds.

■ **PNF shoulder stretch.** Stand straight and let your partner take hold of your hands behind your back. Your arms should be held straight. Get your partner to push your arms upwards with even force. At around shoulder level the stretch/reflex mechanism will kick in. Hold this position for 15–20 seconds, then relax for a couple of seconds before letting your partner lift your arms up further. Don't lean forwards. Hold for 10–15 seconds.

Repeat these PNF stretches five times each.

TRAINING TIP
Stretching one limb at a time (where applicable) can optimise flexibility improvement.

THE WARM-UP AND COOL-DOWN

Warming up

You should warm up before engaging in any form of physical activity. This will inevitably be stressed as part of your induction when you join a gym – and for good reason. A warm-up will prepare you, both physiologically and psychologically, for your workout. The most commonly prescribed warm-up will be as follows: 5–10 minutes of easy CV work, followed by, more often than not, passive stretches for all body parts.

However there are different and potentially better ways to warm up. These relate specifically to particular fitness and sports activities.

It is increasingly being recommended that unless you have particularly stiff joints that can only be mobilised by passive, active or PNF stretching prior to a workout, or if you are new to exercise and have no prior specific and consistently generated exercise-related ROM, that you reduce the amount of static stretching you do in your warm-up and introduce more specific movements. These should relate to the way your chosen fitness activity or sports activity is carried out. I made this connection with dynamic stretching methods, but to provide further examples you could march on the spot prior to using a stepper, jog and perform high knee lifts and lunge walks before running or rowing, and perform some very light weight repetitions prior to weight training. Some of these exercises are covered in Chapter 11

TRAINING TIP

Use it or lose it. If you stop flexibility training you will lose some of the gains you have made. However, the good news is that unlike other forms of fitness training, like weights and CV work, this reduction will be much less marked.

Stretching as part of your cool-down

You should always cool down after your workout; this will safely return your body to its pre-exercise steady state.

To cool down, you should perform some very easy CV work (a minimum of five minutes) and then stretch.

The cool-down is actually a very good time to work on increasing your ROM. At the end of a workout your connective tissue can be in the best condition to be stretched beyond its normal ROM, using any of the methods described previously. Note that you should not do this if you have just performed a particularly exhausting session; this is because your connective tissue will be less responsive to extensive stretching and could be prone to injury – light stretching will suffice.

STRETCHING EXERCISES AND GYM EQUIPMENT

People often perform the same stretches regardless of the equipment they are going to use in the gym. This may mean that they don't stretch the body parts that will be put through their paces by the exercise they are about to perform and could also mean that they will not address any developing tightness in their muscles that results from continued exposure to the same repeated movements, like tight calf muscles from regular running and a stiff lower back from regular rowing. In the following section I've linked specific stretches to common items of gym equipment. You should perform the indicated stretches after you have raised your body temperature with some gentle CV work. Additionally, and crucially, you should also perform some more specific movements, as described previously (marching on the spot, lunges, and so on) as part of your warm-up; intersperse these with the stretches.

Hold all stretches for 20 seconds and perform them five times each, unless otherwise indicated.

For a stretching session in its own right you should choose from all the exercises and stretching methods described in this chapter. Those new to exercise should not perform dynamic stretches.

TRAINING TIP

Although there are different types of warm-up, the one common denominator in them all is that they should all begin with some gentle CV work. This will gradually turn on the physiological processes that will be needed when you begin the main part of your workout.

Stretches for CV equipment

INDOOR ROWER

Rowing is a great form of exercise and works virtually all our major muscles. The lower back and forearms can become tight with regular rowing.

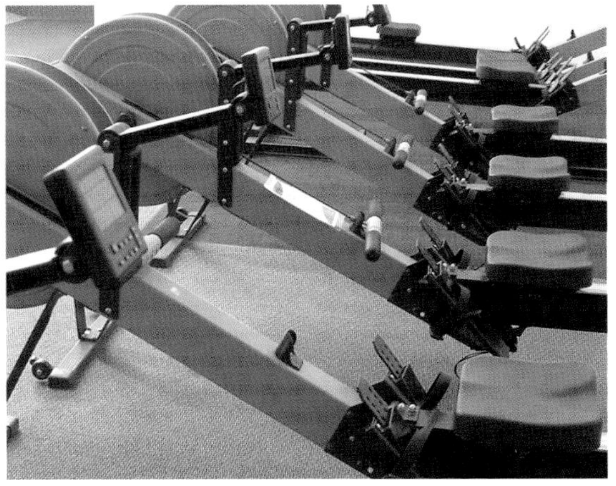

Forearms

Lift your right arm up in front of you so that it is parallel to the ground. Extend the hand upwards – you'll be looking at the back of your hand and your fingers should be pointing upwards. Next, gently ease the hand and wrist back towards your right shoulder by pulling against it with the palm of your left hand. Hold for 10 seconds. This will stretch the muscles on the underside of your forearm.

Next, turn your right hand so that your fingers are pointing down towards the ground – the back of your hand will be facing away from you. Place your left palm against the back of your right hand and gently pull the hand towards your right shoulder to stretch the top of your forearm. Hold for 10 seconds. Repeat with your left arm.

Lunge

For hip flexors, front and rear of upper thighs

Assume a lunge position and support your weight on the flat of your front foot and the balls of your rear foot. Keep your torso upright and look forwards; your hands should be down by your hips. Don't over-extend your front knee past the shin of your front foot, to avoid straining the knee joint. Hold and then swap leg positions to perform on the other side.

TRAINING TIP

Focus on your breathing when you stretch – breathe slowly 'into' the area being stretched; repeat and breathe out when you relax and leave the stretch.

Lower back

Lie on your back. Grasp the backs of your thighs and gently pull both knees in towards your chest. Ensure that you can feel the base of your spine stretch – don't pull your back off the ground, rather concentrate on 'rolling' it in towards you.

The lower back can be prone to stiffness with frequent rowing. This problem can be made worse if you already have poor lower back flexibility, so this is a good stretch to keep your back in good general and rowing condition.

plus;

Shoulders

See stepper, overleaf.

Lying hamstring stretch

See stepper/cycle, overleaf.

Stretches for CV equipment
continued

STEPPERS AND EXERCISE BIKES

Stepping and cycling work the upper and lower legs, while the upper body remains static, holding either the bike's handlebars or the stepper's rails. This does not mean that you should neglect to stretch the area; see the exercises for stretching prior to weight training, on page 41.

For cycling and stepping, perform the lunge and lower back stretch (see stretches for indoor rower on page 37), as well as the following stretches.

Calf stretch

Place your arms out in front of you at shoulder height, pressing your hands against a wall for support. Take your right leg back and push your heel into the ground. Maintain a slight bend at the knee joint. Keep your left foot flat on the floor, your back in neutral spine position (see page 90) and look straight ahead. If you incrementally lift and take the right foot back you'll increase the stretch. Change legs and repeat.

Quadriceps stretch: for front of thighs

As with the calf stretch, you may want to perform this stretch near to a wall to aid balance. Stand tall, with your chest up and head balanced, look forwards. Bend your right leg up behind you. Reach back and, with your right hand, grasp your forefoot, pulling the foot gently up towards your bum. Keep the upper thigh pointed down toward the ground and keep your hips and shoulders front on. Change leg positions and repeat.

Lying bent-knee hamstring stretch: bottom and lower back

Lie on the floor on your back and slide your right leg in towards your bum until it attains approximately a 90-degree angle. Keep your right foot flat on the floor. Lift your left leg up and off the ground towards your body, keeping it straight. Reach forwards and clasp your hands around the back of your left thigh; pull the leg further in towards your body. Hold for 10 seconds, swap leg positions and repeat. You could perform a PNF stretch on your own with this move, although you'll derive more benefit if assisted by a partner.

Shoulders, upper arms (triceps stretch)

Standing tall, raise your right arm and fold it back so that your fingers rest on the top of your right shoulder. With your left hand, support your right elbow. Push the right arm up, letting your fingers come away from your shoulder slightly as you apply pressure to raise your elbow. Hold, then repeat with your left arm.

TRAINING TIP

Stretching after a workout will reduce your chances of subsequent muscle soreness and aid recovery before your next training session.

Stretches for CV equipment continued

RUNNING AND FITNESS WALKING (treadmill or outdoors)

Running and fitness walking, like rowing, involves virtually all our major muscles. Prior to these activities you should perform the same exercises as for rowing and add the following stretch, plus the quadriceps stretch from the stepper and cycle routine.

Achilles stretch

Step forwards to place your right foot flat on the seat of a firm chair, weights bench or similar firm object. Press your knee over your foot, keeping the heel on the ground. By relaxing the calf muscles the tendon will be provided with the right conditions to stretch. Swap leg positions and repeat.

The achilles tendons

Regular running and high-impact fitness classes like step and aerobics can lead to achilles tendon injuries. These tendons are the bands of connective tissue that connect our heel bones to our calf muscle.

The achilles tendons will really benefit from controlled stretching, particularly as part of a cool-down. Bloodflow to these tendons is naturally restricted, but this is not the case after a workout, when they will become more responsive to passive stretching.

TRAINING TIP

Stretching can be performed as part of your warm-up and cool-down, and as a separate workout in its own right.

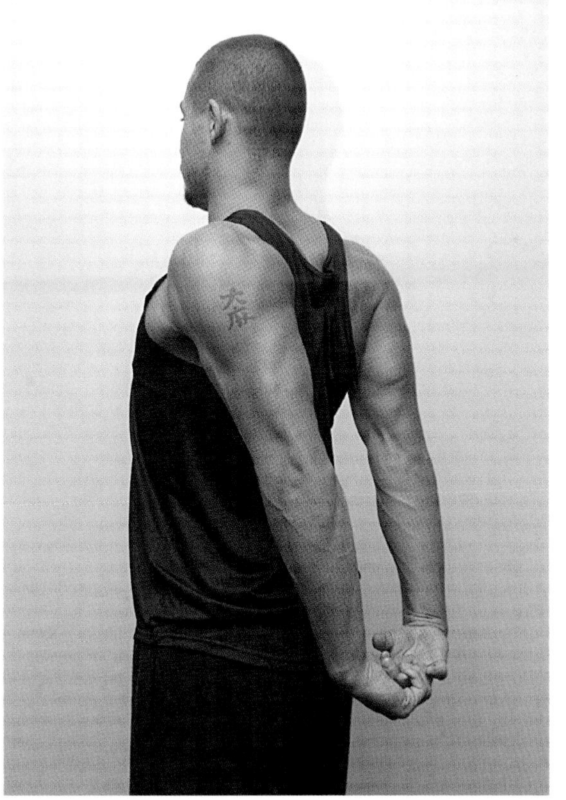

STRETCHES FOR MAINTAINING FLEXIBILITY FOR WEIGHT TRAINING

Here are a couple of specific examples, you should also select from the others described in this chapter.

Chest stretch

This stretch counteracts the tight chest muscles that can be caused by too much bench-pressing and other similar chest exercises.

Place your feet shoulder width apart. Look straight ahead and relax, while keeping your abdominal muscles braced. Clasp your hands behind your back. To stretch your chest, gently lift your arms up behind you. Don't bend your back or force yourself into an overly upright position.

TRAINING TIP

Intermediate and advanced weight trainers could perform some very light repetitions of the exercises they are about to perform to make for a very specific warm-up.

Stretching and weight training

You can perform some light active and passive stretches as part of a weight training warm-up, but it's not recommended that you go all out to improve your flexibility at this time. Research indicates that over-stretching prior to a dynamic activity like weight training can impair performance.

Upper arms and chest

This stretch serves a similar purpose to the one above, but will also keep your biceps elongated, helping you to avoid bowed arms.

Assume a similar stance to that for the chest stretch, but at right angles to a wall. Stand at arm's length from it. Place the palm of your nearest hand against the wall and rotate your body away from your hand. Hold and repeat to other side.

STRETCHING AND FITNESS CLASSES

All fitness classes include stretching in their warm-up and cool-down sections. Certain classes, based on the martial arts or boxing, will require dynamic kicks and punches; your instructor should build up to these (they are very similar to dynamic stretches). If you are new to these movements you might want to hold back a little until you are confident with the required technique, to avoid potential injury. In classes with a flexibility emphasis, like yoga, you should not feel it necessary to go all out to attain certain positions – instead, work steadily and safely and you will progress.

4

CV Training

Cardiovascular (CV) training is perhaps the most important aspect of any fitness programme. Exercising your heart and lungs is not only great for your health but is also an ideal way to burn fat and improve body shape. However, CV training can be a complex and sometimes misunderstood fitness concept. In this chapter I will unravel its mysteries. We'll consider the different ways that your CV system can be trained and will explain how your heart, lungs and muscles respond to this type of training. I'll also provide you with all you need to know about monitoring and progressing your CV workouts. The chapter concludes by providing answers to commonly asked CV questions.

THE HUMAN MACHINE AND ENERGY CREATION

Our bodies are great machines and, like all machines, they need energy to power them. You can generate energy in three ways, by using different energy pathways.

Aerobic training

The majority of people who train their cardiovascular system in the gym do so aerobically: they'll run, row or step, for example, at a comfortable pace for upwards of 15 minutes. Aerobic training is great for calorie burning and will bring about significant health improvements. If it were not for other factors, such as lack of food, overheating and dehydration, our bodies could theoretically continue to exercise aerobically indefinitely.

Aerobic workouts can also be called 'steady state' because, during them, our bodies' energy demand is balanced by its energy supply – hence the steady state.

Understanding cardiovascular training

You could be a bit confused when your personal trainer or gym instructor talks about 'cardiovascular' or 'aerobic' training in the same breath (pun intended!), as these terms are often used interchangeably in the fitness world. Your fitness professional could design for you a 'CV' or 'aerobic' training programme. To avoid potential confusion I prefer to use the term 'cardiovascular' to describe all workouts that train your heart, lungs and oxygen transport system (arteries, veins, muscles and capillaries), as in actuality the CV system can be trained to generate energy 'aerobically' and 'anaerobically'.

Aerobic literally means in the presence of air. Aerobic energy is produced when oxygen combines with glycogen (carbohydrate), proteins and fats, and is broken down by enzymes in our muscles to generate energy.

Table 4.1

The three energy-creation systems

SYSTEM	DURATION	OXYGEN CONTRIBUTION	TYPICAL FITNESS ACTIVITY	CALORIE-BURNING POTENTIAL
Aerobic	Two minutes upwards	Total	Steady-state running and cycling	High
Anaerobic	10 seconds to 2 minutes	Minor initially, but increases rapidly	High-intensity interval training	High
Short-term anaerobic	Less than 10 seconds	None	Weight training and sprinting	Low*

* This type of training will significantly increase your lean muscle mass, which will create the right conditions for increased everyday calorie burning. Plus, the fitter you become, the more repetitions you will be able to complete, which will increase calorie burning during your workout.

TRAINING TIP

Aerobic fitness is the foundation of all other types of fitness. It will, for example, help you to recover much more quickly between shorter, intense efforts like sprints and weights.

Although there are three energy pathways, they are all linked to one another. Depending on how your workout is constructed you can emphasise one over another – don't think that they have to be trained mutually.

The anaerobic energy system

'Anaerobic' literally means without oxygen. Our body can create anaerobic energy in two ways, by the short-term anaerobic (alactic) system (see page 48) and by the anaerobic system. We cannot sustain the energy generated by either of these two systems for very long.

Like the short-term anaerobic system described below, the anaerobic energy system also supplies our bodies with high-powered energy, but for a slightly longer period (up to two minutes). To crank up this system you need to exercise at a very fast, but not flat-out pace.

Have you seen a sci-fi film where a spaceship is about to explode? The film-makers often signpost the impending danger by showing a gauge that gradually moves into the red as the critical state is about to be reached. Thankfully, under anaerobic exercise conditions our bodies will not explode, but the physical sensations and reactions are akin to impending overload. If you push this energy system to the max your muscles will burn, your heart will thump as it reaches maximum output and you'll gasp for breath and sweat profusely. These physiological reactions result from the body demanding more and more oxygen and not getting it as the seconds turn to minutes and as internal chemical reactions begin to short-circuit. An incredible amount of energy is generated in this very short space of time, most of which is derived from chemical reactions taking place in our muscles, which involve stored energy sources: glucose and glycogen, and lactate.

As anaerobic energy production passes the 20-second mark, more and more demand is placed on oxygen; after 30 seconds 20 per cent of the energy produced is done so aerobically and, after 60 seconds, 30 per cent. As you sustain your high-powered effort and as the two-minute mark nears, no amount of oxygen-gulping will save your anaerobic engine and it, and you, will ultimately grind to a potentially painful halt.

See page 59 for more information on lactate.

The short-term anaerobic energy system

The short-term anaerobic system has no reliance on oxygen. It supplies us with energy that lasts no more than 10 seconds. It relies on stored energy sources (phosphates) in our muscles and a chemical reaction that fires it up.

Lifting a set of weights or sprinting 40 metres are examples of this energy system in action, but the first 10 seconds of any activity relies on the short-term anaerobic energy pathway.

Very few gym users exclusively train their CV anaerobic system in the gym; this type of training is more the preserve of athletes like sprinters or tennis players, who need to generate great power for relatively short periods of time (see Chapter 11). However, anaerobic training can be important for general fitness purposes, if you want to optimise your CV and fat-burning potential. This can actually be achieved simultaneously in one workout. If you are at an intermediate or advanced level of fitness you will probably already have done this, although you might not be aware of it. Our bodies, dependent on the effort we put into a run, row or cycle, or other form of CV exercise, actually produce energy through a combination of the aerobic and anaerobic energy systems. Here's an example: if you rowed faster than your normal comfortable steady-state aerobic pace for 30 minutes, due to the fact that your body would not be taking in sufficient oxygen to continue generating exclusively aerobic energy, a percentage of your energy would have to be produced anaerobically. This percentage increases the more you exercise above your comfortable steady-state pace, i.e. the faster you run, row or cycle.

Detailed descriptions of interval training and steady state training can be found on pages 56–57.

Training the short-term anaerobic energy system

If you are after power and speed then you need to train the short-term anaerobic energy system.

Workout examples:

- weight training with one to two minutes' recovery between sets and exercises
- six 40-metre sprints with two minutes' recovery between runs.

Weight training is almost exclusively powered by the short-term anaerobic energy system; avoid it at your peril if you want to achieve a great body.

TRAINING TIP

Long recoveries (one to four minutes) are needed between efforts when training the short-term anaerobic energy system, to allow the body's internal energy stores (phosphates) to replenish, so that quality can be maintained throughout the workout.

How the heart responds to CV exercise

The heart is a muscle, it responds to CV training in much the same way as a skeletal muscle like the biceps does, by growing in size and strength. The key measures of the heart's efficiency are 'stroke volume' and 'heart rate'. The former refers to the amount of blood the heart can pump around the body and the latter the effort that it has to put in to do so.

A world-class endurance athlete or super CV-fit individual's heart could pump 35 to 40 litres of blood around their body per minute and they may have a RHR of under 50 bpm. This contrasts with an untrained individual, whose heart may only be able to pump 20 litres or less, and they may have a RHR of 70 plus during an intense workout.

During our lifetime our heart will pump up to 166.5 million litres of blood and could beat 36.8 million times a year.

TRAINING TIP

Don't train your CV system the same way week in week out if you want the ultimate fitness and fat-burning results – combine aerobic and anaerobic training into your workout programme. Remember, too, that weight training is an anaerobic activity.

Interval training

This provides a great way to optimise your aerobic and anaerobic CV fitness and to boost calorie burning. By manipulating the ratio of work to rest you'll be able to influence how much energy is produced aerobically and anaerobically.

Muscling in on CV exercise

It's important to realise that your heart, although the key determinant, is not solely responsible for improved CV fitness – your oxygen transportation system, including your lungs, arteries, veins, capillaries and, in particular, your muscles, are equally vital components.

After a sustained period of CV training your body will adapt and produce more kilometres of oxygen-carrying motorways (capillaries) in and to your muscles. This will enable an increased quantity of oxygen to get to where it is needed, in turn boosting your CV ability.

TRAINING TIP

This is a tip for you if you are serious about improving your CV fitness. Capillary growth is heavily influenced by the intensity of CV training – the higher the intensity, the greater the potential for capillary growth. The more capillaries you have, the more effective a CV machine you will be.

Muscle fibre type

Muscle fibre will also adapt to improve your CV performance. Muscles are made up of different types of fibre. Aerobic training largely targets the slow-twitch type; these are designed for endurance activity. After a prolonged period of CV training they will increase their ability to use oxygen and generate energy.

Fast-twitch muscle fibre is usually responsible for very short-lived, powerful movements, but it can be trained to improve CV performance.

Personal reflections

Don't fool yourself into thinking that the only way to burn calories is by doing aerobic exercise. I've often had to convince people that this is not the case. To provide them with something that will significantly challenge their potential misconceptions, I often ask them whether they have ever seen an overweight sprinter? The answer is, of course, no (unless the athlete has retired and has no longer kept in shape). Sprinting and sprint training are virtually 100 per cent short-term anaerobic and anaerobic energy system-based activities. These athletes are lean and powerful with little body fat; proof that you do not have to just train aerobically to achieve a great body.

Lactate: that burning sensation

The burning sensation you feel in your muscles after a workout that has taxed your anaerobic energy system is the result of a high-octane chemical reaction that has just occurred in your muscles. Integral to this is blood lactate. You may have heard of it as lactic acid. Lactate is an ever-present feature of the energy creation equation and not the sole consequence of high-intensity exercise, as many people think. It's being used now as you turn the pages of this book. It's only when it cannot be re-used in your muscles to generate energy – due to increasing fatigue and energy demand – that it begins to spill over and compromise your ability to keep going – this is known as your lactate threshold. Regular anaerobic training will improve the lactate-handling capacity of your muscles and improve your endurance potential.

Cooling down (see page 35) is crucial after any workout, but is particularly necessary after intense CV sessions. Gentle CV work (5–10 minutes) and stretching will help disperse lactate from your muscles and will reduce the potential for subsequent muscular soreness and stiffness.

Resting heart rate (RHR)

As identified in Chapter 2, monitoring RHR is a great way to measure improvements in CV fitness. RHR may be determined by recording your heartbeat five minutes after waking in the morning. The fitter you become, the lower your RHR.

Measuring your CV training

Your heart is the barometer of your CV training: the harder it's beating the greater your level of effort. Knowing your theoretical or actual heart rate maximum (HRMax) will enable you to train within heart rate training zones (HRZ; see Table 4.3). Zone training will optimise your CV training returns.

You can determine your HRMax using a heart rate monitor and working to exhaustion (see page 22), but this is not recommended if you are new to exercise or CV training. There are, however, various calculative formulae that can be used to determine a theoretical HRMax.

Probably the best-known calculative method is the '220 minus your age' formula. Thus, for a 30 year old, their HRMax would be 190 (220 – 30).

You may also use the '217 – (0.85 × your age)' formula, which provides a potentially more accurate score. Using this method, our 30 year old would have a theoretical HRMax of 191.5; that's 217 – 25.5 (0.85 × 30).

Although calculative formulae have a real use for those new to exercise, they are prone to considerable inaccuracy (greater than 10 per cent). This is because no two individuals' heart capacities will be the same. HRMax (and sub-maximal heart rate) can be affected by stress, heat, hydration, fitness and motivation levels, and even the type of CV exercise performed. Readings will invariably be higher on a rowing machine or treadmill, and lower on a step machine or cycle, due to the greater amount of muscle involved in generating energy on the former items of gym equipment.

When is it safe to perform a maximum heart rate test?

I recommend that, once you reach a high level of CV fitness, you take an HRMax test. This will allow accurate training zone calculation, which will ensure that you get the most out of your CV training and fat-burning exploits. However, I must stress once again that you should not perform this if you are new to exercise or CV training: just because you are fit for one activity does not mean that you will be for another.

Some criteria for taking a HRMax test:

- you can complete any form of CV exercise for at least 30 minutes at a rate of self-perceived (RPE)* exertion of eight
- you should have been CV training regularly for six to nine months, three to four times a week
- you are in good health
- you should perform the test in the presence of a fitness professional.

* RPE is a self-evaluatory method for CV training and is covered in detail on page 52.

TRAINING TIP

You cannot increase your HRMax – it naturally decreases with age. Having a lower HRMax than your peers does not mean that you are not as fit as, or cannot be fitter than them.

WAYS TO MEASURE YOUR CV TRAINING INTENSITY

Heart rate monitors

Heart rate monitors are relatively inexpensive and are virtually 100 per cent accurate. Most use a chest strap, which relays your heartbeat to a wristwatch-type device that indicates, among many potential functions, how fast your heart is beating. Models vary in their complexity, but the majority will also have a clock and stopwatch function, and the ability to establish target heart rate zones. Some monitors also offer an estimated calorie-counting function. Those models at the upper end of the range can be connected to a computer to allow the download of heart rate data, but unless you are an advanced trainer, perhaps in serious training for a competition, this function is not really worth the additional expenditure.

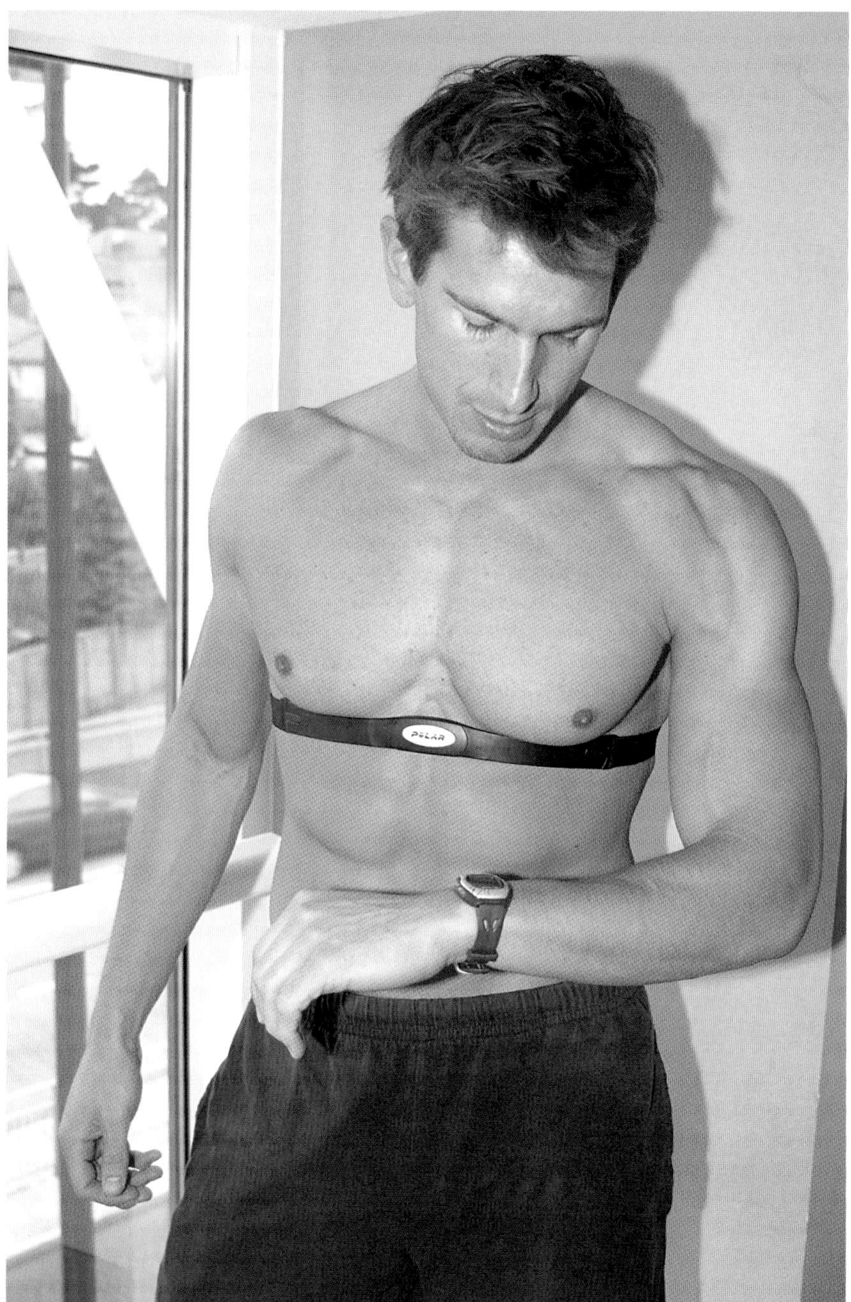

By rate of self-perceived exertion (RPE)

RPE is a great way to measure the intensity of your CV workouts. No kit is involved – only your brain. This method requires you to rate your level of effort against a pre-set scale, as displayed in Table 4.2. (Table 4.2 also links RPE scores to estimated heart rate ranges.)

RPE can have advantages over using a heart rate monitor and training to designated heart rate training zones. If you are having 'one of those days' when your training is not going so well, you might not be able to zip along at your workout's target heart rate for numerous reasons (stress, heat, fatigue, lack of motivation). However, with RPE you should be able to consistently interpret the effort you are putting into your workout and, consequently, continuously adjust your effort to the required RPE. An RPE of five to six will always be an RPE of five to six, provided that you consistently interpret your personal response to exercise. This contrasts with the situation you could find yourself in when using a

Heart rate monitor suppliers

COMPANY	TELEPHONE	WEBSITE
Polar	01926 816 177	www.polar-uk.com
York	01327 701 800	www.yorkfitness.co.uk
Cardiosport	012392 257 388	www.cardiosport.com

Table 4.2
Rate of self-perceived exertion (RPE)

1–10 RPE	SCALE LEVEL	PERCENTAGE OF HEART RATE MAX (HRMax)	HOW DO YOU FEEL?
0	very, very light	40–50%	Able to converse easily
1–2	very light	50–60%	Breathing increases, but still no problems talking
3–4	fairly light	60–65%	Slight feeling of breathlessness, not so easy to converse
5–6	somewhat hard	65–75%	Difficulty talking, sweating prevalent
7–8	hard	75–85%	Breathing and sweating heavily
9	very hard	85–95%	Breathing difficult
10	very, very hard	95–100%	Possible feelings of nausea, unable to continue exercising for very long

heart rate monitor. You might feel obliged to keep up with your workout's predetermined rate, although for that particular workout on that particular day you may not be up to it. Under these circumstances you could push yourself too hard. This could have a negative impact on your subsequent training efforts by leaving you fatigued and demotivated.

Note that research indicates that women are less accurate judges of RPE than men. Using a heart rate monitor may therefore be of particular use when establishing RPE familiarity.

By pulse

You can measure your heart rate manually by taking your pulse. One of the best sites to do this is located at the side of the neck, just below the jawbone. Use the first and second fingers of your right hand to do this; count for 15 seconds and multiply this figure by four to calculate your heart rate over a minute. This method has its limitations, obviously, when trying to record your heart rate mid-exercise.

TRAINING TIP

Always be prepared to adjust your training with regard to how you feel on a day-to-day basis – whether working to a designated RPE or heart rate zone.

Don't train exclusively in one HRZ. Depending on your level of fitness, all zones are available to you as training ingredients in a progressive CV training plan. Emphasise one for a training period and then another. Obviously you'll need to build up so that you can work safely and effectively in the 'tougher' zones.

HEART RATE TRAINING ZONES

If you want to get the most out of your CV training you should work out using heart rate training zones (HRZS).

You will derive a different training effect from working out within different heart rates zones, as indicated in Table 4.3.

Table 4.3

Heart rate training zones

HEART RATE % HRMax	HEART RATE ZONE
50–60	Light to moderate – for the older and untrained individual. Low calorie-burning potential. Primarily works slow-twitch muscle fibre. Energy created exclusively aerobically.
60–70	Everyday fitness zone – this zone enables relatively comfortable and sustained CV exercise to be completed. It is often associated with the misleading belief that it is the best for fat burning (the reasons why this is not the case are explained on page 160). This zone also targets slow-twitch muscle fibre. Energy is created virtually exclusively aerobically. Those with intermediate and advanced levels of fitness could also use this zone for recovery purposes between higher-intensity workouts. It has a moderate to high calorie-burning potential.
70–85	Quality aerobic training zone – this zone is for intermediate and advanced trainers. It offers optimum calorie-burning potential for fat loss and is great for CV fitness purposes. Although the zone predominantly targets slow-twitch muscle fibre, towards its upper end, when you have to increase your speed, it will also involve fast-twitch fibre. These fibres will adapt and contribute towards generating increased CV power. This zone marks the transition into anaerobic training territory and can have a potentially significant post-exercise calorie-burning effect.
85–100	High-intensity training zone – this zone is for advanced trainers and competitive athletes. It's not possible to exercise in it for long – high-intensity interval training provides a great option in this respect (see page 59). All muscle fibre types are involved, although your fast twitch fibres will be relied upon more than in any others. It can burn proportionally high numbers of calories, if it can be sustained, and has a significant effect on elevating post-exercise metabolic rate. Those with more every day fitness goals do not have to train within this zone.

TYPES OF CV TRAINING

Steady-state training

Steady-state training is carried out an intensity that allows your heart and lungs to supply a plentiful supply of oxygen to your working muscles aerobically. It allows us to exercise for a relatively long periods at a comfortable pace. Note that, for the well-trained individual, this could be at a very high percentage of HRMax (e.g. 80 per cent of HRMax). Regular steady-state training will develop a great base of CV fitness and will burn moderate to high numbers of calories – the faster the pace, the higher the heart rate, the greater the number of calories burned.

Walking

Walking is a great fitness option, but with all that flashy gym equipment it can easily be forgotten. With less of the impact associated with running it's not as likely to cause over-use injury. You will have to exercise for longer to derive similar CV benefits to other 'faster-paced' CV options, but not for as long as you may think (see Table 4.4). Further calorie-burning figures for other exercise options are on page 159, and Chapter 9 looks at different fitness class options and provides estimated calorie-burning figures.

Table 4.4

Walking and calorie burning

WALKING SPEED	GRADIENT – CALORIE BURN/HOUR			
	Flat	4%	8%	12%
4.2 km/hour	270	391	526	662
6.4 km/hour	400	579	759	930
8.0 km/hour	530	769	979	1200

Average normal walking pace is 3.2–4.8 km/hour. Figures are based on an 80 kg individual. If you weigh more, you will burn more calories; less and you will burn fewer calories.

TRAINING TIP

As your CV fitness improves, you should increase the effort you put into your steady-state efforts to maintain the level of your energy expenditure. This can be done by increasing the pace or the duration of your workout – but not both at the same time.

Interval training

Don't think that interval training is an advanced training option – it's not. It is in fact a great way to CV train, whatever your fitness level. Interval training can be carried out on any item of CV equipment.

> **TRAINING TIP**
> **High-intensity interval training should only be performed once or twice a week in a 12–18-week training cycle, and then only by advanced trainers, once a suitable base of CV fitness has been established. Expect discomfort – this is one of the few occasions when the maxim 'no pain, no gain' does hold true.**

INTERVAL TRAINING STRUCTURE

The interval

This is the main component of the session, the time when you exercise to a designated HRZ, RPE or HRMax percentage. The interval can be as short as 30 seconds or as long as 20 minutes, and a workout can be designed to have a primarily aerobic or anaerobic affect.

The recovery (active or passive)

At the end of each interval a rest is taken, this can be active or passive.

A passive rest involves walking or standing around for a set time after the completion of each interval. Despite its name, this period should not be totally passive or inactive, you shouldn't just flop down and wait to perform the next interval. Rather, you should walk around and perform some gentle passive stretches. This will maintain your physiological readiness for the next interval.

Active recovery is more regimented and requires you to perform a set period of much less intense CV work between your harder intervals – if you are cycling, for example, you can simply decrease your speed. Active rest can be controlled, by time, RPE or when your heart rate has dropped to a designated level.

Why interval train?

1. Interval training will boost your CV exercise confidence by enabling you to exercise for longer than you would be able to 'in one go'. It offers great calorie-burning potential because of this.
2. Interval training can develop aerobic or anaerobic fitness, or a combination of both when carefully crafted.
3. Interval training can motivate you to new levels of effort, as it can be more mentally (and physically) stimulating than steady-state training.
4. During either an active or passive recovery period, your CV system will still be working to return your body to a more restful state, this involves further energy expenditure and oxygen consumption, which all adds up to improved fitness and calorie expenditure.
5. High-intensity interval training can improve your speed and power, making your slower efforts that much easier. It will improve your running, rowing, cycling and stepping economy, and boost your lactate threshold.

Interval training is based on 'intervals of effort' combined with 'periods of rest'.

Personal reflections

My recent forays into the world of indoor rowing have taught me a great deal about CV training. My experience shows me that no matter what you might think, you can train your CV system to a high level by selecting the right training ingredients and following a structured training programme.

When I first began rowing I couldn't row continuously for more than 10 minutes – for this mode of exercise I was very much 'new to exercise'. My long jump training had provided me with a base of strength and power but not too much in the way of transferable CV fitness. Rowing the 2 km race distance, my goal, relies heavily on the aerobic energy system, while my previous training was largely based around short-term anaerobic training. To get into the required shape to try to row a good time, I had to build up my endurance significantly and train very differently. I had to use steady-state workouts and various types of interval training. I recall finding it very difficult to maintain my mental focus for a couple of minutes on the rower, let alone for the half an hour steady-state efforts that were required – most of my long jump training efforts were over in five seconds!

I trained for indoor rowing six months of the year for four years and managed to row the 2 km distance in 6 minutes 35.2 seconds at the age of 40. This turned out to be a respectable time and even ranked me 46th in Britain out of 700 40–45-year-old men who recorded times in the 2002 Concept2 indoor rowing age-based rankings.

If you establish a goal, train systematically and consistently, and follow a well-thought-out training plan you will achieve great results.

HOW TO GET THE MOST OUT OF INTERVAL TRAINING

In the section that follows, I have provided you with examples of interval training workouts that reflect different intensity levels. This will show you how these workouts can be tailored to different levels of fitness and to different fitness goals. Suggested RPE scores for both the interval and the recovery phase are provided, as is the type of recovery you can use. The broad physiological effect of each workout has been provided, as has information about each workout's suitability for use by those new to exercise or at an intermediate or advanced level.

Use any piece of CV equipment, but ensure that you warm up and cool down before and after completing any of the workouts.

Low-intensity interval training workout, suitable for those new to exercise

- Interval: 3 minutes RPE 3–4
- Recovery: active rest RPE 1–2 for 2 minutes
- Number of intervals: see below

You should continue to alternate between the interval and the recovery phases until a point is reached when you cannot maintain either the required RPE during the interval or the recovery period. As your fitness improves and you are able to push yourself a little bit harder you should increase the required RPEs.

Physiological effect – This level of interval training will prepare the heart, lungs and muscles for more intense workouts. It will also burn moderate numbers of calories – in the region of 200–300 Kcal for a 30-minute workout.

TRAINING TIP

For all levels of interval training, as with HRZ training, don't deviate from the intended intensity of your intervals in terms of planned RPE or heart rate, as this will alter the specific physiological effect that the workout is designed to achieve.

Blood lactate

Lactate is an ever-present feature of muscular action. It plays a crucial role in your body's energy-creation equation, ebbing and flowing in the muscular furnace until, with the heat turned up, through greater exercise intensity, it begins to overflow and gum up your muscular machinery, making further exercise harder and eventually impossible. Technically speaking, this is when your 'lactate threshold' is reached. The more intense your intervals (or a single continuous effort) the greater the concentration of lactate build-up.

MEDIUM-INTENSITY INTERVAL TRAINING

Medium-intensity interval training uses 'long' intervals of 8–20 minutes' duration. Rest periods are kept relatively short, normally three to six minutes. Each interval has to be performed 'strongly': you should attempt to move along at a pace considerably faster than your normal steady-state one.

Medium-intensity interval training workout, suitable for those with intermediate and advanced levels of fitness

- Interval: 10 minutes RPE 7–8
- Recovery: active rest RPE 3–4 for 4 minutes
- Number of intervals: 3

Physiological effect – This type of interval workout will train your heart and lungs to sustain medium- to high-energy outputs for long periods. It will also develop your muscles' ability to cope with the build-up of lactate.

HIGH-INTENSITY INTERVAL TRAINING

High-intensity interval training is only suitable for advanced trainers. It is constructed from short intervals, lasting 30 seconds to five minutes, and uses similarly short recoveries. This workout requires great strength of mind as well as body to complete – take it from me, it will hurt! During the intervals, your heart rate will reach near maximum as you work to an RPE of 8/10.

High-intensity interval training workout, suitable for those with an advanced level of fitness only

- Interval: 5 minutes RPE 8–9
- Recovery: active rest RPE 3–4 for 5–6 minutes
- Number of intervals: 4

Physiological effect – Significantly enhances the CV system's ability to produce energy under very taxing conditions, boosting lactate threshold, maximum oxygen capacity (VO2Max; see page 61), CV exercise power and economy.

High-intensity interval training is a great way to boost your lactate threshold, if you are after serious high-end CV fitness.

Table 4.5

Summary of CV training methods and their effects

Type of CV training and fitness level suitability	Intensity of session (RPE)	Heart rate response (HRMax percentage)	Lactate level increase	'Feelings'	Aerobic /anaerobic
Steady state 1: beginner*	3–4	60–65	Minimal	Easy	
Steady state 2: intermediate/ advanced *	5–6	65–75	Moderate	Having to concentrate, but comfortable	
Lactate threshold effort: intermediate/ advanced ***	7–10	75–100	High (but reached only once)	Breathless, sweating heavily, muscles burning	
Intervals: new to exercise **	1–4	50–65	Minimal	Easy, breathing comfortable	
Intervals: medium intensity ** intermediate/ advanced	5–8	65–85	Moderate–high, accumulating throughout the workout	Relatively breathless, sweating heavily	
Intervals: high intensity ** advanced	8–10	85–100	High, reached on numerous occasions during the workout	Very breathless, feeling weak, sweating heavily, muscles burning	

* Refers to average heart rate over the course of the workout.

** Refers to average heart rate during the intervals.

*** Not mentioned previously, this type of CV training requires you to run, cycle or row as far as you can at a moderate to fast pace for around 20 minutes; you stop when you can't continue for any longer. At this point you will be at or near your maximum heart rate and your body will have produced a significant amount of lactate. Used sparingly, it can boost your aerobic power.

TRAINING TIP

Those beginning a CV training programme could use the stepper or exercise bike, as opposed to the treadmill or rowing machine, to develop preliminary CV fitness and confidence. These machines recruit lesser amounts of your body's musculature and are initially less taxing and are, of course, load bearing, which reduces injury potential.

VO2Max

If you read up more on CV training you'll probably find that training intensity is often expressed as a percentage of VO2Max as well as HRMax.

VO2Max is a measure of aerobic power and specifically refers to the maximum amount of oxygen your body can process per kilogram of body weight per minute, as expressed in millilitres. Elite athletes will tend to train at percentages of VO2Max rather than HRMax or RPE because VO2Max has a greater relevance for controlled training adaptation.

Table 4.6

Heart rate expressed in terms of VO2Max

HEART RATE	PERCENTAGE VO2Max
130	50
150	60
165	75
180/190	90
190 plus	100

Source: Suslov, adapted by Dick (2002).

To give you an idea of VO2max potential, an average 20-year-old woman's VO2max will be between 35 and 40 ml per kg body weight per minute, and that of a top marathon runner 70 ml per kg/min.

Using VO2Max: 70 per cent of VO2Max should be your minimum target for steady-state training and medium-intensity interval training if you are after optimum fat burning and quality CV fitness.

It's estimated that, in 12 weeks, those new to exercise should be able to improve their VO2Max by 5–25 per cent.

The Karvonen method of calculating VO2Max heart rate

The Karvonen formula calculates a heart reading that links to VO2Max and is useful for those who want to know how to train to VO2Max.

To use this formula you need to know both your resting heart rate (RHR) and HRMax. If you wanted to work out at 70 per cent of your VO2Max you would calculate the required heart rate using the Karvonen method, as follows:

Heart rate = (0.70 [HRMax – RHR] + RHR)

So, if you had a RHR of 67 and a HRMax of 190 (actual or estimated) your Karvonen calculated heart rate required for working out at 70 per cent VO2Max would be:

0.70 [190 – 67] + 67 = 153.1

Calculated as follows:

0.70 × 123 = 86.1

86.1 + 67 = 153.1

TRAINING TIP

CV strength can also be developed by running or cycling up hills or into the wind, or by selecting a 'strength' type of programme on CV equipment.

CONSTRUCTING A CV TRAINING PROGRAMME

Constructing a CV training programme is not as difficult as it may sound. Information about most of the tools of the trade has already been provided in this chapter – now it's time for the tricks of the trade. (You should also refer to Chapter 6, which takes an in-depth look at how to plan your training.)

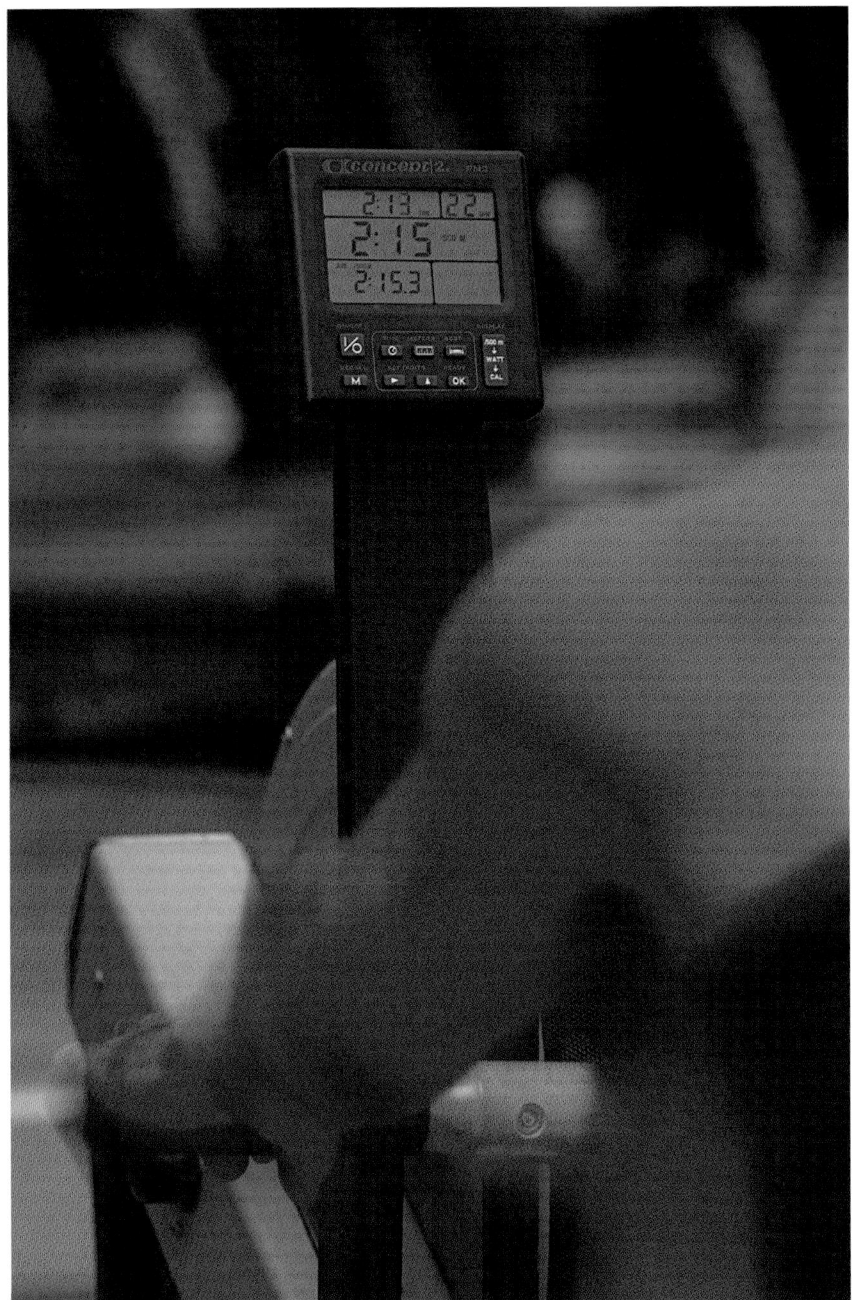

The guidelines

1. Always build a base of aerobic CV fitness, for the next phase to be built on.
2. You should progress slowly and train progressively within training zones to establish consistent CV fitness. Each zone should be emphasised for a period of 6 to 18 weeks in a training phase.
3. You should be prepared to increase or decrease the speed of your training progression as necessary. You don't have to stick rigidly to planned workouts – you will have good and bad days.
4. You should not do the same type of training all year round – emphasise speed over duration, or intervals over steady-state training, for example, during different training phases.
5. Don't expect to stay in peak CV condition all year round. Sometimes you will need to lose or reduce a certain type of fitness to gain a different type, or to progress to a higher level.
6. You must monitor and record your training using a training diary, and use this information to plan your workouts.
7. You should combine CV training with weight training. Stronger muscles are more fatigue-resistant, which makes for more effective CV workouts. This training combination is also the best for great health and fat burning.

I have designed the following CV training programme with the needs of someone new to exercise in mind (see Table 4.7). Those with a higher level of fitness could increase the suggested RPEs by one or two levels for the training sessions to suit their needs. Each phase is designed to build and progress safely and optimally the fitness attained in the previous one.

Always warm up and cool down before and after your workouts; select your own piece of CV equipment.

Table 4.7

Suggested CV training programme

TRAINING PHASE AND NUMBER OF WEEKS	WORKOUTS PER WEEK	WORKOUT AIMS	SESSIONS
Phase 1 1–12	4	Aim to build CV confidence and stimulate basic heart and lung improvement, by means of steady-state and new to exercise interval training.	**Steady-state sessions × 2** Start with 10 minutes @ RPE of 1–2, building up to 20 minutes plus @ RPE of 3–4. Increase the duration of each workout by a minute at the start of each week. Increase your RPE when you feel ready. **New to exercise interval training**. Build up so that the workout lasts for 35 minutes.
Phase 2 12–18	4	Aim to build on the above base, by introducing more 'quality' training, but without pushing too hard.	**Steady-state sessions × 2** 20 minutes @ RPE 3–4 (you could increase the duration of these workouts by a minute a session). **Medium-intensity interval training sessions x 2** 2 × 8 minutes @ RPE 5–6, passive recovery 4 minutes (you could introduce active recoveries to the same time after week 14 if your training is really progressing well @ RPE 1–2).
Phase 3 18–24	4	Aim to increase intensity, while maintaining balance of week's training, between steady state and interval training.	**Steady-state sessions × 2** 1 × 20 minutes and 1× 25 minutes @ RPE of 5–6 (note the increased RPE; if you are progressing well, you could increase these efforts by a minute a week also). **Medium-intensity interval training sessions × 2** (a) 3 × 8 minutes @ RPE 5–6, active recovery 5 minutes @ RPE 1–2 (b) 3 × 5 minutes @ RPE 7–8, passive recovery 5 minutes.

CV exercise equipment

Ever been to the gym, looked at the mass of flashing diodes on the various machine displays and have had no idea how to get started? Well, you're not alone. I recall a couple of occasions with embarrassment, when I thought I'd programmed a piece of kit for a lengthy workout, only for it to run for a minute, stop and congratulate me on a 'great workout'. It can happen to all of us.

GETTING STARTED

Most CV machines are designed with a quick-start function that will enable you to commence exercising immediately without selecting a specific programme or inputting data. During this type of no-nonsense workout, you should also be able to speed up the machine or adjust its resistance mid-flow. However, most machines also have fairly complicated and numerous other workout options: a treadmill could offer steady-state runs, interval training and/or hill programmes or any combination of these. It might also have the option of a 'pace or race'-style programme, which requires you to attempt to keep up with a 'virtual' competitor on the machine's display panel. VO2MAX and maximum power tests may also be available on some machines.

To use these options, you will invariably be asked to enter your weight, age, desired duration and level of difficulty into the machine. This can be a bit of a challenge if you have never used the item before, but once you have completed a couple of workouts you'll have a good idea of the programmes and levels that work for you and of the machine's functions. You should always be able to adjust the programme level by pressing the appropriate buttons on the machine's display, so if the going gets tough, or too easy, you'll be able to make a change.

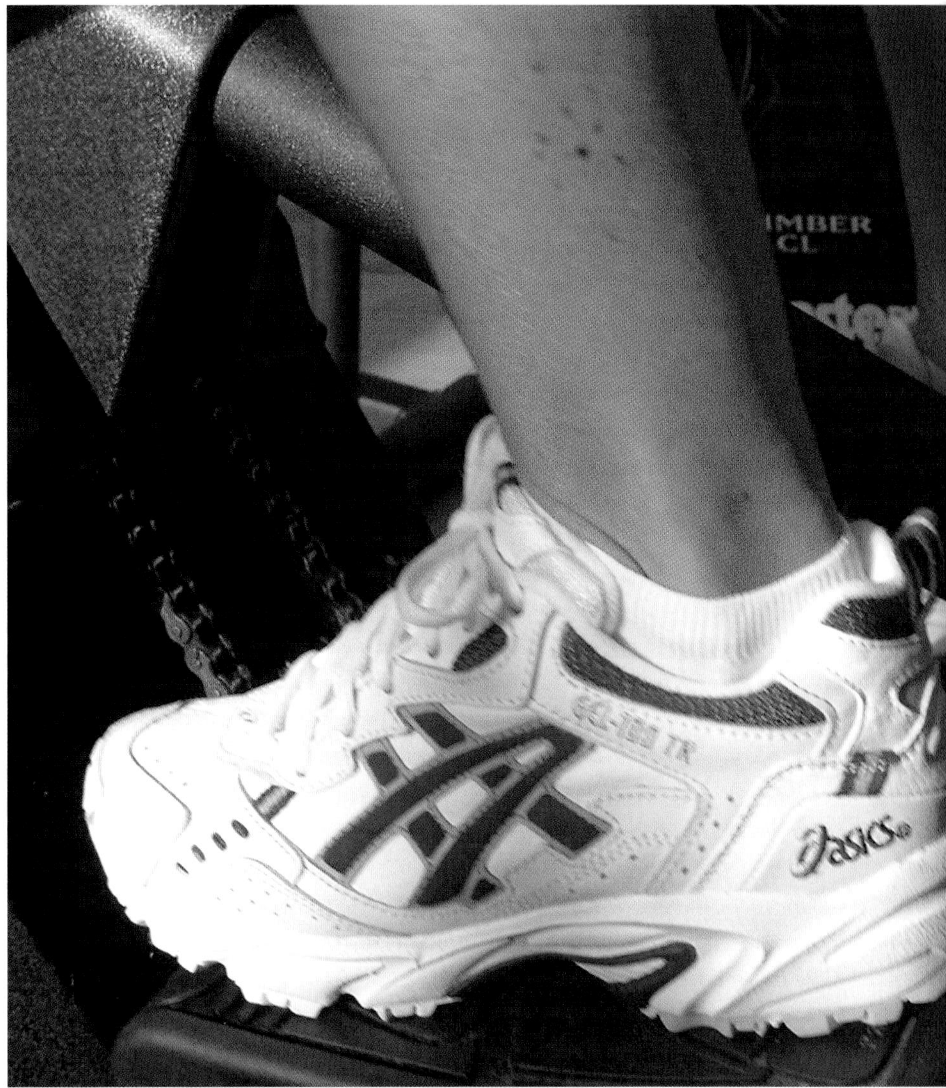

Heart rate compatibility and CV equipment

Most CV machines have heart rate-monitoring capability. This can appear on the machine's display and may be transmitted through sensors placed, for example, in the grips of an upright or recumbent exercise bike. Other machines might require you to select a particular workout option to achieve this function, while others (like the Concept2 indoor rower) have a heart rate monitor interface. This allows you to see your heart rate on the machine's display. Note that you'll need additional kit to achieve this coupling – consult the manufacturer or a member of staff at your gym.

CV equipment: FAQs

Is any piece of CV kit a better calorie burner?

No one piece of CV equipment is a better calorie burner than another, it's all about the effort you put in. Put it in and, no matter what the machine, the calories will disappear. Having said that, most gym users find that they burn more calories and reach higher heart rate levels on treadmills and rowing machines than on exercise bikes and steppers. This is because rowers and treadmills recruit larger amounts of muscle, which increases the effort you have to put in to power the exercise.

Does a high level of running fitness provide a high level of fitness on another piece of CV kit?

There is a limited transference of CV fitness between items of CV equipment, so don't think that because you can run for an hour easily, you'll be able to row just as easily for an hour. CV fitness, like all other fitness elements, is specific. If you want to be 'good' on all types of machine, you'll have to train on them all. A benefit of this cross-training is the reduction in the potential for over-use injuries.

Do CV machines develop strength as well as heart and lung capacity?

All CV machines develop strength endurance and a degree of specific strength in specific muscles groups. For example, rowing will develop back and shoulder strength and leg power, whereas cycling and stepping will have no major effect on the upper body.

Why are some steppers easier to use than others?

Some machines have an independent action and some a dependent one. The former provides no assistance to the stepping action, while the latter does. An independent machine will therefore provide a tougher workout.

TRAINING TIP

CV equipment varies in its difficulty as well as its complexity of use. One manufacturer's stepper's 'level six' may not be the same as another's. If you're not familiar with an item of equipment then always start on a low-level programme – you can always move up if you find it too easy.

Is it better to row on a higher resistance setting than a lower one on a rowing machine?

The most common type of rowing machine in most gyms is the Concept2. It works on the principle of air resistance increasing or decreasing the resistance in the machine's fan. You slide a lever up and down in the fan's cage to do this. A level of resistance from 1–10 is offered; many other rowing machines offer similar levels of variable resistance. It's often wrongly assumed that a high level (actually called 'damper setting') will provide a better workout. I also thought this, until I was told otherwise! In truth you need to experiment and select the level that allows you to master smooth technique and generate optimum power – for most people, this is around level 4 on a Concept2.

Quick fix – take a rowing class, so that the instructor can coach you on proper technique.

Do the legs or the arms dominate the rowing stroke?

Your legs should contribute about 80 per cent of the power generated; the arms only 'finish off' the stroke as the oar passes the knees during the 'drive' (pushing back) phase.

Quick fix – think 'legs, back, arms' as you row.

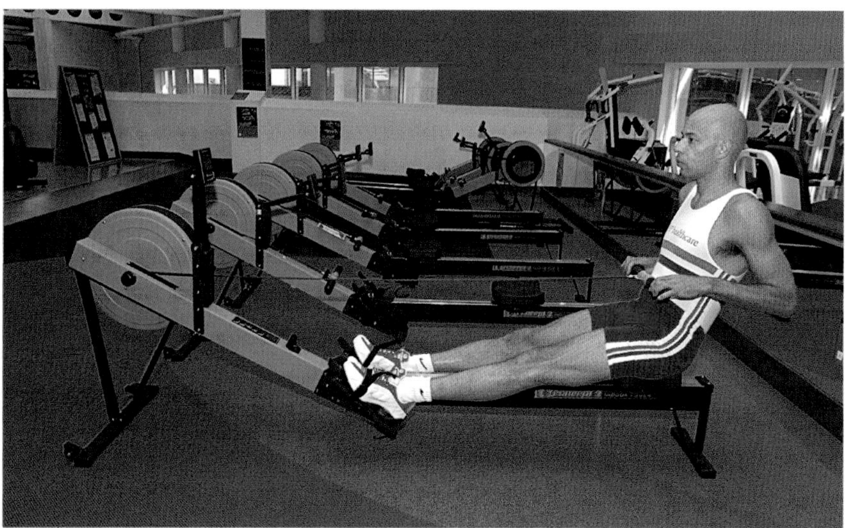

> **TRAINING TIP**
> **If you are in any doubt about how to use a piece of CV equipment ask a member of gym staff, or contact the manufacturer or supplier if you have purchased your own item for home use. Only once you fully understand a machine's capabilities will you be able to get the most out of it – and yourself.**

Recumbent bike

What's the difference between an upright and a recumbent bike?

A recumbent bike recruits the muscles of the rear of the upper thighs in a slightly different way to an upright bike, although the front thigh muscles supply power in much the same way. The main advantage of a recumbent bike is that it reduces the potential for back strain.

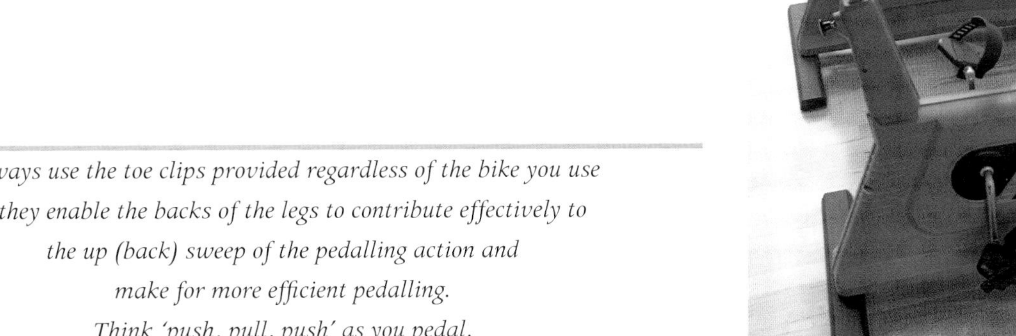

Always use the toe clips provided regardless of the bike you use – they enable the backs of the legs to contribute effectively to the up (back) sweep of the pedalling action and make for more efficient pedalling. Think 'push, pull, push' as you pedal.

Upright bike

How can I improve my running technique on a treadmill (or outdoors)?

The keys to good running technique are:

- relaxed neck and shoulders, head in alignment with your body, chest elevated
- you should look forwards, not down at your feet
- your arms should swing backwards and forwards in time with your legs to assist your speed; keep your shoulders down, not up by your ears, while maintaining a 90-degree angle at the elbow joint; to avoid developing tension, don't clench your fists
- you should strike the ground evenly with your feet, while trying to be 'light' on them
- knee lift should be comfortable and not exaggerated
- keep control of your mid-section and try to avoid inefficient twisting movements that will slow you down.

Is running on a treadmill the same as running outdoors?

Most people find it easier to run on a treadmill, due to the fact that a smooth and constant stride can be maintained and also because of the greater level of cushioning offered. In terms of running technique a treadmill provides a more 'on top of the surface stride' (the result of the belt moving underneath you), while running outdoors generates a more 'across the surface' feeling, as you have to 'push' the ground backwards to propel yourself forwards. Running with a slight incline (2 per cent) on a treadmill will achieve a similar effort to outdoor running.

What's the purpose of a cross-trainer/elliptical trainer?

A cross-trainer, or an elliptical trainer's motion is something of a hybrid between that of a treadmill and a cross-country ski machine. Like running and rowing machines, cross-trainers involve both the upper and lower body, and therefore offer a very effective way to train the CV system and burn calories. Their smooth action also reduces injury potential.

> **Further information**
>
> Calorie-burning figures for common forms of exercise can be found on page 159.
>
> Other types of CV training are considered elsewhere in this book. Chapter 9 considers various fitness class options, which can have a CV effect, and Chapter 5 considers circuit training and circuit resistance training, which can also develop CV fitness as well as muscular strength.

USE IT OR LOSE IT: WHAT YOU HAVE TO DO TO MAINTAIN CV FITNESS

You've taken months developing your CV fitness, what do you have to do to maintain it? Research findings make reasonably pleasant reading: if your exercise intensity is maintained, the frequency and duration of training can be cut back quite considerably without a significant loss of CV fitness. Quality of effort is the key, so two to three training sessions at a high intensity could do the same as six varied lower-level-intensity ones. Note that this will maintain, not improve, your CV fitness.

5 Resistance training

If you are serious about your health and fitness then you need to resistance train. Weight training, circuit training and fit ball exercises are all forms of resistance training. Regular resistance training will reduce the risk of diseases such as osteoporosis and arthritis, improve your functional strength and sports performance, make you less injury-prone, improve your body shape and increase your fat-burning potential.

The chapter is divided into three parts. The first addresses how our muscles work, and considers weight training systems and exercises in detail. The second considers circuit training. The third takes a look at other resistance training options such as fit balls. At the end of it, you'll be armed with all the information you need to construct your own varied and highly effective resistance training workouts.

PART 1: MUSCULAR ACTION AND WEIGHT TRAINING

Progressive overload

Progressive overload is the key to successful resistance training. Your weights or body weight training should develop strength progressively, gradually and systematically over your workouts. You must always be prepared to challenge your muscles if you want to develop more strength and more lean muscle mass, and burn more fat. To achieve this, the last one or two repetitions in each set of weight training exercises or body weight moves should be difficult to complete, but not at the expense of good technique.

Important – Please note that if you are in any way unsure about your suitability to weight train, consult an expert. This applies to those with certain medical conditions, like high blood pressure. It is generally recommended that young people (under 16) do not train with weights, although they can perform body weight exercises.

TRAINING TIP

Those new to weight training should use fixed-weight machines before progressing to free weights once confidence and strength develops.

Types of weight training equipment

Take a look around your gym and you'll see a huge variety of resistance training kit. Fixed-weight machines use cables and weight stacks that are confined within the design of the equipment. Plate-loaded machines allow for the attachment or detachment of weighted discs to increase or decrease the resistance offered. Free weights, dumbbells, barbells and discs allow for a multitude of resistance exercises to be performed, while air or hydraulics provide the resistance for yet more equipment. Each type has its own merits, but all work on the same principle: their external resistance will increase your muscular strength.

Resistance training and fat burning

If you are serious about fat loss you need to weight train. Muscle burns up to three times as many calories as any other body part – the leaner you are (the more muscle you have as opposed to fat) the more efficient calorie-burning machine your body will be.

Facts and figures: increase your lean body weight and burn more fat

0.45 kg of muscle burns 30-50 Kcal a day. If you increased your lean weight by 5 kg, you could increase your daily calorie burn by 500 Kcal at most – that's equivalent to an hour's moderate-intensity running.

Women and resistance training

Women are often put off weight training because they think it will make them 'musclebound' and unattractive. Truth is, it can actually do just the opposite, by creating a more aesthetically pleasing body shape, strengthening, developing and toning 'problem' areas and burning fat.

Women can achieve similar percentage strength gains to men through weight training, without developing large muscles. Men get bigger because they possess more muscle mass than women. But women can weight train as hard as men should they desire; there are no physiological reasons why they should not. I am particularly aware of this as, during my serious athletic training years, I was regularly 'out-lifted' by my female training partners.

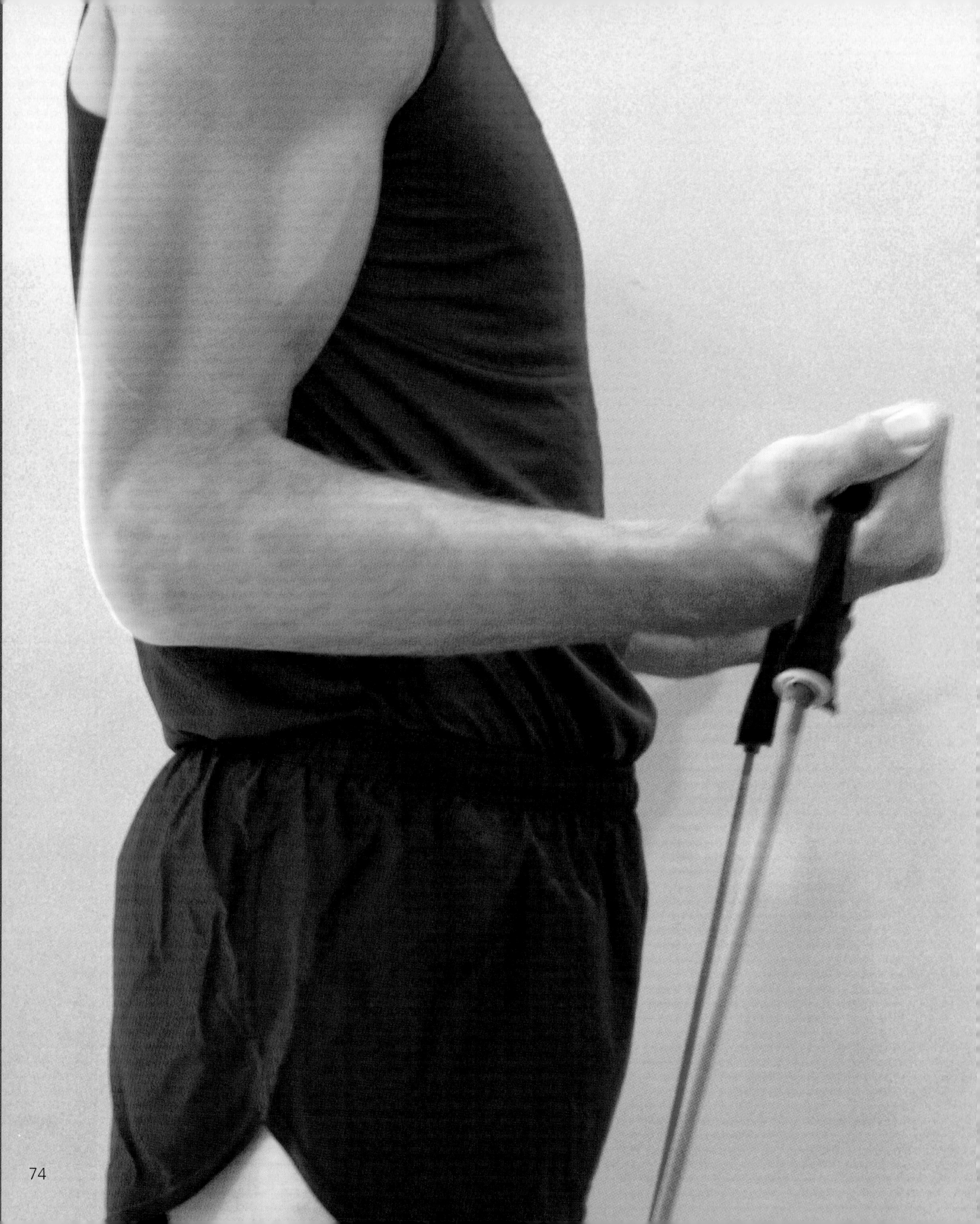

How do muscles work?

We have more than 430 muscles that we can control. Around 75 per cent of muscle is protein, 20 per cent water and 5 per cent inorganic salts and other elements, while the rest is water. Muscles pull and push on our bones through tendons to create movement. Each muscle contains thousands of fibres. Their force is generated via a contraction that acts along the long axis of the fibre. To contract them, an electrical impulse progresses from our brain, through the spinal cord to our muscles stimulating them to contract. A chemical reaction then occurs within them to produce sustained muscular energy.

The majority of resistance training energy is produced via the short-term anaerobic energy system. The only significant resistance-based exception to this is circuit training (see page 108) when your heart and lungs will also have to provide a plentiful supply of energy aerobically, and anaerobically, to sustain exercise.

Slow-twitch muscle fibre

Slow-twitch (or Type 1) muscle fibre has a high aerobic energy capability. When resistance training, it is used to move weights of less than 60 per cent of your 1RM (see pages 76–77). Developing these fibres does not significantly increase the size of your muscles.

Fast-twitch muscle fibre

Fast-twitch (or Type 2) muscle fibre possesses a two to three times greater speed of contraction capacity than its slow-twitch counterpart. In order to fully recruit these fibres you need to weight train above 60 per cent of your 1RM (see overleaf).

This fibre type is sub-divided into Type 2a and Type 2b. Type 2b fibres are the high-power fibres; the turbo chargers in your muscles that are activated to provide a great power boost. Type 2a fibres have a relatively fast contraction speed and can take on the characteristics of Type 1 or Type 2b fibres, depending on the right training.

Strength and power weight training programmes and plyometrics (jumping-type exercises) all increase their short-term power and speed capability, while strength endurance resistance training and CV training will increase their endurance capability.

Training your fast-twitch fibres through resistance training is much more likely to result in an increase in muscle size.

Muscle fibre

Not all our muscle fibres are the same. They are designed to carry out different energy-releasing functions. Some are ready for powerful explosive movements, like sprinting and weight training (fast-twitch muscle fibre), while others are suited to longer-duration activities, like rowing, walking and running (slow-twitch muscle fibre). Contrary to popular belief, these fibre types are fairly evenly distributed throughout the body at birth. People are not born fast or slow. Rather, it is the way you train that determines how your muscles will respond.

Key weight training terms

It's unfortunate, but fitness books can look a bit like an algebra text when it comes to weight-training programmes. If you want to get your weight training sums right there's no other way round it – you'll have to learn the equations.

Making sense of repetitions and sets

Study the following example for the bench press, a common upper-body weight-training exercise (you'll find the majority of weight training routines expressed in this way in this book).

Bench press 3 × 10 @ 60% 1RM

Sets (S) refers to the number of times you perform the exercise in one attempt. In this example you are being asked to complete three sets. You should take a rest, normally one to two minutes, after each set.

Repetitions (R) refers to the number of times you lift a weight or perform a body weight exercise in one set. In the example, you are being asked to perform 10 repetitions, three times.

1 rep maximum (1RM) refers to the maximum amount of weight you could lift only once, on one exercise, for example the bench press. Knowing a real or estimated 1RM is very useful for developing different types of strength (see page 82) and systematically progressing your training.

Percentage of one rep maximum (% 1RM) refers to the amount of weight you can lift expressed as a percentage of your 1RM. Thus, if your best bench press was 100 kg, 75 per cent of your 1RM would be 75 kg, 40 per cent, 40 kg, and so on.

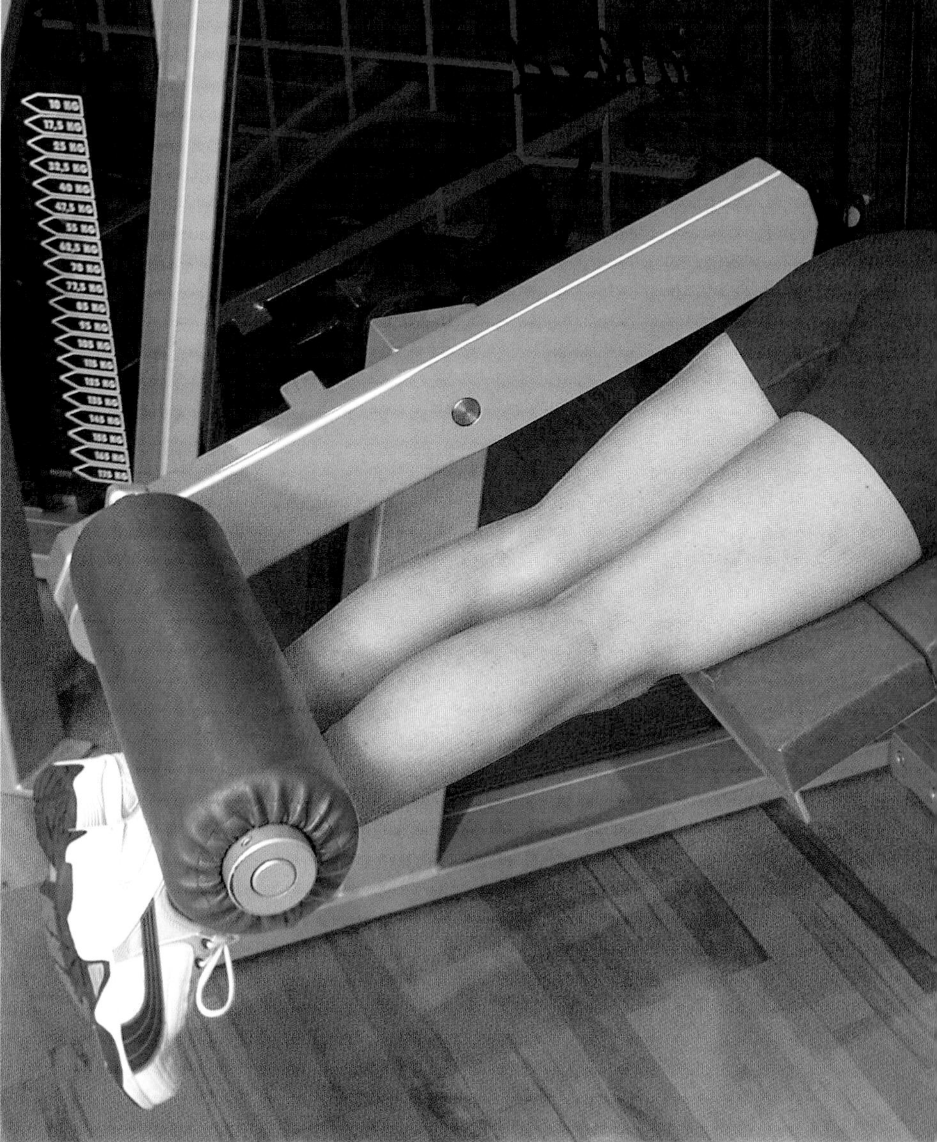

What to lift: what's a heavy, medium and light weight

The following guidelines will give you a good idea of what is a heavy, medium and light weight. These terms are also used to reference weights workouts that appear later in this chapter.

- Light weight (LW) – less than 65 per cent 1RM; this approximates to a weight you could lift 10–15 times before fatigue sets in.
- Medium weight (MW) – 65–75 per cent 1RM; approximates to a weight you could lift 7–10 times before fatigue sets in.
- Medium heavy/heavy weight (MH/HW) – 75–85 per cent 1RM; approximates to a weight you could lift 5–7 times before fatigues sets in.
- Heavy weight (HW) – 85–100 per cent 1RM; approximates to a weight you could lift less than five times.

Note that these are approximations – the number of repetitions you are able to perform will be governed by your current level of strength and fitness.

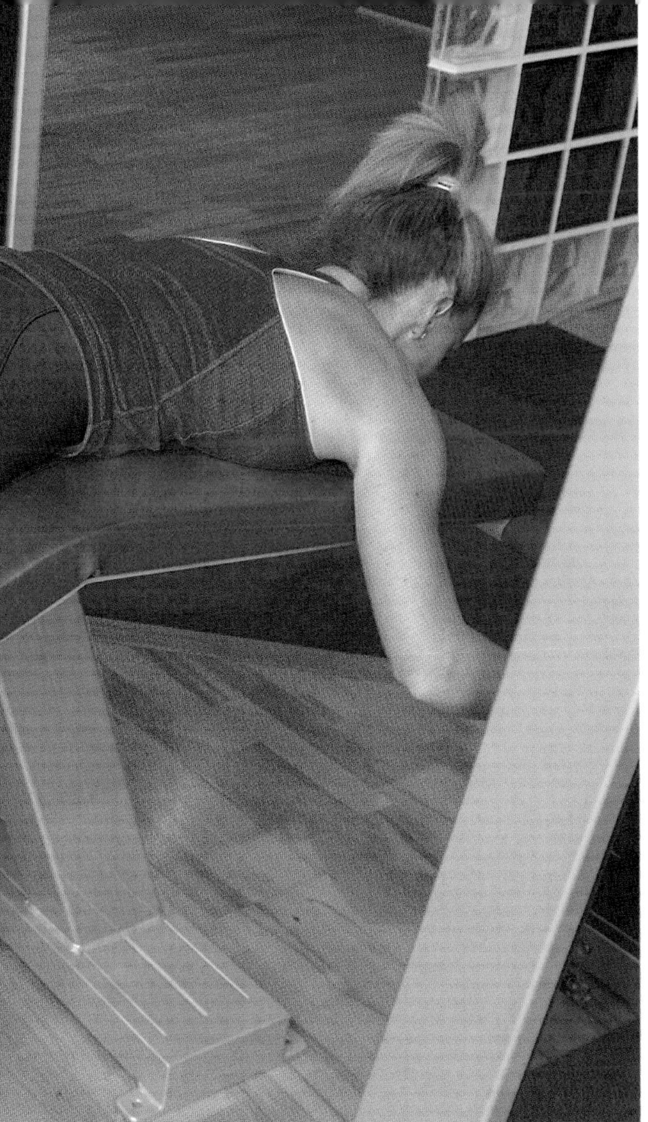

How to calculate your one repetition maximum (1RM)

Those new to exercise should not attempt to discover their 1RM by loading as much weight on to a bar (or machine) in an attempt to discover how much they can lift. Rather, there are much safer methods that you can use, based on calculations made from completing a set of much lower intensity repetitions.

Select a light weight and begin to lift it in a continuous, controlled fashion. You will reach a point when you are unable to complete any further repetitions with good technique. When this point is reached, record the number of lifts and use the figures provided in Table 5.1 to calculate the estimated percentage of 1RM you have been working at.

You'll have to use a bit of trial and error at first to select your 'repping' weight; underestimate what you think you can lift and aim for 12–15 reps.

Table 5.1

Calculating your 1RM

%1RM	MAX REPETITIONS
100	1
95	2
93	3
90	4
87	5
85	6
83	7
80	8
77	9
75	10
70	11
67	12
65	15

Knowing your 1RM will enable you to construct the most effective weight training programme for you.

TRAINING TIP

Lifting heavy weights is no better than lifting lighter ones – each intensity will bring about significant but different muscular adaptation.

MUSCULAR ACTION AND STRENGTH DEVELOPMENT

TRAINING TIP
Varying the type of muscular action you use in your workouts is a great way to maintain variation and muscular adaptation.

Isotonic muscular action

Isotonic muscular action involves movement and incorporates 'concentric' and 'eccentric' actions. Curling and lowering a dumbbell when performing a biceps curl and running are examples of isotonic muscular actions.

Concentric muscular action

A concentric action involves the shortening of a muscle as it contracts to create movement. It's the most common direction of effort for resistance and CV exercise. During a biceps curl the biceps contracts concentrically to raise the bar.

Eccentric muscular action

An eccentric muscular action involves the lengthening of a muscle to create movement. During a biceps curl the biceps extends eccentrically to lower the bar.

Understanding the way your muscles work will significantly assist the way you approach your resistance training. It will provide you with different ways to train and increase your potential to achieve the fitness results you desire.

Isometric muscular action

During an isometric exercise no movement occurs. This is the result of opposing muscle groups working against each other, such as the biceps and triceps, or the muscles of the front and rear of the upper arms. Clasping your hands in front of your chest and pressing them together is an example of an isometric contraction. This type of training is not widely practised, as it is difficult to measure its overall effect on muscle strength. However, it is involved in some way in nearly all everyday and fitness activities; these are focused largely around the trunk, when the muscles to the front and rear (abdominal and back muscles) work with each other to hold us upright, when walking, running, standing or sitting, or in a prone position (as when performing a press-up).

TRAINING TIP

If you are unlucky enough to sustain an injury that prevents you from using one of your limbs for a while, you can maintain a high proportion of its strength by performing resistance training exercises on the non-injured side. This is a neuromuscular response and not a muscular one.

Mental and physical effort: the neuromuscular system

The amount of weight you can lift (or the effectiveness of any movement – sports, fitness or everyday) is not only determined by your strength but also by your neuromuscular system. This is a highly complicated element of your body's operation. Your brain is at the hub of the system; it sends out electrical signals all around your body to invoke an appropriate response. This can be involuntary (i.e. automatic without conscious effort) as in the case of the continued beating of your heart), or voluntary (i.e. conscious) when moving limbs and your trunk to resistance train.

TRAINING TIP

This is a training tip for *intermediate / advanced* trainers. You can specifically train your muscles eccentrically, by concentrating on the lowering or return phase of an exercise. How? Either lift the weight into position yourself, set up a Smith machine accordingly (see page 103) or get a partner to do so. Then lower to a five-second count. Training eccentrically is a great way for intermediate or advanced trainers to push through periods of training stagnation and restimulate muscular adaptation.

MUSCULAR ACTION AND STRENGTH DEVELOPMENT
continued

Isokinetic muscular action

Isokinetic muscular action involves moving a pre-set resistance (concentrically or eccentrically) over a full or part range of movement. Isokinetic resistance training machines exist in some gyms, although the majority of fixed-weight installations are isotonic. Isokinetic machines are often used for injury rehabilitation purposes.

You can perform your own type of isokinetic exercise by slowing down the eccentric and/or concentric part of an exercise in an attempt to keep the force being generated more constant.

Isokinetic machines often use hydraulics to produce a constant resistance

Keep your muscles and your brain on their toes

Resistance training develops the nervous system as well as the muscles. In fact, it's estimated that as much as 20 per cent of the 'strength' required to a perform a common weight training move like the bench press results from nervous activity. In time, an exercise becomes so 'patterned' into your brain (and consequently your muscles) that less effort is required to complete it. This switching on to automatic pilot is great for sports skill development, but not so good for resistance training, when after a while strength improvements will slow and even come to a halt as our neuromuscular system puts in less effort to do the job. This is why, as I stress many times throughout this book, you must constantly change and progress your training.

TRAINING TIP

Muscle does not turn to fat when you stop training. Rather, the gradual return to pre-training levels of strength and muscle mass, and the associated reduction in energy expenditure, increase the likelihood of fat gain – we achieve a negative energy balance (see page 152). Simply put, we eat too much and don't exercise enough.

Plyometric muscular action

Plyometric exercises are very dynamic. Hopping and rebound jumps are typical examples – they are used by sports performers who want to increase speed, power, agility and strength (see Chapter 11).

Plyometric exercises work on the principle that a concentric muscular contraction is much stronger if it immediately follows an eccentric contraction of the same muscle. It's a bit like stretching out a coiled spring to its fullest extent and then letting it go: immense levels of energy will be released in a split second as the spring recoils. Plyometric exercises develop this recoil or, more technically, the stretch/reflex capacity in a muscle.

Personal reflections

Don't overdo it! Be warned. This applies to any training method you use for the first time. I remember my first significant contact with plyometrics. I was 22 and was asked by my athletics coach to perform some bunny (two-footed) jumps. All went well until after the workout my legs seized up. It seemed as if I had lost all strength in them. It was so bad that when I got home I was unable to climb the stairs. I had to sit backwards on them and use my arms to push myself to the top! The next day I had the worst case of muscle soreness I have ever had. Everything was back to normal in about a week, but I learned a valuable lesson: always underestimate what you think you can do when performing any exercise, not just a plyometric one, for the first time.

TRAINING TIP

Change the emphasis of your resistance workouts every 6–12 weeks to maintain physical and mental stimulation. Once you can achieve your repetitions and sets at a given weight comfortably, it's time to move on and to change the weight you lift, or the weight system you are using (see page 86).

Glycogen: muscle fuel

Glycogen is premium-grade muscle fuel. It is stored in our muscles and liver. We can only hold on to it in limited amounts (375–475 g). It needs to be continuously replenished by consuming sufficient carbohydrate (see page 176).

Developing different types of strength

There are three main types of strength that can be developed through weight training: maximum strength, endurance/toning and shaping strength, and power strength. Each is determined by the percentage of 1RM that you work out at and the number of repetitions completed.

Maximum strength weight training

Targets: fast-twitch muscle fibre, and has a potentially significant effect on increasing muscle size.

If you are after an increase in your absolute strength and muscle size then using low repetitions (one to six) with heavy weights (85 per cent plus of 1RM) is the way to go. You should employ anywhere between one and eight sets, depending on the number of repetitions. Recovery must be high (two to five minutes between sets) to maintain quality and intensity. Training for maximum strength is very draining. Correct technique, as for all weight training, is a must.

Sample workouts

1. 4 × 5 @ 80 per cent 1RM
2. 3 × 6 @ 75 per cent 1RM
3. 8 × 1 @ 95 per cent 1RM

Number of exercises: four to six for all examples.

> **TRAINING TIP**
> **You should work out with a training partner when doing maximum strength weight training. It's their job to 'spot' for you (i.e. assist you to return the bar back to its starting position), if you cannot complete your repetitions. Their presence and 'words of encouragement' will also motivate.**

Strength endurance, toning and shaping weight training

Targets: slow-twitch muscle fibre; has little effect on increasing muscle size, but shapes and tones.

Weight training develops strength endurance and has a toning and shaping effect when high numbers of repetitions (15–30) are combined with light weights (30–60 per cent of 1RM).

Keep your recovery to a minimum for strength endurance purposes, as you are seeking to develop the ability of your muscles to sustain repeated contractions under conditions of fatigue. For toning purposes, longer recoveries can be taken. Make sure you perform the exercises rhythmically and with control.

Sample workouts

1. Toning: 2 × 15 @ 40 per cent of 1RM (number of exercises: 6–12, exercises for all body parts); recovery: 60–90 seconds between sets
2. Strength endurance: 5 × 20 @ 35 per cent 1RM (number of exercises: 6–15, exercises for all body parts); recovery: 30 seconds or less between sets

> **TRAINING TIP**
> **Strength endurance weight training provides a great foundation for subsequent power and strength weight training in a training plan.**

Power weight training

Targets: fast-twitch muscle fibre, and has a potentially significant effect on increasing muscle size.

Power weight training is as intense as maximum strength weight training. To develop it you need to work out with weights set between 65 and 85 per cent of your IRM while performing three to eight repetitions. Power weight training differs from strength weight training in that it requires dynamic, but controlled, lifting. As with maximum strength weight training you'll need similar long recoveries to allow you to put in maximum effort.

Sample workouts

1. 3 × 8 @ 70 per cent IRM (number of exercises: six)
2. 4 × 4 @ 80 per cent IRM (number of exercises: four)

> **TRAINING TIP**
> **Power weight training will develop a foundation of specific strength for those involved in power sports such as football, tennis and sprinting (see Chapter 11)**

Moving weights quickly but with control will develop power

WEIGHT TRAINING SAFETY

Follow these tips to weight train safely.

Fixed-weight machines

1. You may find that some fixed-weight machines are not ideally suited to your body type, particularly if you are either very tall or quite short. In these cases you should make a decision as to whether using that particular machine will compromise correct exercise technique sufficiently to put you at risk of injury. If you are unsure, speak to a gym instructor or personal trainer. Invariably there will be an alternative exercise that you can do that will work the same muscle group in a similar way.
2. Watch your fingers! Don't put them anywhere near the weight stacks, pulleys or cables.
3. Don't bang the weights together in the stack. Control the weights when lifting and lowering.

Free weights

1. Always make sure that the collars are securely fastened on to the bar or dumbbells.
2. Always use a squat rack or Smith machine when lifting medium and heavy weights on to or from your shoulders.
3. Weight training gloves can be worn if you want to protect your hands, although you'll get a better grip without them.
4. Weight training belts are not a necessity. If you lift technically correctly and develop good core stability they should not be required.
5. Make sure there is plenty of space around you when lifting.
6. Don't lift heavy weights outside of a Smith machine without a training partner, coach or fitness professional in attendance. If you get into trouble you'll need someone on hand to take the bar.

RESISTANCE TRAINING SYSTEMS

There are many ways to combine reps, sets and %1RMs into a weights routine to create a weight training system. In the examples provided in the text so far, all the sample workouts use the 'simple set' system. You'll most probably be set this type of workout when given your first weight training programme by your gym instructor or personal trainer at your gym. Despite its name, though, it's a very effective method of training.

Descriptions of other systems are provided below, together with information about their suitability for those of you with different fitness experience. Reference is also made to the type of strength that the examples provided develop.

Note that the type of strength developed in our examples is not exclusive to that particular system: variation in %1RM, set and repetition numbers will vary the output of the workouts and therefore the type of strength developed. To simplify, the pyramid system can develop strength, strength endurance, power and maximum strength, depending on how it is designed.

> **TRAINING TIP**
> **If you vary the repetitions, sets and %1RM at which you work out using the knowledge provided here, you'll be able to construct a multitude of different strength outcomes from the weight training systems available to you.**

Pyramid system

Suitable for intermediate and advanced trainers.

Session example

- 1 × 8 @ 70 per cent 1RM
- 3 × 4 @ 80 per cent 1RM
- 2 × 2 @ 90 per cent 1RM

Type of strength developed in the example: maximum strength and power.

The pyramid system requires you to perform increasing or decreasing sets of repetitions, with an increasing or decreasing weight. In the example, long recovery periods (two to three minutes) should be taken between sets to allow for quality lifting.

Super-set system

Suitable for intermediate and advanced trainers.

Session example

- 10 @ 60 per cent 1RM on biceps curl + 10 @ 60 per cent 1RM on triceps push-down × 3 sets

Type of strength developed: various (note that this system does not readily lend itself to maximum strength or power strength development, as quality will be compromised by the way it recruits muscle fibre; it can, however, promote increased size, particularly with heavier weights).

Re-read the session example above closely and you'll see that the super-set system combines two different exercises in the same set. This provides an intense level of muscular stimulation.

There are different types of super-set, but the most common involves combining two exercises that work opposing muscle groups, like the biceps and triceps (as in the example) or quadriceps and hamstrings. No rest is taken between each exercise, but you should rest for two minutes between each super-set; the heavier the weight the longer the recovery should be, and vice versa.

Matrix system

Suitable for intermediate and advanced trainers.

Session example

Using the leg extension as an example, repetitions are as follows:

- from start position to halfway up @ 70 per cent 1RM
- from halfway up to full leg extension @ 70 per cent 1RM
- full-range leg extensions @ 70 per cent 1RM

This example will contribute to the development of maximum strength and strength endurance – it's a tough workout.

The matrix system is designed to stress a muscle intensely over different ranges of movement and, as described, requires the performance of full-range, half-range, and eccentric and concentric repetitions.

Some fixed-weight machines and Smith machines can be set up to achieve these specific ranges of movement, but if this is not possible you'll have to move the weights into position yourself by raising or lowering the fixed or free weights into the appropriate position. You could, of course, get a training partner to help you.

Complex training system

Suitable for intermediate and advanced trainers (and those involved in power sports).

Session example

- 10 × jump squats (body weight) + 10 x @ 70 per cent 1RM squats × 3 sets

Type of strength developed: power.

Complex training is based on the principle that a weight training exercise, when combined with a plyometric one in the same set, will increase the ability of our fast-twitch muscle fibres to generate power. It's a great sports training system.

You should take two to three minutes' recovery between each set of paired exercises, and 30 seconds between each exercise. Select exercises that work the same muscle groups.

Weights and resistance training exercises

In this section, you'll find detailed descriptions of some of the most effective weights and body weight exercises. Each exercise has a detailed technique guide, which identifies the main muscles the exercise works (written in normal type) and those on which it has a secondary effect (in italics).

Breathing and resistance training

Take a breath prior to lifting, and exhale while lowering yourself or the weight. For isometric and plyometric exercises, continue to breathe as normally as possible.

Muscular soreness and resistance training

It's almost inevitable that you will suffer some residual muscle soreness when resistance training, especially when you perform an exercise or system for the first time (witness my own experience, as described in the 'Personal reflections' box on page 81).

This soreness, properly known as DOMS (delayed onset of muscle soreness), occurs through structural damage to our muscles, caused by training. The symptoms of DOMS are loss of strength, and decreased range of motion and neuromuscular function. DOMS is usually at its worst 24–72 hours after the completion of the activity that caused it. Gentle CV exercise, stretching, massage, ice, hot baths and supplementing with vitamin E can all reduce DOMS. The other good news is that the one bout of exercise that caused the soreness in the first place can 'inoculate' against further soreness for a period of up to six weeks.

Certain types of muscular action can generate more soreness than others – notably eccentric and plyometric training.

Exercises for the chest and arms

LAT PULL-DOWN

sides of upper back (latisimus dorsi), chest, *biceps*
(All levels)

Starting position

Adjust the machine's pads so that they secure you comfortably into its seat. Stand up again, and take a wide over-grasp (wrists on top of the bar) grip. Sit back down. Keep your back in a neutral position (see page 90) and lean slightly backwards to a 20–30-degree angle.

Action

Pull the bar in to a point just above mid-chest level and control it on its return.

Points to note

The lat pull-down is a great move for anyone looking to increase the width and strength of their upper torso.

> **TRAINING TIP**
> **Maintaining a smooth pull on the bar during both the concentric and eccentric phases, together with the declined back position will ensure that your latissimus muscles are worked evenly over their full range of movement.**

BENCH (CHEST) PRESS

chest, *triceps, shoulders*
(Fixed-weight machines all levels; free weights intermediate and advanced)

Starting position

Lie flat on your back on the bench, knees bent and your feet on the floor.
Fixed weights – take hold of the machine's grips. Free weights – take an even grip on the bar, remove it from its rack and lower it to a position a couple of centimetres from your chest. For both versions, the bar or machine's grips should be positioned over your mid-chest.

Action

Free and fixed weights – extend your arms upwards until they are nearly locked, then lower the weight with control to the starting position. Raise and lower the bar in a straight line over your chest.

Points to note

Fixed weights – don't bounce the weights in the weight stack; this reduces the effectiveness of the exercise.
Free weights – don't let the bar rest across your chest during the lowering phase (this is very dangerous as it could restrict your breathing), and don't bounce the bar off your sternum, which is equally dangerous and could also lead to injury.

Free weights are the advanced resistance training option because they require balance as well as strength to press or lift a weight – they use more of your smaller stabilising muscles in consequence.

TRAINING TIP
Don't flatten your back when performing bench presses or other weight-training exercises that support your back on a bench. Maintain neutral spine position.

Back safety and neutral spine position

With every exercise option, not just weight training, there is a potential injury risk to the back. This can be minimised if you make sure you perform each exercise technically correctly and don't try to progress your training too quickly. You should also focus on keeping your back in neutral spine position while weight training. Neutral spine position will optimally distribute the forces that your back is subject to.

How to attain neutral spine position

Stand with your heels touching, or nearly touching, a wall so that your bottom and shoulders brush against it lightly. Keep this posture in mind and adhere to it when weight training. You should even apply it to your everyday activities in order to preserve good posture.

TRAINING TIP

Working out with dumbbells is a great way to develop a symmetrical body shape.

DUMBBELL FLYES

chest, *front of shoulders*
(Intermediate/advanced levels)

Starting position

On a flat bench, hold a dumbbell in each hand, palms facing inwards. Lie back on the bench, extending your arms upwards until your hands are in line with your shoulders. Keep your feet flat on the floor and your head back on the bench.

Action

Take both arms out and away from your chest in an opening movement. When the dumbbells reach a position parallel to the floor, return them to the start position using a closing movement.

Points to note

If you are unable to put your feet on the ground, try placing a gymnastic mat under them to attain the best starting position.

TRAINING TIP

Concentrating on 'squeezing' your chest muscles together will focus your mind on maintaining good form.

PEC DEC

chest, *front of shoulders*

(All levels)

Starting position

Place the inside of your lower arms against the machine's pads and keep your upper arms parallel to the ground. Sit firmly back on the machine's seat while maintaining neutral spine position.

Action

Pull the pads across your chest in a closing movement to lift the weight, and then open them to lower the weight.

Points to note

Keep your chest open and control the return movement so that the machine's pads do not pass behind your shoulders, to prevent injury.

> **TRAINING TIP**
>
> **Many people hunch their shoulders forwards on the pec-dec machine in an attempt to impart additional impetus to the move. This dilutes the contribution the chest muscles make and should be avoided. Doing this also indicates that you are attempting to lift too heavy a weight.**

STANDING BICEPS CURLS

biceps

(All levels)

Starting position

Fixed weights – this exercise can be performed using the low pulley machine and a straight bar attachment.

Free weights – this exercise can be performed with a barbell or dumbbells. For all variations, you should use an undergrasp (palms under the bar) grip. Keep your hands shoulder width apart and let your arms hang down by your sides. If using a barbell or low pulley machine, allow the bar to touch the front of your thighs. Dumbbells should rest by your hips.

Action

Curl the weight towards your chest, making sure that you keep your elbows in and your arms close to your sides. Control the bar on its downward path. Maintain neutral spine position and don't lock out your knees or elbows.

Points to note

Don't swing the bar. This is a very common fault that reduces the effectiveness of the exercise.

TRAINING TIP

Imagine that your elbows are pinned to your sides. If using dumbbells you can turn your hands so that they (and the dumbbells) are parallel to your body to perform a 'hammer curl'; this places a different emphasis on the biceps muscle.

SEATED DUMBBELL SHOULDER PRESS

shoulders, *triceps, trunk*
(All levels)

Starting position

Grasp a dumbbell in each hand and sit on a weights bench, with your feet firmly on the floor. Adjust the backrest to a 10- to 20-degree incline. Lift the dumbbells up to shoulder level, so that they are approximately in line with your ears, and have your palms facing forwards. Maintain a neutral back position.

Action

Press the weights upwards and slightly in front of your head. As you finish the press, bring the dumbbells together. Don't straighten your arms out fully on extension, and ensure that you lower the weights under control.

Points to note

Performing the seated shoulder press takes away the contribution the legs could make to the move if you performed it standing up. All resistance training exercises develop core (abdominal and back strength) stability, some more than others. The seated shoulder press is very useful in this respect as you have to 'work through' your core to maintain stability on the bench.

> TRAINING TIP
> **Concentrate on keeping your hands in line with your shoulders throughout the move. Don't let them 'flop apart'.**

TRICEPS PUSH-DOWN

triceps
(All levels)

Starting position

Attach either the short straight bar or the triangular attachment to a high pulley machine and hold with both hands, knuckles on top. Keep your elbows in and forearms at right angles to the ground. Push the weights down so that your arms are in front of your thighs and your elbows almost fully extended.

Action

Raise the weights under control so that you attain a near 90-degree angle at the elbow joint; then push the bar back down to the starting position.

Points to note

Don't rock your body backwards or forwards to add momentum.

TRAINING TIP

As with the biceps curl, imagine that your elbows are pinned to your sides. If your gym has a triangular attachment then you should use this as it will help to keep your wrists in the right position throughout the exercise.

Abdominal and back exercises

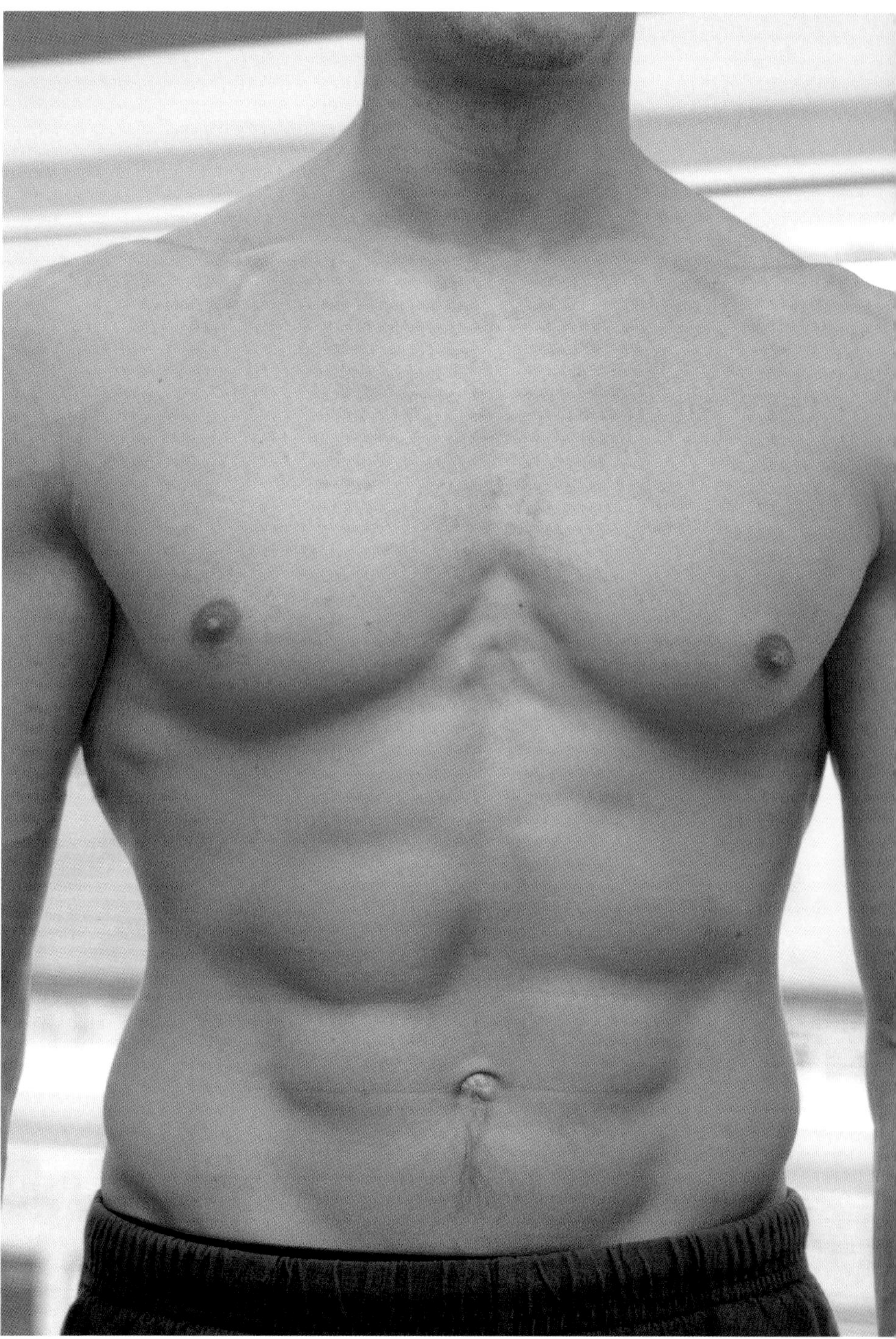

The six-pack

The six-pack washboard stomach is a very desirable, if elusive, body commodity to have. Many gym users fall into the trap of believing that performing hundreds of crunches (or other abdominal exercises) day in day out will do the job. It won't. Achieving chiselled abs relies on an all-encompassing approach that incorporates all aspects of the fitness lifestyle. You'll need to burn fat by performing CV work and to increase lean muscle mass using resistance training, otherwise your abs will be shrouded in a fatty overcoat. Additionally, you'll have to adhere to a healthy eating regime to make sure that your body burns fat optimally. All this must be underpinned by a workable and realistic training plan (see Chapter 6). If you don't do this, then that elusive six-pack will remain just that. Elusive.

TRAINING TIP

If you're after the ultimate abs then you must concentrate on correct abdominal exercise technique. It's far more effective to perform fewer repetitions with perfect form than hundreds with poor technique.

CRUNCH

abdominals

(All levels)

Starting position

Lie flat on your back and lift your feet off the floor – your upper thighs should form a right angle to the ground with your lower legs parallel to it. Place your hands by the side of your head, elbows back.

Action

Contract your abdominal muscles to bring your torso towards your knees.

Points to note

To avoid straining your neck, don't grab on to your head or behind your neck with your hands. Keep your elbows pointing out to the sides with your outstretched fingers in line with your earlobes. If you experience discomfort in your neck, incline it further forwards. Don't think that you have to lift your trunk a long way forwards to get the most from the exercise – contracting the abdominals to move the torso just a few centimetres from the floor is sufficient.

TRAINING TIP

If you are new to exercise you can cross your ankles in order to create greater stability and ease when performing the crunch (you can also place your lower legs on a chair of suitable height).

REVERSE CURL

abdominals

(All levels)

Starting position

Lie flat on the ground. Place your outstretched arms by your sides, palms facing down. Lift and 'fix' your legs at a 90-degree angle to the floor.

Action

Contract your abdominal muscles to achieve a couple of centimetres of daylight between the floor and your bum. Maintain control and lower.

Points to note

Although the large slab of muscle on the front of your torso (the rectus abdominus) is one muscle, the reverse curl can recruit more muscle fibre from the lower part.

> **TRAINING TIP**
> **Concentrate on performing the exercise with your abdominals – don't feel tempted to rock and push your hips into the air.**

SIT-UP WITH TWIST

abdominals, internal and external obliques
(All levels)

Starting position

Place your left foot flat on the floor with a 90-degree angle at the knee. Cross your right leg over your left – right ankle resting on the top of your left thigh just behind your knee. Place your hands by the side of your head as for the crunch.

Action

Bring your left elbow to your right knee by contracting your abdominals.

Points to note

This exercise will strengthen the outer muscles of your trunk, the obliques, as well as the rectus abdominus.

> **TRAINING TIP**
> **You should include exercises that target different abdominal muscles (and parts of them) to achieve optimum core stability. You'll find more abdominal exercises in the circuit training part of this chapter.**

Lower body exercises

DUMBBELL SPLIT SQUAT

front and rear of thighs (quadriceps, buttocks and hamstrings)
(All levels)

Starting position

Hold a dumbbell in each hand in line with your sides and step forwards with your right leg into a lunge position. Keep the heel of your right foot flat on the ground. Your left leg should be extended behind you with your weight supported on your toes. Keep your torso facing the front, head looking forwards and spine in neutral.

Action

Lower your body by bending your right knee to a 90-degree angle. Don't let the knee extend past your ankle, to avoid injuring the knee joint. Push back up to return to the starting position. Complete your repetitions, swap leg positions and repeat.

Points to note

The split squat can also be performed using a barbell supported on the shoulders or straddled between the legs – these are intermediate or advanced trainer options.

> TRAINING TIP
>
> **Concentrate on dropping your bottom down towards the ground to maintain good technique.**

LEG PRESS

quadriceps, buttocks and hamstrings
(All levels)

Starting position

Sit in the leg press machine's seat and place your feet evenly on the plate. To get into the correct starting position, adjust the seat so that you achieve a 90-degree angle at your knee joint. Look straight ahead and hold the machine's grips by your side.

Action

Push the plate away from you with your legs until your legs are virtually straight, then bring them back towards you under control.

Points to note

Don't lock your knees out on the push, to avoid damage to the joints.

> **TRAINING TIP**
>
> **Bringing the weights back slowly, while not allowing them to touch the others resting in the stack, will maintain muscular tension; this will increase the contribution the hamstrings and bum muscles make to the move.**

LEG EXTENSION

quadriceps
(All levels)

Starting position

Sit back in the leg extension machine's seat with your back in neutral position. You should adjust the backrest so that you are sitting upright or leaning slightly backwards. Next, adjust the foot pads so that they rest just above your ankles. Grasp the sides of the bench or the handles provided.

Action

Extend your lower legs upwards; don't lift them off the bench. Lower the weight under control.

Points to note

The leg extension is a great exercise for those who have had knee problems as it can strengthen the knee joint (always consult your GP or physiotherapist for exact advice).

> **TRAINING TIP**
>
> **If you are an intermediate or advanced trainer you could perform single leg repetitions. This will promote better-balanced strength and muscle development.**

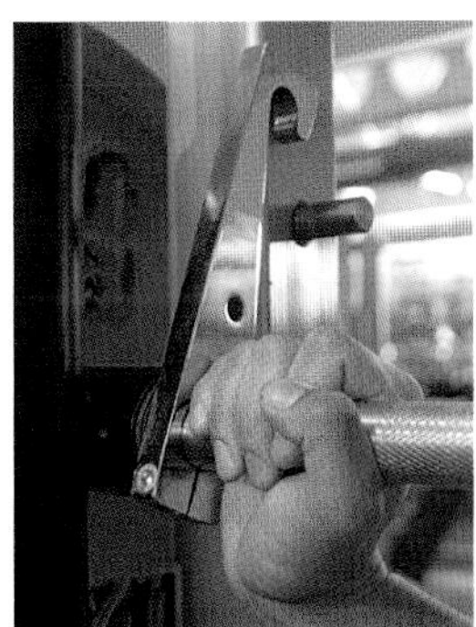

Rotating the bar with your wrists will secure it safely in the Smith machine.

SQUAT, WITH BARBELL AND SMITH MACHINE

quadriceps, buttocks, hamstrings, *calf muscles, core*
(Intermediate and advanced levels)

Starting position

Adjust the height of the bar in the Smith machine so that you can step under it and straighten comfortably to remove it from its rests – this is done by rotating the bar forwards with your wrists. The bar should rest across the fleshy part of your shoulders. Hold it with an equally spaced knuckles-on-top grip. Keep your back in neutral, feet shoulder width apart and heels firmly on the floor.

Action

Bend your knees to lower the bar and extend back up to complete one rep. See 'Training tip', below, for information on how deep to squat.

Points to note

A Smith machine provides a secure environment for the performance of a number of free weight exercises, like the squat, bench press and split squat, as at any point during the move you can place the bar back in to the machine.

TRAINING TIP

As you become stronger and more confident, you can gradually increase the depth of squat to a half-squat (thighs parallel to the ground) position. Squatting to a three-quarter squat position is a viable exercise in its own right, but will have less effect on your bum and hamstrings.

INNER AND OUTER THIGH EXERCISES

adductors and abductors
(All levels)

Starting position

Many gyms have similar-looking pieces of equipment specifically designed to exercise the muscles on the inside and outside of the thighs. For both inner- and outer-thigh exercises you should sit upright in the seat, holding on to the machine's grips.

Inner thigh

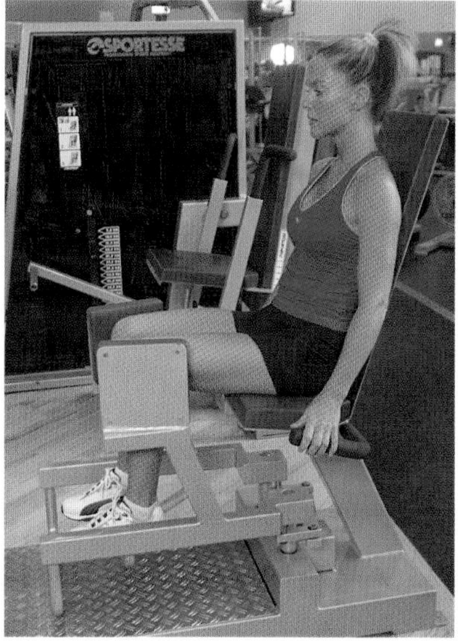

Outer thigh

Inner thigh

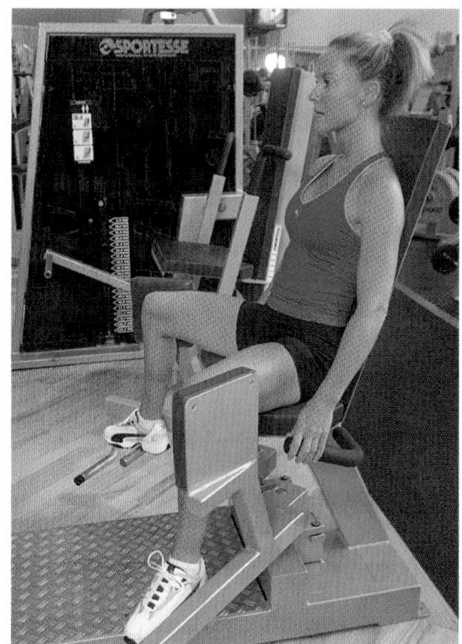

Outer thigh

Action

Inner thigh machine – draw your legs together.
Outer thigh machine – push your legs away from each other.

Points to note

Many women perform these exercises in the hope of reducing cellulite – unfortunately it's not physiologically possible to spot-reduce this unwanted fat by these exercises alone. To tone your thighs – or indeed any body part – you need to develop increased lean muscle through these and other weight-training exercises. You should also CV train to burn substantial numbers of calories, and adopt calorie control.

> **TRAINING TIP**
> **Don't rush the exercises, make sure that you control the movement of the machine. This will ensure that you really work your muscles and create the best conditions for strength gain.**

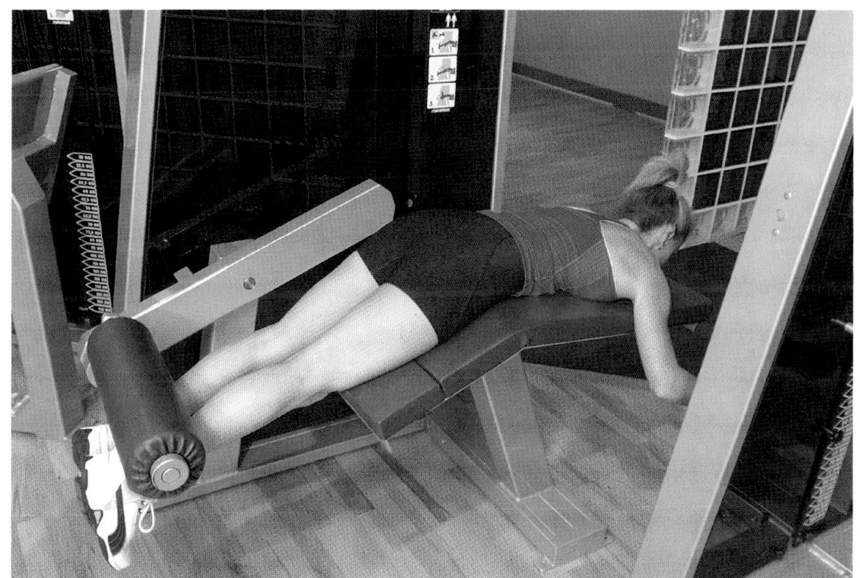

LEG CURL

hamstrings
(All levels)

Starting position

There are a couple of different types of machine that can be used to perform this exercise. For the first, lie face down on the machine. Hook your heels under its rolls – these should sit comfortably towards the lower end of your calf muscles. Hold on to the machine's grips. For the second (not shown), sit upright or slightly back in the machine's seat and place the back of your calf muscles, just above the ankles, over its rolls.

Action

If using the first type of machine, pull your heels back towards your bottom using a controlled smooth action. Just before they come into contact with it, stop the pull and then extend your heels away from your body to lower the weights. If using the second type of machine, pull your heels back towards the bench, then lift them under control to complete one repetition – don't lock out your knees.

Points to note

If using the first type of machine, keep your hips in contact with the bench (the decline in the bench on the machine in the picture is designed to do this). Leg curls are a great way to achieve shapely and defined legs. There's a tendency, as with all exercises, to concentrate on the muscles you can see – those at the front – rather than those that you can't, at the rear. The hamstring curl is therefore a great exercise for enhancing your rear view.

TRAINING TIP

Always start with a light weight as, like the inner and outer thigh muscles, the hamstrings are often relatively weak and will need time to develop a good level of strength. If you find your hips coming away from the bench, you are lifting too heavy a weight.

CALF RAISE
calf muscles
(All levels)

Starting position
Stand straight and step under the calf raise machine's pads so that they rest on your shoulders. Look straight ahead and keep your back in neutral. Rest your toes on the footplate and make sure they are lined up with one another and are hip width apart.

Action
Extend your ankles to lift the weight and lower them to return the weight.

Points to note
The standing calf raise machine places a greater emphasis on the gastrocnemius calf muscle as opposed to the soleus. This is the reverse of the seated calf raise that can be performed on another piece of fixed-weight equipment (not shown here). If you want well-defined calf muscles then you should incorporate both exercises into your training schedule.

> **TRAINING TIP**
> **Keep your ankles, knees and hips aligned to ensure correct technique and safe exercise performance.**

WEIGHT TRAINING PROGRAMMES

INDIVIDUAL WORKOUTS

You'll probably come across numerous weights workouts in other fitness books specifically designed for body parts like the legs, the abdominals or the shoulders. I have avoided this because it's unnecessary for everyday fitness. What you need is a balanced weight training programme that targets all parts of your body.

Progressing your weight training

Again, rather than go into great detail with specific workouts, I believe that it's much more advantageous to provide you with the information that will enable you to progress and develop your workouts for yourself. So, as in the CV chapter, I have provided an example that, although designed for someone new to exercise, is adaptable to those at all fitness levels. It displays how to develop a resistance training programme over a number of weeks (see Table 5.2).

More tips to get the most out of your weight training

Some weight training guidelines are as follows.

- Always warm up and cool down before and after your workouts.
- Select different exercises for each workout and leave at least a day's recovery between each.
- Take 1 to 2 minutes' recovery between sets and exercises.
- Remember that, to progress your weight training, you should experience some discomfort on the last couple of repetitions of your sets.
- Always lift with correct technique.
- Be prepared to adjust your training, up or down, with regard to how you feel on a particular day, but make sure you record all your workouts in your training diary.

TRAINING TIP

If you want to keep improving you must constantly change and cycle your resistance training workouts.

Table 5.2

A 21-week weight programme suitable for those new to exercise

WEEKS	TYPE OF WEIGHTS WORKOUT	COMMENTS
1–3	**Simple sets** 6–8 exercises for all body parts. 10–12 repetitions %1RM estimated @ 30 per cent 1RM ('a light weight') 2 sets Two sessions a week.	The first few weeks are all about attaining weight training familiarity. You'll have to experiment during your first couple of workouts to find the right weight. At the end of the third week, you should complete a 10-repetition test on your main exercises to estimate your subsequent %1RMs (see page 77).
4–6	**Simple sets** 6–8 exercises for all body parts. 10–12 repetitions estimated @ 50 per cent 1RM 2 sets Three sessions a week.	This is when you really begin to train. Re-test your maximums as above at the end of the sixth week.
7–9	**Simple Sets** 6–8 exercises for all body parts 10–12 repetitions estimated @ 40 per cent 1RM 3 sets Three sessions a week.	At the end of week nine you should re-test as above. Note that the weight lifted drops slightly as an additional set is added.
10–13	Sessions 1 and 3: **simple sets** 3 × 8 reps @ 60 per cent 1RM Session 2: **simple sets** 3 × 12 @ 40 per cent 1RM	Your weights are now heavier and are designed to develop more lean muscle and shape. Re-test as before at the end of week 13.
14–17	Session 1: **pyramid session** 8 @ 50 per cent 1RM 6 @ 60 per cent 1RM 2 × 4 @ 70 per cent 1RM Session 2: **simple sets** 3 × 8 reps @ 65 per cent 1RM Session 3: **pyramid session** 2 × 10 @ 60 per cent 2 × 6 @ 70 per cent	These workouts are designed to improve body composition rather than develop bulk. Re-test as before at the end of week 17.
18–21	Session 1: **pyramid session** 8 @ 60 per cent 2 × 6 per cent @ 70 per cent 1RM 2 × 4 @ 75 per cent 1RM Session 2: **simple sets** 4 × 12 @ 55 per cent 1RM Session 3: **pyramid session** 2 × 15 @ 40 per cent 1RM 2 x 6 @ 65 per cent 1RM	Following on from weeks 14–17, this period further channels your strength endurance and maximum strength gains through a combination of sessions that will continue to tone, shape and develop lean muscle.

PART 2: CIRCUIT TRAINING

Circuit training combines body-weight and weight-training exercises with a potentially large CV component. Unfortunately, some of us can have negative perceptions about it from our school days. I did. I remember when my PE teacher would 'force' my class to do 'circuits' as a punishment for bad behaviour. Many years later, I now appreciate that circuit training should not be regarded as a punishment and can actually be enjoyable. It's a highly effective all-encompassing way to get fit that can be done virtually anywhere – at home, on holiday or in the park.

A well-designed circuit will increase your CV ability, your strength, strength endurance, agility, fat-burning potential and, if so desired, your sports performance.

Circuit resistance training (CRT)

CRT is another great form of circuit training. It combines light weight-training exercises (@ 30 to 60 per cent of your 1RM), and body-weight moves. Because of the weights component it is more effective at increasing your lean muscle mass than a body-weight only circuit.

If you want to construct your own CRT workout, select 8–12 weights and/or body-weight exercises that cover all body parts. Aim for 10–20 repetitions of each; try to select an achievable target figure. Your number of sets will depend on your level of fitness, as will your recovery.

You can expect an increase in lean muscle mass of between 1 and 3.2 kg and a reduction in body fat of between 1 and 3 per cent as a result of regular CRT.

Different ways to circuit train: rotational and in-parallel circuit training

Although circuit training permutations are literally endless they can all be seen to derive from two basic circuit styles: 'rotational' and 'in parallel'. They are characterised by the way you progress from one exercise to the next.

Like weight training, circuit training uses repetitions and sets, as well as percentages of 1RM (where weight exercises are incorporated). Repetitions can be performed on either a time-on and time-off basis (e.g. 30 seconds on, 40 seconds off), or to a designated target number of repetitions. Each set of exercises is carried out at a 'station'.

Rest is perhaps the most important training variable when designing a circuit; allow too little and the circuit will grind to a painful premature halt, allow too much and your training gains will be limited. As with CV interval training, your rest periods can be active or passive. A passive recovery for a circuit would involve walking around for the designated recovery period between each station or at the end of each circuit, while an active one would involve performing some low-intensity CV work between each station or at the end of each circuit – this is more taxing, increases the CV aspect of the circuit and should only be used by intermediate and advanced trainers.

The number of circuits you perform will depend on your fitness and your training goals.

All the exercises contained in the circuit training examples that follow are described on pages 111–121.

TRAINING TIP

If you take part in a circuit training fitness class at your gym, bear in mind that all members will have different levels of ability. Don't think that you have to keep up with the fittest. Work comfortably and progress slowly – you will catch up as you take more classes.

ROTATIONAL-STYLE CIRCUIT TRAINING

Rotational circuit training requires you to move from one exercise station to the next, with or without a rest, until you complete all the exercises in the circuit.

Rotational circuit training example suitable for those new to exercise

Press-ups • Sit-ups • Squats •
Triceps dips • Star jumps • Crunches

- Number of repetitions: timed for 20 seconds at each station
- Number of sets: 2 (times round)
- Recovery: 30 seconds between each station
- Recovery at the end of each circuit: passive (two minutes' easy walking)

IN-PARALLEL CIRCUIT TRAINING

In-parallel circuit training requires you to perform all your sets of the same exercise, one set after the other, at the same station with very limited recovery, before moving on to the next station. This is the tougher circuit training option as it allows very little recovery time for muscles at each station.

In-parallel circuit training example suitable for intermediate and advanced trainers

	No. OF REPS	No. OF SETS	RECOVERY
Press-ups	10	4	10 seconds
Sit-ups	10	4	10 seconds
Squats	10	4	10 seconds
Triceps dips	10	4	10 seconds
Star jumps	10	4	10 seconds
Crunches	10	4	10 seconds
Calf raises	20	4	10 seconds

Recovery at the end of each circuit:
active (four minutes' cycling RPE 3–4)

FAT BURNING AND CIRCUIT TRAINING

All forms of circuit training are great fat burners as they consume large numbers of calories and can increase your metabolic rate through post-exercise calorie burning and increases in lean muscle mass.

LACTATE THRESHOLD AND CRT

Circuits are primarily designed to develop strength endurance. They target your slow-twitch muscle fibre. Lactate is a critical feature in your body's energy-creation process (see page 50). During a circuit training workout lactate levels will increase as your muscles fatigue. As specific circuit training fitness improves, your muscles (and heart) will improve their lactate-using function, providing you with more usable energy to perform more repetitions and circuits. This will increase your calorie-burning potential.

CRT WILL MAKE YOU STRONGER

CRT will increase strength, but not to the same extent as maximum strength or power weight training. Those new to exercise could expect a potential increase of 10–30 per cent in 1RMs after a 12-week period of regular CRT using weights set at 40 per cent of 1RM.

TRAINING TIP

If you are an intermediate or advanced trainer, have a heart rate monitor and are seeking a high level of CV fitness from your circuit training, you should aim to keep within 75–85 per cent of HRMax, or work to an RPE of 7–8 during your circuits. Those new to exercise should work to an RPE of 5–6 for at least six weeks, circuit training twice a week, before gradually increasing the intensity of their workouts.

TRAINING TIP

Although all circuits have a CV component, some deliberately attempt to emphasise this element and can significantly improve your CV fitness. These versions require you to run/cycle/step/row between stations and/or during the rest period at the end of each circuit. In a test, participants in a circuit that involved three minutes of aerobic activity followed by five weights exercises (@ 40–50 per cent of 1RM) performed five times (45 minutes of continuous effort) increased their VO2Max (a measure of aerobic power; see page 61) by 18 per cent. This compares favourably with the CV gains made from an aerobic only based training programme.

Body-weight circuit-training exercises

In this section you will find descriptions of some of the most popular circuit-training exercises.

THE PRESS-UP

chest, *triceps, shoulders, trunk*
(All levels)

Starting position

Assume a prone position – support your weight on your toes and through your hands, which should be placed shoulder width apart. Keep your torso braced and your head in alignment.

Action

Lower your torso to the floor and then extend your arms to push back up to complete one repetition.

Points to note

Keep your trunk braced. This will avoid poor technique and develop core stability.

> **TRAINING TIP**
>
> **Those new to resistance training can make the exercise easier by performing the move from a kneeling position (see picture). This is a great way to gain the necessary confidence and strength required to perform the full prone press-up. Place a mat under your knees for cushioning, lean forwards on to your hands and perform the exercise as described above.**

Body-weight circuit-training exercises

continued

SIT-UPS

abdominals

(All levels)

Starting position

Lie on the floor, legs bent to an approximately 90-degree angle, heels flat on the floor. Don't flatten your back, keep it in neutral. Place your hands by your ears and incline your neck forwards.

Action

Contract your abdominal muscles to lift your upper body from the floor. Lower under control and repeat.

Points to note

You will not develop more abdominal strength by lifting your body more than 12–15 cm off the ground.

> **TRAINING TIP**
>
> **Concentrate on maintaining a flat-footed contact with the ground at all times. This will isolate the abdominal muscles and prevent your hip flexors (the muscles at the top front of your thighs) from providing assistance. Perform each repetition to a four count.**

TRICEPS DIP

triceps, *rear shoulders*

(All levels)

Starting position

Sit on a bench or step. Place the palms of your hands on the bench behind you, either side of your bum, fingers facing forwards. Walk your feet about 50 cm away from the bench/step and position them so that they are parallel to each other and a couple of centimetres apart. Keep your knees at a 90-degree angle. Extend your arms to lift your body off the bench/step and maintain a neutral spine position as you look forwards.

Action

Lower your body to achieve a 90-degree angle at your elbow joints and then push back up.

Points to note

The triceps dip is a great move to incorporate into a home circuit as it can easily be performed on your stairs or using a strong chair.

TRAINING TIP

If you want to increase the size of your upper arms target the triceps – they're already a naturally bigger muscle than the biceps.

Body-weight circuit-training exercises

continued

STAR JUMPS

quadriceps, buttocks, hamstrings, calf muscles
(Intermediate/advanced levels)

The star jump is a plyometric exercise (see page 81). Plyometric exercises are often included in circuit training workouts as they can rapidly cause fatigue and elevate heart rate. Other examples include squat jumps, split jumps and tuck jumps.

Starting position

Stand with your feet just over shoulder width apart, while maintaining a neutral spine position. Look forwards and let your hands hang by your sides.

Action

Bend your knees and spring up into the air. In the air, open your arms and legs to form a star shape then bring them back together before you land.

Points to note

The star jump is great for developing leg power and will benefit most sports performers. However, like other plyometric exercises, it is best avoided if you have knee or lower back problems.

> **TRAINING TIP**
> **Land lightly on your feet and with a slight knee bend to absorb the impact. Looking straight ahead will help you to keep your back in the right position. Always wear well-cushioned trainers, and perform the exercise on a sprung floor or firm non-slip gym mat.**

ALTERNATE ELBOW-TO-KNEE SIT-UP ('CHINNIES')

abdominals and obliques

(All levels)

Starting position

Lie on your back and place your hands by your head, as for the sit-up (see page 112).

Action

Bring your right knee in towards your left shoulder, while curling up and twisting at the trunk. Then push the knee away to straighten the leg while simultaneously lowering your trunk. Repeat in reverse fashion and continue in this alternating way.

Points to note

Chinnies are a great way to develop specific running core strength, due to the exercise's single-leg and rotational aspects.

> **TRAINING TIP**
> **Perform the move slowly and with control to develop sound technique before increasing speed.**

Body-weight circuit-training exercises continued

SINGLE-LEG SQUATS

quadriceps, hamstrings and buttocks
(Intermediate/advanced levels)

Starting position

Stand on your right leg, foot flat on the floor. Maintain a slight bend at the knee joint. Bend the left leg, tucking your heel up towards your bum. Keep your chest up, head looking forwards and your arms by your sides (don't force your shoulders back). Balance.

You can also perform body-weight double-leg squats – use the same technique as described for the weight training version on page 103 (obviously omitting reference to the bar). Place your hands on your hips, or hold them straight by your sides. Body-weight squats are a great exercise for developing strength endurance and lower body tone.

Action

Lower your body 'through' your right leg to a three-quarter squat position. Maintain control and then push yourself back up. Complete your repetitions, swap legs and repeat.

Points to note

All single-limb exercises are more intense options than double-limb moves.

TRAINING TIP

Don't let the heel of the standing foot come off the ground. If you find it difficult to balance, support yourself against a wall or on the back of a suitable-height chair. As you gain in strength, gradually lower the depth of squat so that you can attain a 'thighs parallel to the floor' position when lowering.

Inner thigh

Outer thigh

INNER (ADDUCTORS) AND OUTER (ABDUCTORS) THIGH MOVE

(All levels)

Starting position

For both exercises you'll need to lie on your side on the floor. Support your head with your right hand and allow your left arm to fall across the front of your body in front of your hips to permit balance when exercising the inner right thigh and outer left thigh. Reverse the start position when you exercise the outer right thigh and inner left thigh.

Inner thigh move – additions to start position: lift the left leg and bring it in towards your body while placing the left foot flat on the floor over your right leg.

Inner thigh

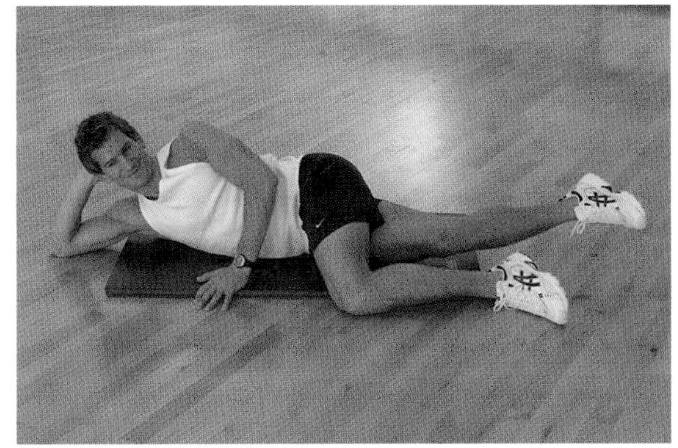

Outer thigh

Action

Inner thigh move – lift the right leg up and lower under control to work the muscles of the inner thigh. Keep the foot in an 'almost parallel to the floor' position.

Outer thigh move – to work the left leg, simply raise and lower it under control.

Points to note

You should perform these exercises slowly to really target the inner and outer thigh muscles. Resist the temptation to 'roll out', especially on the outer thigh move. For both exercises you should complete all your repetitions on one side before changing legs.

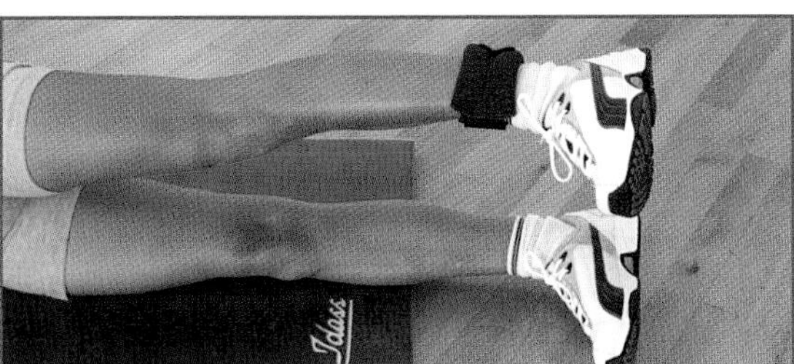

TRAINING TIP

Once you have become confident with the exercises you can increase the difficulty by using ankle weights.

Body-weight circuit-training exercises
continued

LUNGE WALK

quadriceps, buttocks and hamstrings
(All levels)

Starting position

Stand tall, with your spine in neutral and your head looking forwards.

Action

Step forwards on to your right foot into a lunge position. Then step forwards on to your left foot to achieve the same lunge position, but reversed. Progress in alternating lead-leg fashion to complete your repetitions. You can keep your arms on your hips throughout, or co-ordinate them with your leg movements, as illustrated.

Points to note

Try to move 'through' each lunge, rather than 'lift and step' into the next. Walking lunges are also great for hip flexibility.

> **TRAINING TIP**
> **Go for controlled, deliberate movements and pause each lunge for two seconds before moving on to the next to really target your hamstrings and bum muscles.**

STEP-UP DRIVES

quadriceps, calf muscles, *hip flexors*
(All levels)

Starting position

You'll need a low bench or step to perform this exercise. Stand up straight, about 75 cm from it.

Action

(Note that the exercise is completed in one smooth movement.) Step up on to the bench with your left foot. Extend up on to your toes while simultaneously driving the right thigh up, so that it reaches a position parallel to the ground. Keep your chest up, look straight ahead and co-ordinate your arms with your legs. To complete the repetition step back with the right foot and place it firmly on the ground before bringing the left leg back down to join it. Repeat with the right leg leading.

Points to note

Co-ordination and balance are required to perform this exercise. This enhances its strengthening ability.

> **TRAINING TIP**
> **Focus your gaze on a point straight ahead of you to assist your balance.**

Body-weight circuit-training exercises

continued

SINGLE-LEG CALF RAISE

calf muscles (in particular, the gastrocnemius)
(All levels)

Starting position

Stand tall, look straight ahead and maintain the natural arch in your back; balance on your left foot.

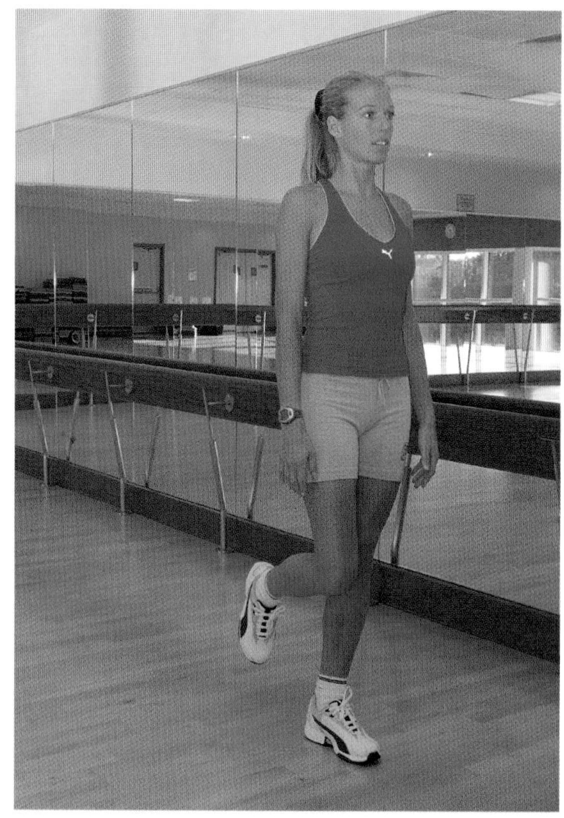

Action

Fully extend from your ankle to lift your body upwards, and then lower slowly to return your body to the start position. Perform all your repetitions on the left side before switching to the right foot.

Points to note

You may need to put an arm out against a wall to assist your balance until you become confident with the exercise.

> **TRAINING TIP**
>
> **Perform the exercise over the end of a low bench or step, to increase the range of movement. Those new to exercise should start with double-leg calf raises (see page 106 for a technique guide using the weight-training version).**

BRIDGE

abdominals, lower back, *shoulders, legs*
(Intermediate/advanced levels)

The bridge (sometimes called the plank) is an example of an isometric exercise; despite looking relatively simple it's actually a tough exercise that involves many muscle groups.

Starting position

Assume a prone position and support your trunk on your elbows. These should be placed under your shoulders with your hands a few centimetres apart, just in front of your head.

Action

Lift your body off the floor by straightening your legs. Keep it in alignment and brace your core muscles to hold the elevated position.

Points to note

As this is an advanced move, begin cautiously by holding the bridge for no more than a couple of seconds at a time, before increasing the time of the hold.

TRAINING TIP

Although you will feel the strain of the exercise the longer you hold the bridge, try to remain mentally relaxed.

Cross-training challenges and 'Ultra-FIT Magazine'

Cross-training involves combining different fitness methods or sports activities in a specific training session or training programme. Combining weights and CV work in a workout, or doing circuit training and playing tennis in a training plan, are all examples of cross-training.

Great reasons to cross-train

- Cross-training can prevent over-use injuries due to the varied nature of the training.
- Cross-training can reduce workout boredom.
- Cross-training can provide optimum fitness for health and fat-burning purposes – especially if you combine resistance training and CV work. You'll burn calories and strengthen your heart from the CV aspect and will increase your lean muscle mass, fat-burning potential, functional strength and muscle tone from the resistance part.

Cross-training challenges

It's because of these great reasons that *Ultra-FIT Magazine* has championed the cause of cross-training since it was first published over 14 years ago. The magazine runs numerous cross-training challenges in the UK, Europe and Australia. Our main event is the *Ultra-FIT X-Training Challenge* (XT-C), which has discovered various clubs', regions' and nations' fittest men and women. The XT-C has been described as a 'gym decathlon' as it combines 10 weight-training, body-weight and CV exercises into one gruelling challenge.

Potentially less intense but equally motivational is the *Ultra-FIT Club Sport Challenge*. This involves five exercises and has three event levels (gold, silver and bronze) and three age categories. It's designed so that *Ultra-FIT Magazine* readers and gym users can test, rate and improve their fitness against that of their peers.

PART 3:
OTHER RESISTANCE TRAINING OPTIONS

FIT BALLS

Don't just kick those oversize footballs that you might find scattered around your gym out of the way as they offer a great way to improve posture, core stability, flexibility and strength. In this section I'll show you how to get the best out of them.

How to select a fit ball

Ensure that:

1. it is burst-resistant to a minimum of 500 kg (static)
2. it is, preferably, made from PVC
3. it meets British or international standards
4. it has anti-burst properties
5. you purchase a product that comes with an exercise instruction booklet, video or CD
6. it is correct for your size (see Table 5.3).

Table 5.3

What size of fit ball do you need?

YOUR HEIGHT (cm)	BALL SIZE (cm)
152–168	55
168–188	65
188-plus	75

FIT BALL EXERCISES

Fit Ball Flexibility

TOP OF THE WORLD

stretches the whole body

Starting position/action

Sit on the ball in an upright position and walk your feet away from you so that the ball rolls under your back. Next, stretch your arms up over your head and balance by placing your hands on the floor behind you. Relax your neck and extend your toes. Hold for 20 seconds.

Fit balls are also a great home workout option.

ROLLING PIN

back, shoulders

(All levels)

Starting position/action

Kneel on the ground with the ball against your chest. Push it away from you, but retain contact with the top of it until your torso is parallel to the floor. Hold this position for 10 seconds and then roll the ball back towards you.

Repeat three times.

Fit ball body-strength exercises

Press-up (version 1)
chest, shoulders, *abdominals, back*
(All levels)

Starting position
Kneel facing the ball. Place your palms on the sides of the ball and keep your body in alignment, looking straight ahead of you. Fold your feet and lower legs behind you to tip forwards into the starting position.

Action
Lean into the ball, maintain a braced position and lower your chest towards it. When your chest almost makes contact with the ball, push back with your arms until they are nearly fully extended.

Points to note
Keeping relaxed will assist your ability to perform the move; additional tension will increase the instability of the ball.

TRAINING TIP
Place a firm non-slip gymnastic mat under your knees.

PRESS-UP (VERSION 2)

chest, shoulders, *abdominals, back*
(Intermediate/advanced levels)

Starting position

Assume a normal press-up position, but with your hands just under your shoulders on the outer mid- to top extremities of the ball. Squeeze the ball to stop it from moving.

Action

Lower your chest towards the ball and then press yourself back up.

Points to note

You will really have to work your arms and chest hard to stop the ball rolling away from you while you raise and lower your body.

TRAINING TIP

You can combine this exercise with the normal press-up (see page 111) and fit ball press-up version 1, opposite, to form a super-set (see page 87) that will really target your chest and shoulders. Perform 10 repetitions of each exercise and move straight on to the next. Complete three sets.

Fit ball body-strength exercises
continued

SQUAT
buttocks, hamstrings, quadriceps, *core*
(All levels)

Starting position
Place a fit ball between your lower back and a wall.

Action
Bend your thighs to a half-squat position and extend back up to complete one repetition.

Points to note
Imagine that a straight line is drawn from your knees to your ankles and don't allow your knees to extend in front of it.

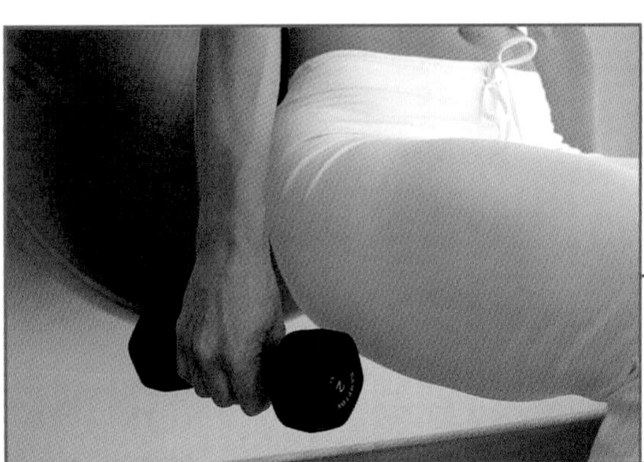

TRAINING TIP
Always be conscious of pushing the ball into the wall when you raise and lower your body. Once you have mastered the exercise you can increase its difficulty by adding dumbbells. These should be held at arm's length by your sides.

HAMSTRING ROLL

hamstrings, *back, pelvic stability*
(Intermediate/advanced levels)

Starting position

Lie on your back and place your heels on top of the ball. Keep your arms outstretched by your sides and your bottom on the floor.

Action

Push your heels into the ball to raise your bum a couple of centimetres from the floor; pull the ball towards you and then push it away. Lower your hips back down.

Points to note

The pushing and pulling of the ball towards and away from your body will require considerable active stabilisation work on the part of your pelvic and back muscles, which, if done regularly, will enhance your core stability.

TRAINING TIP

The degree of pelvic stability required can be increased by raising your forearms to an approximately 90-degree angle to the ground.

Fit ball body-strength exercises
continued

BENCH PRESS WITH WEIGHTED BALL
chest, shoulders, *triceps, buttocks, hamstrings*
(All levels)

Starting position
Support your upper back, neck and head on the fit ball. Make sure you are braced with your feet firmly on the floor. Have a partner pass you a medicine ball and grasp it with both hands, one on either side of it.

Action
Lower the medicine ball to your chest and then press it away, like a normal weight-based bench press.

Points to note
This exercise displays the full scope of what can be achieved with a fit ball. The starting position requires all-over strength, balance and co-ordination, while the press develops strength in the chest and shoulder muscles.

> **TRAINING TIP**
> **Brace your abdominals to maintain your stability on the ball.**

FIT BALL HYPER-EXTENSION

back

(All levels)

Starting position

Kneel down and lean forwards on to the fit ball. Raise both your arms, folded at the elbows, up and over your head and a little to the side. Keep your knees on the floor (put a gym mat down to act as a cushion) to support you during the move.

Action

Lift your back up and away from the ball, hold for two seconds and lower under control.

Points to note

The fit ball focuses the emphasis of the exercise on to your lower back, and minimises the contribution your bottom and hamstring muscles can make to the movement.

> **TRAINING TIP**
>
> **Do not over-extend your back when you lift from the ball, to avoid injury.**

Other resistance options

Before concluding this chapter I'll take a brief look at other types of resistance training equipment you might find at your gym. Many, like fit balls, can be the basis for great home workout ideas.

Resistance tubes

Resistance tubes are ideal for those who want to keep fit on the move, because they are so easy to transport. Different levels of resistance can be provided by different tube strengths; tube strength is usually signified by the colour of the tube or its grips. Many upper- and lower-body weight-training exercises can be replicated with them.

The shoulder press can be performed easily with a resistance tube

> **TRAINING TIP**
> **Unless you have a particularly strong resistance tube, it's best to perform high-repetition (15 plus), short-recovery (15–30 seconds between exercises) workouts with them. This will develop strength endurance and muscle tone. You should pay particular attention to the lowering phase when using a resistance tube, as due to their elasticised nature they can create a 'whip' effect, which can lead to a loss of control over the exercise.**

You can used weighted balls to perform or add resistance to numerous body-weight exercises.

Weighted balls

Weighted (or medicine) balls have become a bit unfashionable of late, but they are still a very useful training option. Modern balls are made with a rubber shell as opposed to the leather of the older type. They can be pressed and pulled to perform controlled exercises, or thrown to develop dynamic strength (intermediate/advanced exercisers only). They can also be used to add resistance to body-weight or fit ball moves. The walking lunge (see page 118), for instance, could be performed holding a weighted ball.

Other resistance options
continued

BOSU boards

BOSU boards are a recent addition to the resistance training world. BOSU is an acronym and (sort of) stands for 'both sides up'. This obviously means that you can perform exercises using either the flat or the curved side; three examples of BOSU moves are pictured. All types of upper, core and lower body exercises can be performed on this versatile piece of kit. As they require balance, BOSU boards are great for developing core stability. Contact your local gym to see if classes are available.

Prone side to side platform tilt

Prone balance

Double leg V sit balance

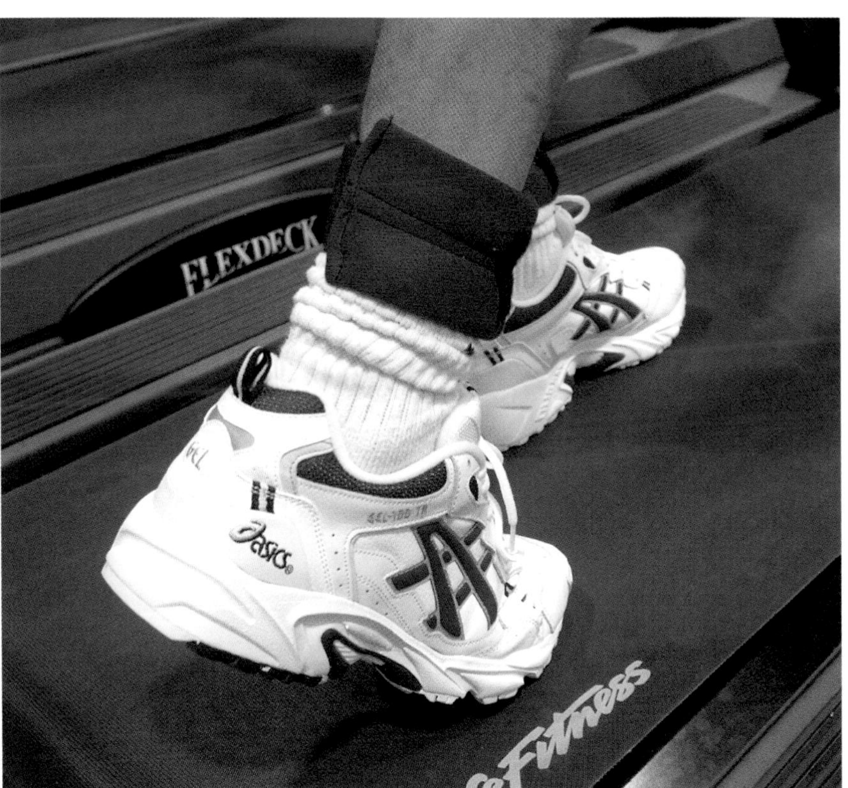

Adding ankle weights to your CV training can increase calorie expenditure.

Ankle and wrist weights

Ankle and wrist weights can increase the resistance offered by many body-weight exercises and, like resistance tubes, can be used to replicate many weight-training exercises. They can also increase the calorific expenditure and strength component of CV training: try power walking on a treadmill wearing wrist weights.

TRAINING TIP

Ankle and wrist weights should not be used if they interfere with correct CV exercise or sports technique.

USE IT OR LOSE IT? MAINTAINING THE STRENGTH GAINED FROM RESISTANCE TRAINING

As with CV training, it's easier to maintain your resistance training strength gains than attain them. Two sessions a week where you lift near to your 1RM can help you to hold on to a high portion of the strength you have developed. If you are a circuit trainer, then two hard circuits a week will serve a similar purpose. Note that although these sessions will maintain your fitness, they are unlikely to promote further gains.

6 Planning
your training

Many people go to the gym with no real idea of what workout they are going to do – perhaps they'll just use what equipment is available at the time. This non-planned approach can also extend itself to fitness classes where selection may be made solely on the basis of what class is starting at the time of arrival. Although a great deal better than not doing any fitness activity at all, this haphazard approach will not maximise your fitness, sport or fat-burning training. In this chapter I'll show you how to achieve the maximum by learning how to construct a relevant and systematic personal training plan. You'll gain vital information on how long it takes the body to significantly respond to training, how to avoid stagnation and boredom and the importance of rest and recovery for your fitness lifestyle. This chapter pulls together the information contained in the practical training chapters. It will allow you to optimise your training efforts and put you well on the way to becoming your own personal trainer.

ESTABLISHING A TRAINING PLAN

It's crucial that you realise that you will not continue to get fitter or burn more fat if you just keep following the same old training routines. If you don't develop the fitness or body shape you desire you will become disillusioned. But, by developing and following the right training plan, you will maximise the potential to achieve your goals.

Adaptation

Adaptation is the term used in the fitness and sports world to refer to the positive changes that occur to your body when it is consistently subject to regular training.

Personal trainers

Even though I want you to be able to take as much responsibility for your own training as possible, there is still a role to be played by a personal trainer (PT). This is obviously the case when you are new to exercise, when a PT will get you working out to a relevant and safe training plan within a very short period. However, as your fitness and fitness knowledge improve (or if you are at an intermediate or advanced level) then I see no real reason why you cannot take on an ever increasing responsibility for your workouts. At this stage, a PT can perform less of a hands-on and more of an advisory role. They could:

- help you plan and put together your training pyramid (see page 138)
- perform fitness tests
- look in on the occasional workout to motivate you and ensure that you are adhering to good technique and have not developed any bad habits.

See page 237 for information on choosing a personal trainer.

TRAINING TIP

Creating a training plan is in reality no different from following a recipe. All you need to do is select the right (fitness) ingredients for your training goal, and prepare and blend these together in the best possible way (via a training plan) to achieve optimum fitness results.

TRAINING TIP

You should always be prepared to change your training plan to take into account everyday factors that can be a negative influence, like stress and fatigue. At times like these you should not push yourself so hard or force yourself to train; instead you should wait for your energy levels to return to normal before recommencing your training. Training should be fun and not a further source of stress.

You will not continue to get fitter or burn more fat if you follow the same old training routines over and over again. Your body needs to be continuously stimulated with fresh workout ideas to continue gaining in fitness.

THE TRAINING PLAN VARIABLES: QUANTITY, QUALITY, DURATION AND REST

These variables – quantity, quality, duration and rest – are fundamental to constructing a progressive training plan. They will inform and shape your individual workouts and your overall plan. You need to constantly reference these variables to your short- and long-term goals and your fitness level to produce the best training plan for you.

Quantity

Quantity refers to the amount of training we do, either in a particular workout or as part of particular training phase. It can be measured by the number of kilometres covered for CV training, or total weight lifted, repetitions or sets completed for resistance training.

Quality

Quality usually reflects the intensity of a workout and may usually be judged as follows.

For CV training

The speed at which a steady-state CV effort or set of intervals during an interval training session are completed. A quality interval workout, for example, will allow for longer recoveries to permit the intervals to be performed at a high intensity, with little drop-off in speed caused by fatigue.

For weight training

The amount of rest we allow ourselves between repetitions and sets. The longer the recovery, the better the quality (intensity), as this will enable us to lift as strongly and dynamically as possible without experiencing fatigue.

Duration

Duration primarily applies to CV training (although it could be applied to a circuit training session). It refers to the length of a workout or particular aspect of it (such as an interval) and is inextricably linked to quantity and quality. Duration is measured in hours, minutes and seconds. Longer-duration workouts tend to have less of a quality aspect than shorter-duration ones. However, this need not always be the case: if you were preparing to run a marathon, you might perform 'quality 20-mile runs' in your training – these long-duration efforts (well in excess of two hours, depending on your ability) would be performed at a high-quality pace as part of your specific marathon preparation.

Note that duration can also apply to the length of a training phase (see the training pyramid on page 139).

Frequency

Frequency refers to the number of times we train over a week, month or other designated time span.

Rest

Rest is often neglected as a training variable, but it is in fact just as important as the training you do. It's when you are not at the gym that your body adapts and grows stronger, and profits from the CV or resistance training that it has been subjected to. Without sufficient rest these adaptive processes will not optimally take place. Rest days, rest periods and the carefully constructed use of light, medium and tough workouts should all form part of a balanced training plan.

As you will see in Chapter 8, diet also plays a crucial role in aiding recovery and promoting positive fitness adaptation.

Putting together your training pyramid is the first step towards constructing a training plan. It will provide the blueprint for achieving your fitness goals.

The training pyramid

You'll see from Table 6.1 that a training pyramid incorporates a number of specific training phases. Each has an in-built fitness focus and builds on the fitness achieved in the previous phase. The overall aim of each is to take you closer and closer to your ultimate fitness goal, by allowing your body to adapt systematically. The training pyramid can be applied to any fitness or sports-specific training target. Each phase should be long enough (usually between 6 and 18 weeks) to allow you to develop a specific fitness aspect, like strength endurance, or the ability to row for 40 minutes. In all, you should allow at least three to six months to reach the top of the pyramid and achieve your fitness goal. Make sure you reference your body type and select the best training methods for it for your pyramid (see page 15).

Make sure you reference your body type and select the best training methods for it for your pyramid (see page 15).

TRAINING TIP

What to emphasise in a training phase (selected examples) – see also Table 6.1:

- **develop a base of CV fitness in phase 1 to promote optimum fat burning in the next phase through the use of higher-intensity workouts**
- **use circuit resistance training in phase 1 to maximise strength and muscle size in the next phase, which will involve using heavier weights and more advanced weight-training systems**
- **develop a base of speed and agility in phases 1 and 2 to improve football fitness for the next phase (playing season).**

Make sure you record all your workouts in a training diary (see page 148).

Table 6.1

The training pyramid

A training pyramid provides the framework in which to place the right workouts for your training goals, in the right order to create the right environment for optimum fitness adaptation.

> **TRAINING TIP**
> **Relevant fitness tests should be scheduled in at appropriate times in a training pyramid – the beginning, middle and end of each training phase are good times to assess your progression.**

TOP (YOUR GOAL)

PHASE 4

Key characteristic

This is a recovery or relaxed fitness phase, which you use before returning to restart the training cycle. It's designed to allow your body and mind time to regenerate.

Suggested workout options and progression ideas

During this phase you could involve yourself in new fitness activities, classes or sports, but this should only be on a very low-key basis.

Duration 2–4 weeks

PHASE 3

Key characteristic

This phase usually emphasises quality as you reach your fitness goal. You'll be able to complete workouts that you would only have dreamed about previously.

Suggested workout options and progression ideas

Progression to higher-intensity fat-burning sessions by increasing the RPE of your workouts, perhaps to an RPE of 7–8. Progression to high-intensity interval-training workouts, by reducing the rest period, or switching from passive to active recovery. Progression to higher-level fitness classes. Progression to lifting heavier weights, using more advanced training systems, like pyramids.

Duration 6–8 weeks

PHASE 2

Key characteristic

You become much fitter than you were in phase 1 and can handle more advanced training options and workouts. Duration and quantity are greatest at the beginning of this phase, but normally decline as phase 3 approaches. Quality increases as the phase progresses.

Suggested workout options and progression ideas

You could change the weight training system you use and/or increase the amount of weight lifted, while reducing the number of repetitions, if seeking ultimate strength and power. You could also introduce more specific and complex exercises. Quality (speed, heart rate and/or RPE levels) of CV workouts is increased. You could take more advanced fitness class options.

Duration 6–12 weeks

PHASE 1

Key characteristic

This phase is all about building a base. It normally emphasises the progressive development of training quantity – you 'train to train'. This will allow you to successfully tackle harder usually more quality-orientated workouts in the phases that follow. For those new to exercise this phase is all about getting accustomed to working out slowly and safely, and developing confidence.

Suggested workout options and progression ideas

CV trainers, whatever their level, should increase the duration of their workouts. Resistance trainers should increase the number of their repetitions and sets, incorporating mainly general but some specific exercises into their workouts. You should take introductory fitness classes You should establish a good level of flexibility, with regard to the needs of your specific fitness goals.

Duration 6–18 weeks

The training pyramid
continued

How to select the right workout options for your training pyramid

I identified suitable workout options relevant to specific phases in the training pyramid in Table 6.1. These will act as pointers for you when you construct your own pyramid and progressive training plan. They'll serve to further your understanding of how to progress your training from phase to phase. Elsewhere in this book you'll find detailed examples of progressive training plans (see pages 63, 107 and 173); you should also refer to these to help you construct your own specific personal training plans. You can put this together once you have designed your training pyramid.

The training pyramid has three distinct training phases, and one rest and recovery phase. You could design a pyramid with more training phases if you desired, if your training goal was specific enough to warrant this. But for most general fitness purposes three training phases are sufficient. To increase your understanding of what to include in the pyramid training phases, see Table 6.1.

You don't have to train with the same fitness goals in mind cycle after cycle. Changing your goals will keep you motivated. Try aiming for a high level of CV fitness in one training cycle, optimum fat burning through cross-training in another and even sports-specific ability in another.

> **TRAINING TIP**
> **Training needs to be progressive, specific and cyclical to get the most out of it.**

TRAINING TIP

Remind yourself why exercise can improve your health and increase your chances of living a longer, more fulfilling life. This should make it a great deal easier for you to adopt a fitness lifestyle. Don't think that you have to train like an Olympian to reap the benefits, as a relatively moderate amount of regular exercise will have a significant effect: two to three workouts a week that mix CV exercise and resistance training is all that is needed.

What do you do when you achieve your fitness goals?

This is a great position to be in, but once you have finished celebrating or showing off your new body shape or level of fitness, it's time to re-evaluate and re-focus your fitness efforts and establish another set of fitness goals and another training pyramid. This process of planning, achievement and re-evaluation is called the 'training cycle' – applying its principles will enable you not only to achieve your specific fitness goals, but continually to do so. The cycle will reduce boredom and keep you motivated to train year in year out.

Rest if you want to get fitter

When you exercise, muscle tissue is broken down. It can take between 36 and 48 hours for it to regenerate fully. It's during this period that your body increases its fitness. If you don't provide it with sufficient recovery time, and keep 'beating it up' with heavier and more intense training, positive adaptation will be minimal, if not non-existent.

TRAINING TIP

If you are an advanced trainer, you should take at least one day off in a seven-day training cycle and two in a ten-day cycle to avoid over-training and to maximise your fitness adaptation.

It's easier to maintain fitness than achieve it. You can cut back by up to 50 per cent on the training that achieved your goals if you want to maintain rather than gain (see pages 69 and 133).

Table 6.2
Exercise options

Note that the suggested training frequency has been provided over a week for ease of understanding, but you could use a 10- or 14-day cycle, for example, so that you could include all the workouts you would like to in your training over a more manageable perioid.

FITNESS GOAL	FITNESS LEVEL	EXERCISE OPTIONS AND THEIR PLACE IN THE TRAINING PYRAMID
CV TRAINING Building a CV base and establishing a positive (weight loss) energy balance	New to exercise	**Option** Steady-state CV efforts: RPE 3–4 progressing to RPE 5–6 over 12–18 weeks. **Duration** Building from 10 minutes to 45 minutes plus. **Frequency** 2–3 times a week. **Where?** Phases 1/2
	Intermediate/advanced	**Option** Steady-state CV efforts: RPE 5–6 or 7–8. **Duration** 20 minutes to 1 hour plus. **Frequency** 2–3 times a week. **Where?** Phases 1/2
	Intermediate/advanced	**Option/Where?** Introductory (phase 1) and intermediate aerobic and step classes (phase 2) **Frequency** 2–3 times a week
Maintaining a CV base – also for use as recovery sessions between harder CV workouts	Intermediate/advanced	**Option** Steady-state efforts: RPE 5–6 **Duration** 20 minutes to 1 hour plus **Frequency** 2–3 times a week **Where?** All phases For recovery: sessions should last no more than 30 minutes
Maintenance of a positive energy balance for general fitness and fat-loss purposes	New to exercise	**Option/Duration** Steady-state efforts or new to exercise interval training at an RPE and duration determined by your fitness level **Frequency** Each option 1–2 times a week **Where?** Phase 1
Achievement of a positive energy balance leading to optimal fat loss, which will also develop a high level of CV fitness	New to exercise	**Option** Steady-state efforts at an RPE and duration above that achieved in phase 1 **Frequency** Twice a week **Where?** Phases 2/3
	New to exercise	**Option** Medium-intensity interval training: interval 5–6 RPE with 3–4 RPE active recovery **Duration** Interval 10 minutes, recovery 5 number of intervals 2 **Frequency** Twice a week **Where?** Phases 2/3
	Intermediate/advanced	**Option** Steady-state CV efforts: RPE 7 **Duration** 20 minutes to 1 hour plus **Frequency** 2–3 times a week **Where?** Phase 2
	Intermediate/advanced	**Option** Medium-intensity interval training: interval 7-8 RPE with 3–4 RPE active recovery **Duration** Interval 8 minutes, recovery 4 minutes, number of intervals 4 **Frequency** Twice a week **Where?** Phase 2/3
	All levels	**Option** Intermediate/advanced fitness classes **Frequency** 2–3 times a week **Where?** Phase 2/3

FITNESS GOAL	FITNESS LEVEL	EXERCISE OPTIONS AND THEIR PLACE IN THE TRAINING PYRAMID
Quality CV training for competition purposes (will also optimise post-exercise calorie burning)	Advanced	**Option/Duration** Lactate threshold efforts where you perform a CV activity at a pace that would force you to stop around the 20-minute mark (RPE 8–10) **Frequency** Once a week **Where?** Phases 2/3 **Option and Duration** High-intensity interval training • Interval RPE 8–10, active recovery RPE 5-6, interval duration 6 minutes, recovery same or less • Number of intervals 3–6 **Frequency** 1-2 times a week **Where?** Phase 3
	Intermediate/advanced	**Option** Advanced cycling/rowing fitness classes **Frequency** Twice a week **Where?** Phase 3
RESISTANCE TRAINING Strength endurance	Intermediate/advanced	**Option** High repetition, LW (less than 60 per cent 1RM), short recovery weight training **Frequency** 1–2 times a week **Where?** Phase 1/2 **Option** Weight-based fitness or circuit-training classes **Frequency** 1–2 times a week **Where?** Phases 1/2
Body shaping and toning	New to exercise and intermediate	**Option** High-repetition, LW, good recovery weight training **Frequency** Twice a week **Where?** Phases 1/2
	All levels	**Option** Fit ball and BOSU board exercises **Frequency** 1–2 times a week **Where?** All phases **Option** Yoga and Pilates classes **Where?** Phases 1–3 (as you progress your class skill and fitness) **Option** MW weight training (60–80 per cent of 1RM). **Frequency** 1–2 times a week **Where?** Phases 2/3
Increasing strength and muscle size	Intermediate/advanced	**Option** Medium- to low-repetition (8–4), M/HW or HW weight training (60–70 per cent/70–85 per cent/85–100 per cent 1RM respectively). Also, use of more advanced weight training systems like the pyramid and matrix systems **Frequency** 1–2 times a week **Where?** Phases 2/3
Developing strength and power, lean muscle mass and, if required, specific power and speed for relevant sports; these options will also increase muscle size	Intermediate/advanced	**Option** Medium-repetition (6–10), M or HW weight training (70–85 per cent 1RM) performed dynamically **Frequency** Twice a week **Where?** Phases 2/3 **Option** Plyometrics **Frequency** Twice a week **Where?** Phases 2/3 **Option** Complex training: 3 weights exercises and 3 paired plyometric exercises 4 sets of 6 repetition of each, weights M/HW (70–85 per cent 1RM) **Frequency** Twice a week **Where?** Phases 2/3. Note: don't perform more than two complex training or plyometric workouts in a week

LINKING EXERCISE OPTIONS TO TRAINING GOALS

After you have decided on what to emphasise in your training pyramid you need to start selecting some specific workout options for your training plan. Table 6.2 matches selected workout options to selected fitness goals, and indicates the phase in the training pyramid they should fit into. More detail is now being added as you start to construct a specific and detailed training plan. Ultimately, you should develop these ideas into individual workouts, which you should record in your training diary.

How to use the table

1. Decide on your desired training goal.
2. Reference it to your fitness level.
3. Develop individual workouts (select from the workout examples or devise your own).
4. Slot them into the place indicated in your training pyramid.

Specific workouts should be written in your training diary.

Note that there is obviously a huge array of fitness goals, too many to cover here, so I have selected some of the most common. All workout options described in Table 6.2 have been explained in detail in the practical chapters.

> **TRAINING TIP**
>
> **Although we tend to base our lives around the seven days of the week, for training purposes it can be more beneficial to use a 10-, 12- or even 14-day cycle. This will avoid the problems associated with trying to cram all our workouts into a week, which, given the pace of modern life, is a relatively short period. In a week it might be difficult to fit in two weights sessions and four running workouts, but this would be a much more realistic proposition over a 12- or 14-day period.**

Adding the detail

Here's how you could progress two specific workout options through the pyramid training phases.

OPTION	PHASE 1	PHASE 2	Phase 3
Resistance training to increase strength and size in the chest and shoulders 2 sessions per week, all phases	Fixed-weight machine bench press Simple sets 3 × 12 bench press @ 40 per cent 1RM 3 × 12 press-ups	Free-weight bench press 3 × 6 @ 60 per cent 1RM Dumbbell bench press 3 × 12 @ 45 per cent 1RM	Dumbbell bench press pyramid session 4 × 70 per cent 1RM 3 × 80 per cent 1RM 2 × 90 per cent 1RM Barbell bench press from fit ball 3 × 15 @ 60 per cent 1RM
CV exercise progression: rowing 4 sessions per week, all phases	Steady-state rowing, building from 10 minutes to 30 minutes – RPE increasing from 3–4 to 5–6	Medium-intensity interval training 4 × 10 minutes @ RPE 7–8 with 4 minutes' passive recovery Steady-state efforts 30–45 minutes @ RPE 5–6	Medium- and high-intensity interval training High 5 × 5 minutes @ RPE 8–9 with 6 minutes' active recovery @ RPE 3–4 Medium 3 ×10 minutes RPE 7–8 with 4 minutes' active recovery @ RPE 3–4 Recovery steady-state efforts 20–30 minutes @ RPE 3–4

Selected guidelines for planning your training

1. Medium- and high-intensity interval training should follow steady-state training.
2. High-intensity interval training should be built on steady-state CV training and a period of medium-intensity interval training, and should be used sparingly in a training plan because of its very taxing nature.
3. Strength, power and the development of larger muscles is normally built on a base of strength endurance weight training and circuit training.
4. Plyometric strength is usually built on circuit training, power weight and strength endurance weight training and, where relevant, sports-specific training.
5. All fitness options should be emphasised in training phases that last a minimum of 6 weeks and a maximum of 18 weeks.
6. Although each training phase is progressive, you still need to balance the content of each phase, emphasising the rest variable to ensure that you do not overdo it. To avoid over-training you should schedule in easier workouts and groups of workouts in a training period. Don't think that every individual workout needs to be tougher than its predecessor.

Over-training, rest and recovery

Although exercise is good for you, there are times when too much of it can have a detrimental effect and potentially lead to over-training syndrome (OTS). A carefully constructed training programme incorporating sufficient rest and recovery should avoid OTS. But if you do suffer from some of the symptoms listed below and have been in hard training for a while you could be suffering from OTS. If you think you are, you should take at least a week off training, before returning to your workouts and then at a lower level than when you stopped. If the symptoms persist consult your doctor.

Over-training syndrome symptoms:

- lack of desire to want to train
- continuously feeling fatigued and listless
- decreased maximal heart rate
- greater susceptibility to illness – particularly upper respiratory tract infections
- mood swings
- feelings of anxiousness and stress
- an increase in RHR (resting heart rate)
- sleep problems
- lack of appetite.

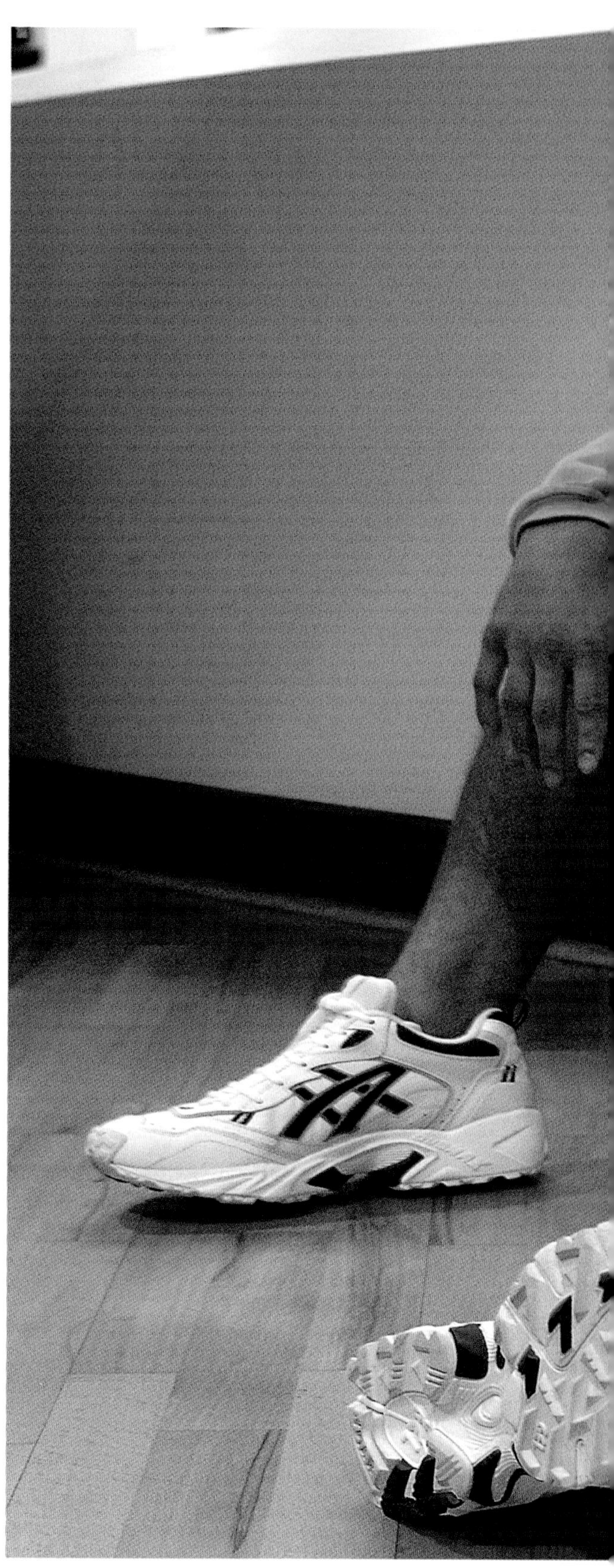

TRAINING TIP

CV trainers need to be particularly aware of the dangers of OTS. Research indicates that those who predominantly CV train at very high exercise intensities are much more likely to suffer from OTS than weight trainers or those who train at lower CV levels. It's therefore very important that you need to make sure that you incorporate adequate rest and recovery periods into your training plans.

TRAINING TIP

Research from the sports psychology world indicates that if you think positively about your workout and focus on its content and its desired goals some time in the day prior to completing it, you'll improve your chances of having a successful workout.

Early riser or late starter? What's the best time of the day to train?

The time that you train can affect your training. Although some of you will have no option but to train in the morning to get your workout out of the way before the rest of the day takes over, research indicates that training in the mid- to late afternoon or evening is more effective. At this time our bodies will naturally be better physiologically prepared to deal with harder, heavier and faster workouts.

Proving the point

A group of cyclists who all thought they trained better in the morning performed 16 km time trials in the evenings for a set period. To their surprise, their later rides brought about significantly better scores than their 7 am rides – the evening workouts were in fact an average of 89 seconds faster than the morning ones.

Keep a training diary: a great way to plan and motivate

Recording your training in a paper or electronic diary will help you to plan, evaluate and motivate. Your diary will enable you to record your long- and short-term goals, and all your specific training that you complete along the way to achieving them.

As the number of entries builds up, you'll be able to flick back through its pages (or onscreen) and see at a glance where you started off and just how much you have achieved and improved.

Table 6.3

Workout rating table

A great way to evaluate your training is to use a 1–5 scale such as the one shown below.

1. Not a good workout, virtually complete non-attainment of workout goal.
2. Disappointing partial completion of workout target.
3. Average workout, perhaps you couldn't quite get into it, or finish off a set of weights lifts, but your main goals were accomplished sufficiently well enough.
4. Good workout – achieved all targets.
5. Excellent workout – surpassed workout goals and felt great.

How to set out a diary entry

Choose the headings that are the most applicable to you from those listed.

Planned workout and individual workout goals

You should record in your diary your intended workouts at least a week to two weeks in advance.

Actual workout

Record how your workout actually went, using relevant markers such as RPE, heart rate zone used, calories burned, distance covered, or number of repetitions completed and weight lifted.

Date and time

As you have seen, the time at which you train could significantly influence your workout. Make a note: it could explain why you had a better workout, or perhaps why you didn't.

Goals

You may have set a short- or longer-term goal for a specific workout day, such as 'to go for a best 2 km row time' or 'to increase weights by 5 per cent' or 'to change from simple to super sets' or 'to have dropped 2 per cent body fat by now'. In some cases, tests will be required, so make sure you plan these in advance.

Venue

You may train at home or at different gyms, or you may be working out while on holiday, so make note of this. This can explain potential differences in your workout outcomes. As mentioned in the CV training chapter, not all equipment is identical, so recording if you are using a different stepper from the one you usually use will explain any discrepancies.

Workout/weather conditions

Obviously the weather can influence your training. A note in your diary will explain why your 5 km run took longer than normal if it was run in wet and windy weather, or why the mild sunshine allowed you to zip along to a best time. Don't think that weather conditions only affect outdoor workouts: in the summer you might not be adequately hydrated to get the most out of your indoor gym training (see page 185).

Feelings about your workout

Reflect on your workout and make useful comments. Simply writing 'felt great' or 'need to re-test 1RMs in a week's time' may be all that is needed (see Table 6.3).

Calories, diet and eating plan

In your diary you may decide to record your actual daily calorie consumption and expenditure, and whether you achieved a positive, negative or balanced energy balance (see page 152). You may even decide to write down what you intend to eat on a particular day to construct an eating plan.

Sample training diary page

GOAL:
Development of increased CV fitness and lean muscle

DATE/TIME:
18 February/11 am

VENUE AND WORKOUT CONDITIONS:
Ultra-fit Gym – not too crowded

PLANNED SESSION

WARM-UP
5 minutes on exercise bike
Work on lower back flexibility

CV
20-minute row @ RPE of 5–6 with 5 minutes passive recovery
15 minutes on cross-trainer, RPE 5–6

COMMENTS
Felt really good, had to hold back, but managed my furthest ever distance on rower: 3000 m.

RESISTANCE TRAINING: WEIGHTS
3 x 12 @ 60 per cent 1RM on bench press, leg press, shoulder press, biceps curl, super set of abdominal moves, 3 x 15 x 2
Last set of bench-press reps felt easy, will need to re-test 1RM next week

COOL-DOWN
5 minutes on bike

CALORIES AND DIET

EXERCISE EXPENDITURE
200 Kcal on the rower, 150 Kcal on cross-trainer – CV total weights estimated total 150 Kcal
Session total 500 Kcal

CALORIE CONSUMPTION
Breakfast 600 Kcal, snack 150 Kcal, lunch 600 Kcal, snack 150 Kcal, post-workout snack 300 Kcal, evening meal 700 Kcal
Total 2500 Kcal

ENERGY BALANCE
Positive – 100 Kcal*

FEELINGS ABOUT SESSION
Very good – had day off work, so felt fresh

RATING
5/5

* See page 158 for how to work out the number of calories you need on a daily basis and page 159 for the calorie expenditure of common exercise forms.

7 Fat burning

the real deal

Improving body image and losing weight are often the main reasons why we join a gym and decide to adopt a fitness lifestyle. Almost daily we are subject to celebrity diets and wonder exercise routines, drug treatments and even the option of cosmetic surgery. While all offer potential solutions to achieving that ever-so-desirable fat-free body, some make false promises and can even do more harm than good. In this chapter I'll outline the fat-burning strategies that will work – these are based on the scientific reality of fitness training and dietary knowledge. This chapter should specifically be read in conjunction with Chapter 8, 'Fuelling your fitness lifestyle'.

HOW DO YOU LOSE WEIGHT AND GET FIT? IT'S SIMPLE: ACHIEVE A POSITIVE ENERGY BALANCE

Losing weight and burning fat is theoretically very simple: all you need to do is burn more calories than you consume – if you do this you'll achieve what's known as a 'positive energy balance' (see Table 7.1). To do this, you should restrict your calorie consumption by diet, and adopt a fitness lifestyle that increases your energy expenditure.

Table 7.1

The energy balance equation

KCAL INTAKE	KCAL OUTPUT	EFFECT ON YOUR WEIGHT	ENERGY BALANCE*
1600	1600	None	Balanced
2000	1600	Increase	Negative
1600	1900	Decrease	Positive

* Refers to the calorific balance between calories in and calories out.

A positive energy balance will result in fat loss.

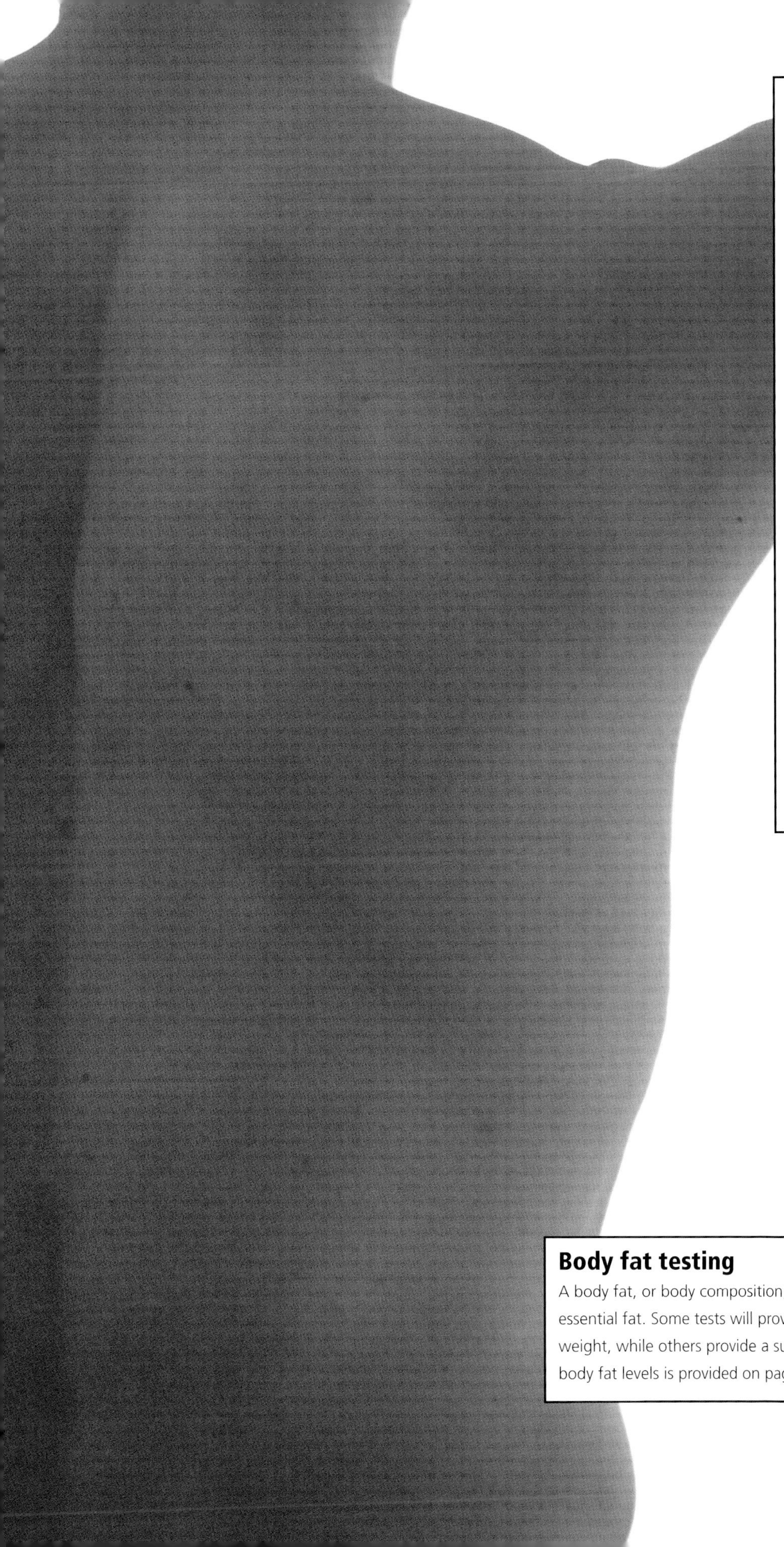

BODY COMPOSITION

Our bodies are composed of different tissue types. Gaining an understanding of these types puts fat-burning training into context.

Lean body tissue

Lean body tissue is made up of muscles, bones, blood and organs. It's metabolically active. Muscle plays a very important role in the fat-burning equation. It burns up to three times as many calories as any other part of the body – basically the leaner you become, the more effective a calorie-burning machine you will be.

Fat tissue

Fat tissue is made up of the following components.

Essential fat

This is stored in bone marrow, heart, lungs and liver, and other vital organs, and supports life.

Storage fat

This acts as a sort of cushion that protects the body's vital organs. It's also spread around the body below the skin's surface (subcutaneous fat).

Non-essential fat

Non-essential fat is the fat we want to burn. It is lazy, has no real purpose and is detrimental to our health if we store too much of it.

Body fat testing

A body fat, or body composition, test can tell us whether our bodies have too much non-essential fat. Some tests will provide us with a body fat percentage for our lean versus fat weight, while others provide a sum of skinfolds (see page 24). Information on acceptable body fat levels is provided on page 167.

What is a calorie?

If you're like me, you could have been, or are, potentially confused by the different methods used to express the energy value of food. Pick up a food product, look at the nutritional information on the label and you'll invariably see that the energy value is expressed in kJ (Kilojoules), j (joules) and/or Kcal (Kilocalories) and cal (calories).

Understanding food energy

Kcals and calories

Metric: 1 Kcal = 1000 cal

Imperial: 1 calorie = 1000 c

A Kcal and a calorie supply the same amount of energy (that's why the terms can be used interchangeably).

Kilojoules

The Kilojoule is the international standard for energy.

1 kJ = 1000 j

A kJ is not the same as a Kcal (or calorie) in terms of its energy provision. To facilitate your fat-burning and dietary calculations, and to ease your understanding of food labels, you can convert kJ into Kcal and vice versa by using these calculations:

- to convert kJ into Kcal: divide by 4.2
  – thus 200 kJ = 48 Kcal (200÷4.2)
- to convert Kcal into kJ: multiply by 4.2
  – thus 100 Kcal = 420 kJ (100 × 4.2)

1 cal is the amount of heat required to increase the temperature of 1 gram (g) of water by 1 degree centigrade. It's a very small amount of energy, hence the general use of the bigger Kcal unit.

Food

Food provides our bodies with energy. Carbohydrate, fat and protein release different amounts of energy (see Table 7.2). Carbohydrate (in the form of glycogen) is your main energy provider when you are active, but fat and protein can also supply your body with energy. The majority of food and drink we consume contains a mixture of carbohydrate, protein and fat (and vitamins and minerals). How this affects our ability to exercise is covered in more detail in Chapter 8.

Table 7.2

Energy release from different food types

Food type	CARBOHYDRATE	PROTEIN	FAT
Energy in Kcal/g	4	4	9

DIETARY TIP

Fat is lazy fuel. It is calorie dense and doesn't like to provide much energy. Although we need fat to survive, saturated (hard) fats are much more likely to increase our non-essential fat than protein and carbohydrate.

Where do all those calories go? The importance of exercise for fat burning

This section explains how it is possible to achieve a negative, positive or balanced energy balance through your daily eating habits and activity levels. You burn energy day and night; understanding where all this goes will put into context just how important working out is for fat burning.

Total daily energy expenditure (TDEE)

Our bodies use energy throughout the day and night to keep us alive; this is our total daily energy expenditure (TDEE).

Resting metabolic rate (RMR)

A very significant proportion (60–75 per cent) of TDEE is used to maintain our resting metabolic rate (RMR). RMR encompasses all those unseen and un-thought-of essential bodily functions, such as heart, lung and mental functioning. Calculations of RMR are made over a 24-hour period, but do not include the calories burned while you are sleeping.

Activity

The high percentage of calories used to maintain RMR may come as a surprise to many, as it's often assumed

> **TRAINING TIP**
> Circuit resistance training (see page 109) is a great way to burn calories, trim fat and develop CV fitness and strength.

that exercise and other physical activity burns the majority of our energy. The reality is that only 15 per cent at most of our TDEE actually goes on any activity, let alone exercise. But don't be discouraged by this, as this seemingly small percentage can make a huge difference to our efforts to burn fat, lose weight and achieve a positive energy balance.

Thermic effect of feeding (TEF)

The thermic effect of feeding (TEF) makes up the remaining 10 per cent of our daily energy expenditure. When you eat and digest food, energy is burned. This, in part, explains why eating five to six moderate meals spread throughout the day, can have a better fat-burning effect – by keeping our metabolic rate elevated – than eating two or three large meals or, worse still, crash dieting.

Calculating the number of calories you need each day

Working out the number of calories you need each day is relatively simple, as is calculating the number of calories you expend during exercise. The following four steps show you how to do this.

Step 1: calculate your RMR

Age 18–30
multiply your weight in kg × 14.7 and add 496

Age 31–60
multiply your weight in kg × 8.7 and add 829

Examples

65 kg individual
65 × 14.7 + 496
= 1451.5 RMR

65 kg individual
65 × 8.7 + 829
= 1394.5 RMR

80 kg individual
80 × 14.7 + 496
= 1672 RMR

80 kg individual
80 × 8.7 + 829
= 1525 RMR

> **TRAINING TIP**
> **Many pieces of CV equipment, and some heart rate monitors, have built-in calorie counters that will assist your calculations.**

Step 2: estimate your daily activity requirements in calories

Multiply your RMR by your daily activity level as indicated in Table 7.3

Table 7.3
Calculating your daily activity requirements

ACTIVITY LEVEL	DEFINED AS	
Not much	Little or no physical activity	RMR × 1.4
Moderate	Some physical activity, perhaps at work, or the odd weekly gym visit	RMR × 1.7
Active	Regular physical activity at work and/or at the gym (three visits per week)	RMR × 2.0

Examples

18–30 year old (65 kg)
Moderate activity level 1451.5 × 1.7 = **2466.7 Kcal**

31–60 year old (80 kg)
Active activity level 1525 × 2.0 = **3050 Kcal**

Source: Bean (2002).

Step 3: work out the number of calories you burn through exercise

I recommend that you average out the number of calories you burn by way of your workouts over a week and then divide by seven to determine your daily average. To assist you in this process, Table 7.4 provides you with an estimate of the number of calories used by common forms of exercise, while Table 7.5 also accounts for exercise intensity. (See page 56 for walking and calorie-burning figures.)

TRAINING TIP

A little goes a long way. There are 3500 Kcal in 0.45 kg of fat. But don't lose heart – although this may sound an incredible number, when compared to the calories you can burn by way of exercise, regular workouts can make a big difference. Here's why. If you burned 300 Kcal a day through your chosen exercise method in a year, you could theoretically remove 13.6 kg of fat from your body.

Step 4: the final calculation ...

Add your daily required number of calories to the number of calories you burn through exercise (see Table 7.4) to work out the total number of calories you need per day. This will provide your Kcal energy balance figure.

Table 7.4

Fitness activities and calorie burning

ACTIVITY	KCAL/HOUR	APPROX. KCAL/MIN
Aerobics high intensity	520	8.5
Boxing (sparring)	865	14
Cycling 16 km/hour	384	6.4
Cycling 8.8 km/hour	250	4.2
Rowing (moderate)	445	7.4
Swimming (fast)	615	10.2
Weight training	270–450	4.5–7.5
Swimming for fitness	630	10.5
Treadmill running (5.6 min/km)	750	12.5
Treadmill running (3.8 min/km)	1000	16.6

The above figures are based on a 65 kg individual. If you weigh more, you'll burn more calories; if you weigh less you'll burn fewer calories.

Table 7.5

Exercise intensity and fat burning

Exercise intensity in RPE*	Percentage of Kcal from carbohydrate	fat	Energy expenditure (Kcal) per min	after 20 mins
Low RPE 3–4	33.4	66.6	9.6	192
Moderate RPE 5–6	50.7	49.3	12.2	244
High RPE 7–8	84	16	15	300
Very high RPE 8/9–10	100	0	20.2	404

* See page 53.

Carbohydrate versus fat calorie burning at low to high exercise intensities

How hard you work out – your 'exercise intensity' – can make a big difference to fat burning (see Table 7.5).

TRAINING TIP

Paradoxically, very intense training can slow RMR, if insufficient calories are consumed to meet increased energy needs.

The myth of the fat-burning CV zone

The term 'fat burning zone' (FBZ) is often used to refer to relatively low-intensity CV workouts that last for more than 20 minutes. You might see reference to 'the zone' on posters in your local gym, or hear about it from your personal trainer and gym instructor. Unfortunately, the concept of the FBZ is misleading and could result in you exercising ineffectively for optimum fat loss.

How did the FBZ gain popularity?

The idea of a specific FBZ developed because: (1) CV workouts carried out at a moderate intensity are both sustainable and achievable by those new to exercise; and (2) because lower-intensity CV workouts seemingly burn more fat calories. You'll see from Table 7.5 that at a low RPE, 66.6 per cent of calories are derived from fat and 33.4 per cent from carbohydrate. Armed with this information, it's not too hard to see how low-intensity CV exercise, as advocated by the FBZ, can be championed as the best fat burner. However, in reality fat burning and attaining a positive energy balance is best accomplished by training at higher CV intensities. This is because total calorie burn is what really counts and is the most significant driving force behind achieving a positive energy balance. This intensity also has some potentially other significant fat-burning effects; these include post-exercise calorie burning and a constantly elevated increased calorie-burning metabolic rate.

TRAINING TIP

To get the best fat-burning returns, develop your CV fitness so you can consistently CV train at medium to high exercise intensities. This level of exercise includes power walking, a good-paced jog or a one- to two-hour cycle – it's not slow, plodding exercise nor a superfast workout burn-up: you're looking at an RPE of 6–8.

Set-point theory

It's argued that there's a control mechanism in our brain's hypothalamus that maintains a 'predetermined' level of fat and weight for each of our bodies. If you have a 'high' set point then your body's fat content could naturally be higher than someone's whose is lower. The good news is that research indicates that this mechanism can be challenged, particularly by higher-intensity exercise, but not apparently by dieting alone; although a low-fat diet in combination with exercise can prove successful.

Personal reflections

I have my own experience of set-point theory. When training for indoor rowing competitions, I would often obliterate huge numbers of calories, sometimes as many as 1000 in one workout (and this figure does not include the potentially high post-exercise calorie burn). I was training four to five times a week and found that I had real, over and above, normal food – and in particular fat – cravings. It was as if my body, or more precisely my brain, was telling me that I had to increase my fat and calorie consumption. The increase in my appetite was obvious in these circumstances, but less so was the fact that my set point was probably influencing my body's need for increased fat, to maintain its 'normal' percentage.

TRAINING TIP

Train to maintain! Once you achieve the body fat percentage you have been striving for, or simply like the look of your 'new' body shape, you can 'train to maintain'. You can ease back and stop trying to run further or lift heavier and heavier weights, and just train to the level you have achieved – or to a lower level (see pages 69 and 133). Controlled calorie consumption will still be a must but, in combination with your leaner fat-burning physique, you should be able to stay trim, toned and trained with less effort.

The calorie factor: dos and don'ts

Don't reduce your daily calorie consumption by more than 15 per cent

If this figure is increased, you run the risk of slowing down your metabolic rate as your body hangs on to the reduced number of calories it gets (this is sometimes known as 'famine/starvation mode'). Huge calorie cuts can reduce metabolic rate by as much as 45 per cent. This will significantly impair your workout (and everyday activity) performance.

Don't yo-yo diet

Rapid increases and decreases in calorie consumption can throw your metabolism out of kilter, and can again increase the risk of metabolic slow-down.

Do continually monitor the number of calories burned by exercise

As your fitness improves, your body will become more exercise-efficient. This means that you'll have to increase your workout intensity to continue to burn as many or more calories than you did when you first started. (For safe training progression, don't increase intensity and duration at the same time.)

Don't overly concern yourself with where the calories you burn during your workouts come from

As I have already indicated, what really matters – within relatively large parameters – is total exercise calorie burn.

Don't believe that a specific 'fat burning zone' exists

All exercise options – CV and resistance – can burn fat and help you achieve the body you desire.

Don't skip meals

Calculate your calorific needs and eat frequently (five to six times) during the day. Research indicates that those who eat the most and train the most are the leanest and fittest. For what to eat on a typical training day see page 184.

Weight train to burn fat

As I've stressed continuously throughout this book, weight training should form a significant element of a fat-burning strategy. Muscle burns more calories than any form of body tissue just to exist – this means significant calorie burning even with your feet up. A 0.5 kg gain in muscle can increase your weekly calorie burn by 350 Kcal. Three months of regular resistance training is all that is needed to really start reaping these calorie-incinerating benefits.

DIETARY TIP

For ideal refuelling, aim for 2 grams of carbohydrate per kg of body weight immediately after your workout, to ensure optimum glycogen replacement. If you weigh 65 kg, this would mean that you would have to consume 520 Kcal of carbohydrate (130 grams).

Muscle is the major component of your lean mass.

Another great reason to weight train to burn fat

Here's another reason why increasing your lean muscle mass will turn you into a brilliant calorie-burning machine. As you age, you lose 0.5 percent of lean muscle mass for every decade after the age of 30, this can lead to a 0.5 per cent decrease in RMR per year. A sustained weight training programme will offset this age-related decline, boost your RMR and keep you in prime lifelong fat-burning condition.

TRAINING TIP

Weight train before your CV workouts to get the best out of them both. The exceptions are when performing high-intensity CV workouts or quality sports-specific training when, in the former case, you won't want to resistance train afterwards (!) and because you'll need fresh and responsive muscles for the latter.

At an advanced training level, stuck in a rut and unable to lose more realistic weight? Here's how ...

Aim to achieve a positive energy balance two to three days of the week only, and ensure a balanced energy balance on the other three to four days. At this fat-burning training level you'll need to consume optimum numbers of calories to sustain your exercise and to prevent RMR slow-down, and will not be burning as much fat as you did when you first started training. Cutting back, just slightly, two to three days of the week could lead to further fat loss – as long as this is a realistic target. You'll keep your metabolic rate up and adequately fuel your exercise needs.

Carbohydrates should amount to 55–60 per cent of your total daily energy consumption, fat 25–30 per cent and protein 15–20 per cent.

TRAINING TIP

Cross-training is the ultimate fat-burning combo. Combine weight and CV training into your workouts and train at least three times a week for the ultimate in fat burning and a great body.

Post-exercise calorie burning

Post-exercise calorie burning is the result of your RMR remaining elevated after a workout. During this time more calories are burned to aid recovery. RMR can be increased by 8–14 per cent by those who train regularly and intensely – that's equivalent to 143–286 Kcal a day, virtually another workout seven days a week.

Carbohydrate boosts fat burning

When you exercise, carbohydrate – in the form of glycogen stored in your muscles and liver – supplies energy. Your body can only store this great fuel source in limited amounts, on average only 375 g – enough to run or walk about 25 km. After a workout, your glycogen stores need to be topped up by carbohydrate and that is why this food source is so important. Without it you could be running on empty, which will lead to your metabolism slowing down.

If fat could exclusively fuel a workout

Even if a workout could be devised that gained all its metabolic power from your body's fat supplies and didn't touch your glycogen stores, there would still be a problem, as your body cannot create an endless supply of glycogen from carbohydrate – much of this excess would be stored as fat.

TRAINING TIP

CV exercise that involves large muscle groups – like walking, running, rowing and cycling – offers great fat-burning potential. However, no one piece of CV kit is a better calorie burner than another: the effort you put in and the duration of your workout is what really matters.

It's all in the mind: the mental approach to fat burning

Psychological strategies are increasingly being combined with fitness training and dietary advice by suitably qualified personal trainers and fitness professionals to optimise results – the power of the mind cannot be overlooked. Neuro-linguistic programming (NLP), for example, is commonly used to mentally bolster clients' adherence to a workout programme and to motivate them to further fitness gains and fat loss.

See Chapter 12 for more detail on making the right choice of personal trainer and for advice on how to set realistic goals.

TRAINING TIP

Tired exercise routines bore your body and stunt fat burning. Try to alter the emphasis of your training every 8–16 weeks. Here are some examples. You could change from slower to more intense CV efforts and/or emphasise weights, or take up a different fitness class. This will stop your mind and body getting bored from performing the same training and will constantly stimulate your fat-burning efforts.

Having a positive mental attitude, allied to realistic goals, will strengthen your resolve to maintain a fat-burning lifestyle.

TRAINING TIP

Don't get complacent. You should constantly check to see whether some of your training gains are being cancelled out by an increase in the more sedentary aspects of your life or by poorer eating habits. Cutting out junk food or getting off the bus one stop earlier and walking to work could be all that is needed to tip your fat-burning scales back to a positive energy balance.

Why quick weight loss can be disappointing in the long run

Take a look at the following two scenarios and consider whether you should be happy with the results.

1. You go on an intense calorie-restrictive diet and, three weeks later, you check your weight. It's down by 3 kg.
2. You jump on your scales after a run and a smile appears across your face as you see that you've lost half a kilo.

The answer to both these scenarios is that you shouldn't be happy, although you might think that you should. In scenario 1, insufficient calorie consumption to sustain your daily and activity energy levels can result in your metabolic rate slowing down. You'll hang on to more calories that you need and the long-term result could be easier weight gain when calorie restriction ceases.

In scenario 2, the body finds it much easier to burn glycogen rather than fat as a fuel source. Fat weighs much less than glycogen, so the chances are you'll be lighter after a workout due to glycogen usage (and water loss) rather than fat loss. As your body restocks with glycogen and rehydrates, your weight will return.

To achieve fat loss you should carefully and systematically control your calorific consumption while exercising two to three times a week. This combination will maintain your energy levels and restock your glycogen stores, burn calories, increase lean muscle mass and create the key to fat loss: a positive energy balance.

Filling fat cells: putting on weight

It will help you to understand weight loss if you first understand weight gain. The body has billions of fat cells. These fat cells can become fatter (fat cell hypertrophy) or can increase in number (fat cell hyperplasia) through lack of exercise or poor dietary control. Your genetics, the last trimester of pregnancy, the first year of life and adolescence are further reasons for a fat cell increase and potential weight gain.

Obesity refers to being over-fat and overweight, it can be expressed as a percentage of body fat. The massively obese can have a body fat percentage in excess of 60 per cent.

Can fat cells be killed off?

Until recently it was thought that this was impossible, but now exercise scientists believe that exercise and calorie control can get rid of fat cells permanently. In the past it was thought that we could not reduce the number of fat cells we had, rather that exercise and calorie control could only reduce their fat content, so that they'd lie dormant waiting for calorie control to cease or exercise levels to drop, which would fill them with fat and increase weight again.

Table 7.6

How many fat cells do we have?

Non-obese person	25–30 billion
Moderately obese	60–100 billion
Massively obese	300 billion

Table 7.7

Borderline obesity expressed in terms of body fat percentage

AGE	17–50	50+
	Men: 20 per cent	Men: 25 per cent
	Women: 30 per cent	Women: 37 per cent

Don't become obsessed with your body fat readings.

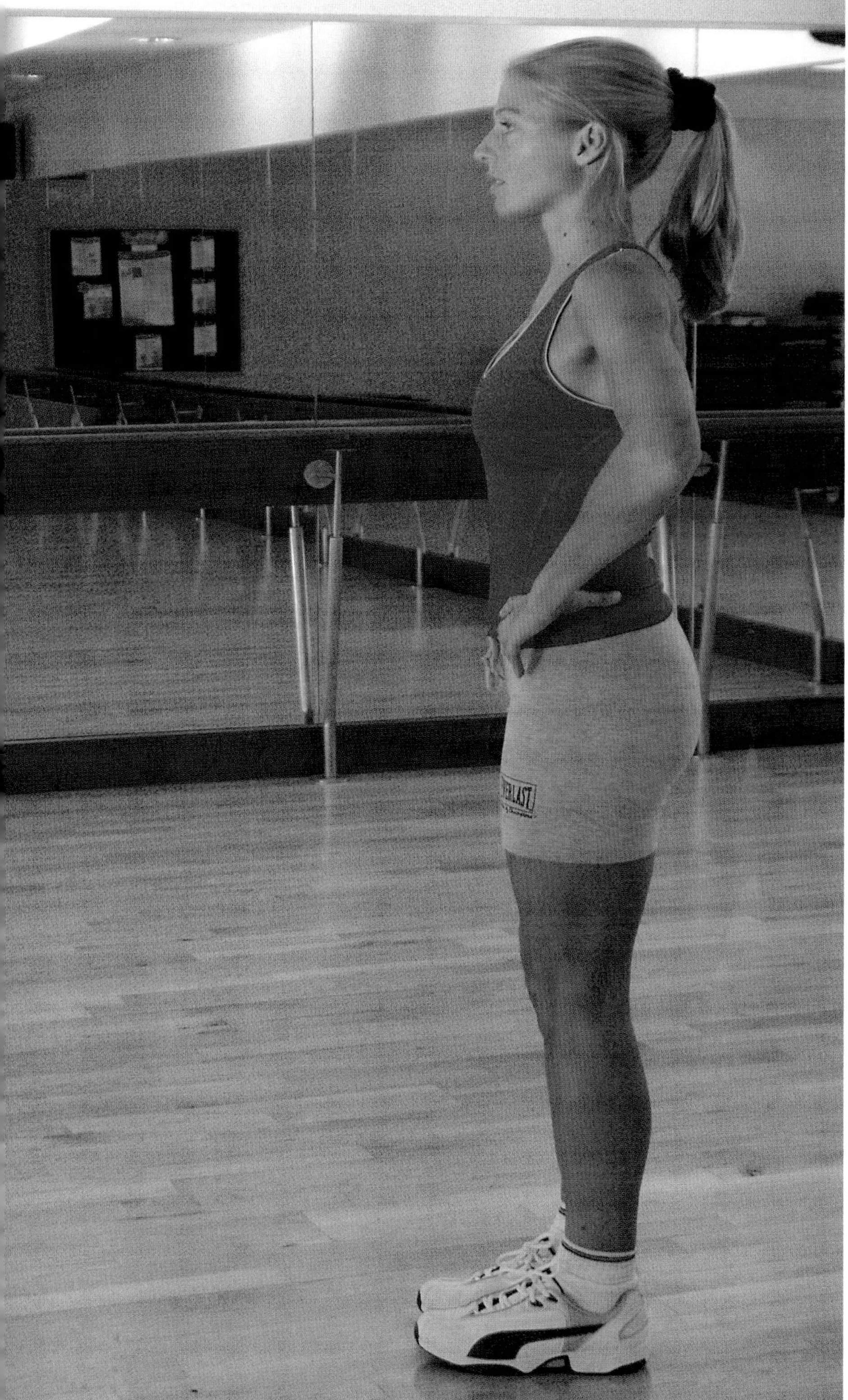

How much body fat is acceptable?

It's not good to become overly preoccupied with body fat readings. This is because you can easily become disappointed if they have not dropped as much as you would like. The pressure to look good can result in constantly checking and worrying about body fat readings. Although there is a place for the periodic use of body fat testing as an aid to monitoring training and fat-burning progress, I believe that it can be much more motivating and perhaps less frustrating, to determine your fat-burning progress by other measures of fitness such as an increase in CV ability and/or strength, and visible changes in muscle tone and muscle size. Improved feelings of vitality and adherence to a healthy eating plan are further indicators of successful training and fat-burning progress.

Table 7.8
Acceptable body fat levels

AGE	MEN	WOMEN
21–30	12–18%	20–26%
31–40	13–19%	21–27%
41–50	14–20%	22–28%
51–60	16–20%	22–30%
61+	17–21%	22–31%

Note: if you attempt to reduce your body fat levels any further than the figures indicated you run the risk of damaging your health.

Women, fat loss, cellulite and menstruation

Menstruation

Regular high-intensity training and reduced body fat levels (less than 20 per cent) can cause a temporary cessation in the menstrual cycle. Most women's normal cycle will return within three months of training less intensely and/or when their body fat levels return to pre-exercise levels. Women who have not menstruated for more than six months can suffer from accelerated bone deterioration due to low levels of the female hormone oestrogen. If you are in this category then you should consult your doctor.

Fat loss

Women face greater difficulties than men when it comes to fat burning. Research indicates that not only are their bodies designed for greater fat storage than men's, they also have their exercise-related ability to burn fat hampered by their body's desire to hold on to the fat they have. Men naturally, initially at least, have less body fat on average and posses a greater ability to burn fat due to their metabolic and hormonal functioning. But women can overcome these barriers by training sensibly and by adopting a healthy eating programme – provided that they have established realistic fat loss goals and a relevant training programme for their body type.

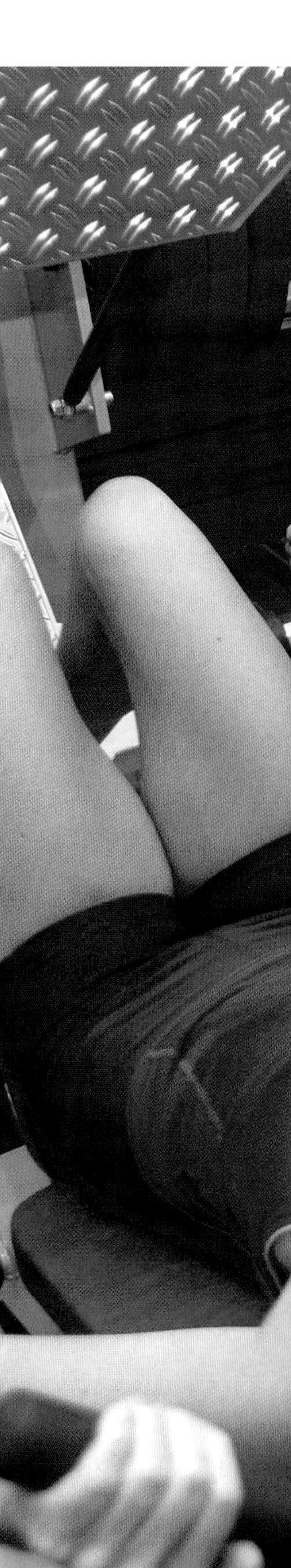

TRAINING TIP

Don't think that targeting a specific body part with a specific exercise will burn fat or remove cellulite from that region ('spot reduce'). Fat is actually mobilised in consequence to an all-body-part and varied training programme, and then usually (initially) from the site of its greatest concentration.

Cellulite and spot reduction

Over 95 per cent of women report that they have cellulite. Cellulite is the name given to the dimpled looking skin found around the inner and outer thighs, caused by trapped fat. Women naturally store more fat in this region than men, in response to their hormones and as a form of fertility protection. The right working programme can tone, shape and burn fat from the thighs and other 'problem' areas.

A key factor often overlooked by women is weight training. Fitness weight training will not result in bulky muscles, but will increase lean muscle mass and increase fat burning.

EIGHT-WEEK FAT-BURNING WORKOUT FOR THOSE NEW TO EXERCISE

The workout aims

This eight-week fat-burning programme (see Table 7.9 on page 173) will burn calories and increase your lean muscle mass. The programme will also develop a sound base of CV fitness (via both interval and steady-state training) and muscular strength. It really is designed with the needs of someone with little or no exercise experience in mind, as the intensity levels are very low. Your choice of CV kit (stepper and cycle) has been made; these are in themselves easier options for someone who might be carrying a little too much weight. For the weight-training elements you should select your own weight-training exercises (see Chapter 5) and fit them in to the designated simple-set weight-training system (indicated 'SS' in Table 7.9). Select six to eight exercises, two or three each for the upper and lower body and two for your core. I've indicated the number of sets and repetitions that you should perform. The weight you should lift should be a light weight (see pages 76 and 77), around 30–40 per cent of a notional one repetition maximum. The intensity of the weights workouts increases over the course of the eight weeks, as do the durations and intensity levels of the CV workouts. You should take a day's recovery between workouts.

You will burn calories

By the end of the eight weeks you should have burned well over 3500 calories, which equates to at least 0.45 kg of fat (figures based on a 65 kg individual, you'll burn more calories if you weigh more, and fewer if you weigh less or if you can safely up your exercise intensity). The calorie-burning figures should only be used as a guide and they further underestimate the potential for total fat loss, as they do not include calories burned during your warm-up and cool-down, and as a result of post-exercise calorie burning, nor the effects of an increase in RMR created by improved lean muscle mass and regular training. So, in reality, you should lose a lot more fat.

If you find the workouts too easy then adjust the intensity accordingly by lifting heavier weights or increasing the referenced RPEs for the CV sessions – the latter can be achieved by increasing the length of your workout or the speed at which you perform them.

> **TRAINING TIP**
> **Don't turn up at the gym with a 'got to do half an hour on the bike to burn 300 calories' attitude. It'll make your training seem like work. Instead, enjoy your workouts, think long term not short term, and the positive adaptations will come.**

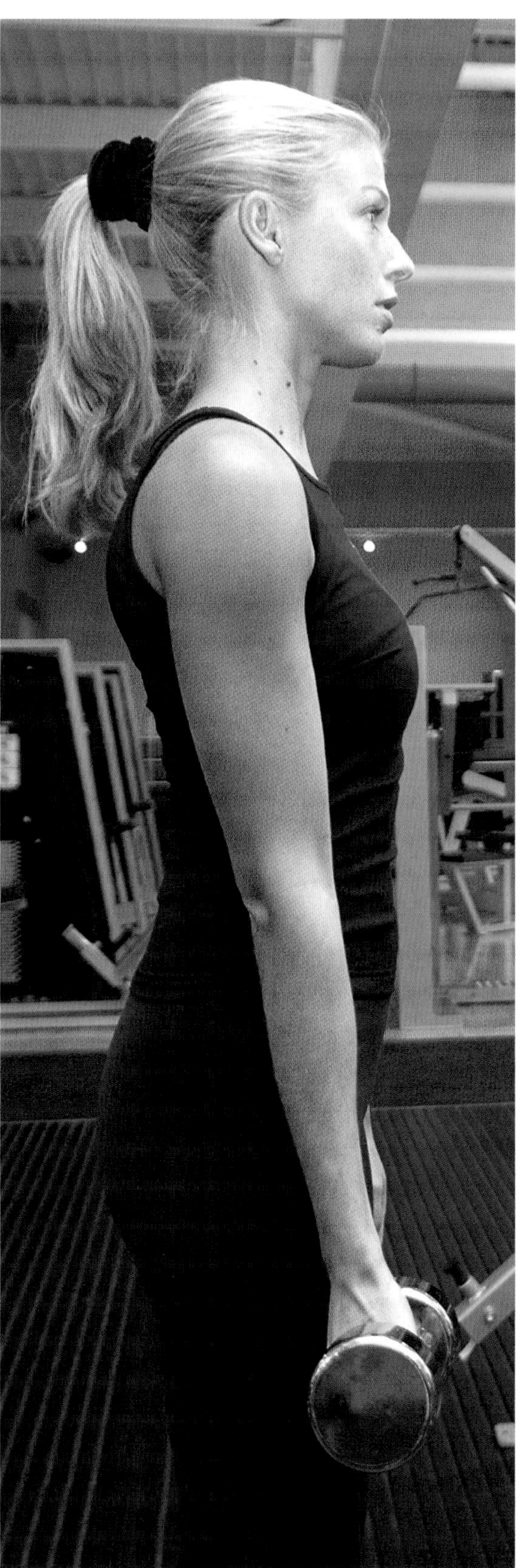

TRAINING TIP

Don't get comfortable if you want to achieve optimum fat loss. If you always use a treadmill, then switching to a rowing machine will immediately boost your calorie-burning potential, as you'll have to work harder to become exercise-efficient on the new machine. You'll get the same effect if you switch from aerobics classes to cycling classes.

The workout

Always warm up and cool down before and after your workouts.

Combine the workout programme with a healthy eating programme. Reduce your calorie consumption by no more than 15 per cent per day and ensure you consume an optimally balanced diet.

Always work out within your limits and take into account how you feel on a particular day. Don't train or push yourself if you don't feel so good.

Full descriptions of interval training, steady-state and weight training are provided in Chapters 5 and 6.

More detail on a balanced diet is contained in Chapter 8.

What to do at the end of the eight weeks

Repeat the last four weeks of the programme as follows.

- CV: increase the RPEs by one level for each workout, thus a RPE 5–6 session, becomes a RPE 7–8 one.
- Weights: increase the amount of weight you lift, you could progress to 3 × 8 reps with a medium intensity weight (60–70 per cent 1RM). The heavier weight will encourage greater lean muscle mass development, but because it is heavier you will have to cut down on repetitions and sets. Remember that the last few repetitions of a set must be difficult to perform but not at the expense of good technique.

WEEK	SESSION 1	SESSION 2	SESSION 3	SESSION 4	APPROXIMATE CALORIES BURNED
1	CV 10 mins RPE 3–4 stepper	Weights SS – 2 sets, 12 reps	CV 12 mins RPE 3–4 cycle	Weights SS – 2 sets, 12 reps	332
2	Weights SS – 2 sets, 12 reps	CV 14 mins RPE 3–4 stepper	Weights SS – 2 sets, 12 reps	CV 16 mins RPE 3–4 cycle	380
3	CV 16 mins RPE 3–4 cycle	Weights SS – 2 sets, 12 reps	CV 20 mins RPE 3–4 stepper	Weights SS – 2 sets, 12 reps	416
4	CV 20 mins RPE 3–4 cycle	Weights SS – 2 sets, 12 reps	CV 2 × 8 mins RPE 5–6 new to exercise interval training 5 mins active recovery @ RPE 1–2 stepper	Weights SS – 3 sets, 10 reps	495
5	20 mins RPE 3–4 cycle	Weights SS – 2 sets, 12 reps	CV 2 × 10 minutes RPE 5–6 new to exercise interval training 5 minutes active recovery @ RPE 1–2 stepper	Weights SS – 3 sets, 12 reps	570
6	25 mins RPE 3–4 stepper	CV 20 mins RPE 3–4 cycle	CV 2 × 10 minutes new to exercise interval training first interval RPE 3–4, second 5–6. active recovery 5 minutes @ RPE 1–2 stepper	Weights SS – 3 sets, 12 reps	638
7	Weights – 3 sets, 12 reps	2 x 15 minutes new to exercise interval training first interval RPE 3–4, second 5-6 active recovery 5 minutes @ RPE 1–2 stepper	Weights SS – 3 sets, 12 reps	Weights SS – 2 sets, 12 reps	750
8	Weights SS – 3 sets, 14 reps	CV 25 mins RPE 3–4 stepper	Weights SS – 3 sets, 14 reps	CV 25 mins RPE 5–6 cycle	750

Table 7.9

An eight-week fat burning workout for those new to exercise

Body fat monitor manufacturers

Company	Telephone	Website
Maltron	01268 778251	www.maltronint.com
Tanita	01895 438577	www.tanita.com
Bodystat	01624 629571	www.bodystat.com

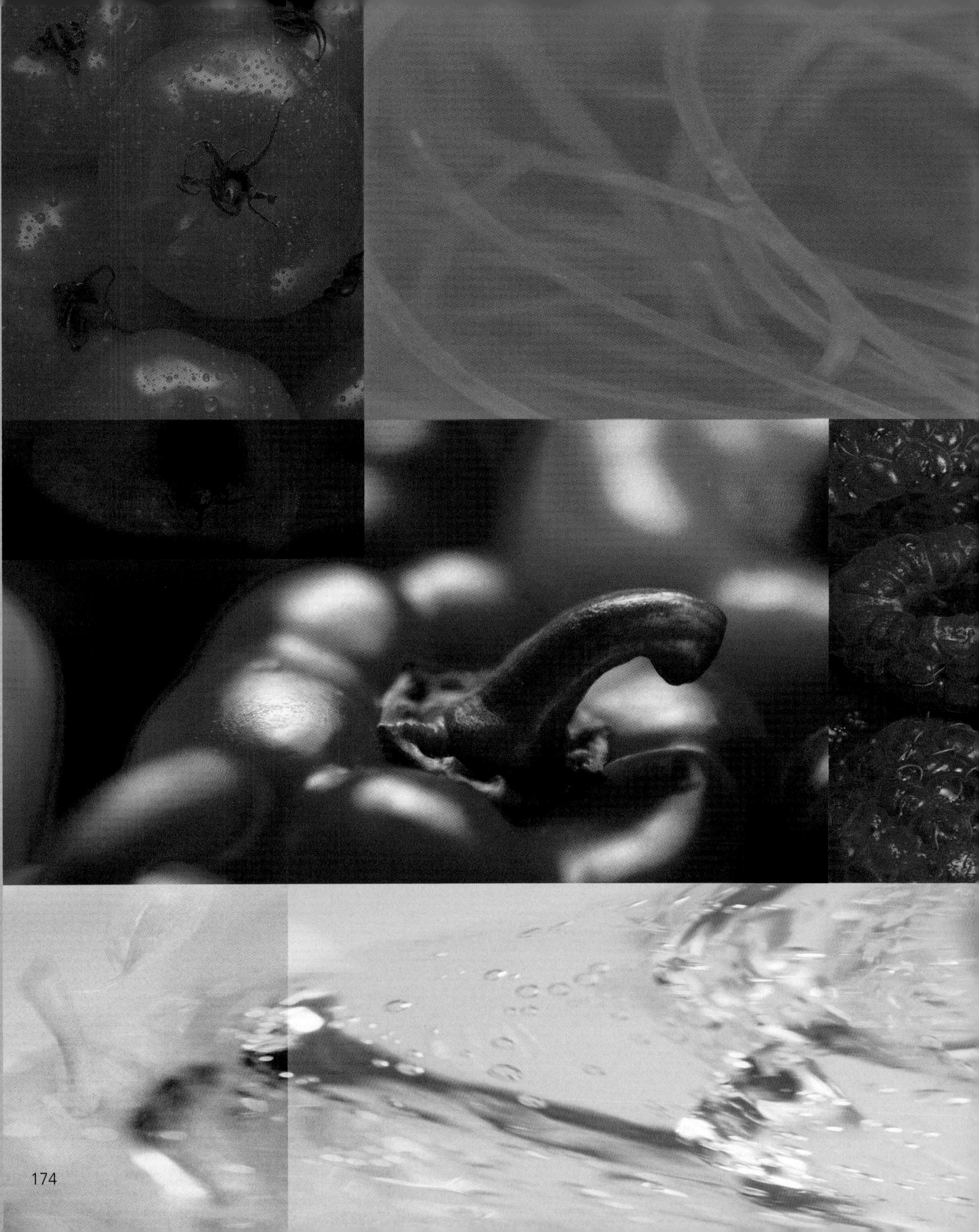

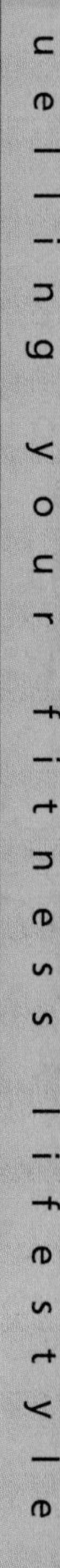

8 Fuelling your fitness lifestyle

To get the best from your fitness training, you need to get the most from your diet. What you eat can boost your CV performance, increase your lean muscle mass, speed up your metabolism and help you burn fat. Trouble is, many of us believe that we are too busy to calorie count or select and prepare the best foods to optimally fuel our fitness and weight control goals. We're also overloaded with information from the 'diet industry', which tells us that this food is 'bad' for us, this food is 'good' for us, and that we should supplement our diets with various vitamins and minerals. All this conspires to make the simple process of eating seem complex. In this chapter I'll demystify 'nutrition' and will provide you with straightforward explanations as to how to get the best out of what you eat. I'll tell you how and when to eat and drink, and what vitamins, minerals and fitness supplements can enhance your fitness lifestyle.

MAKING THE RIGHT FOOD CHOICES

CARBOHYDRATE, FAT AND PROTEIN

You won't maintain your energy levels, recover between workouts or burn fat optimally if you don't make the right food choices. You derive your food energy from carbohydrates, protein and fat.

Carbohydrate

Carbohydrate should constitute 55–60 per cent of your daily food consumption.

Carbohydrate is your body's prime fuel source when you are physically active; on digestion it increases blood sugar levels and provides you with energy – as you will see later, some sources of carbohydrate do this more quickly than others. Carbohydrate is also stored in your muscles and liver as glycogen. As I've mentioned previously, glycogen is premium-grade muscle fuel and our bodies can only store it in limited amounts. It needs to be constantly replenished for you to remain in optimum workout condition.

Carbohydrate energy is released through a series of chemical reactions that use glycogen, glucose and oxygen as the starting materials.

DIETARY TIP

Keep a food diary. It will provide you with a great starting point for making dietary changes. Be honest: write down everything you eat over a period of at least five days. You'll soon see how much you're snacking, how much saturated fat you're eating and whether you're going for low- or high-GI foods (GI stands for glycaemic index; see page 117) and what your daily calorific intake is. With the information provided in this chapter you'll soon be able to make the right changes.

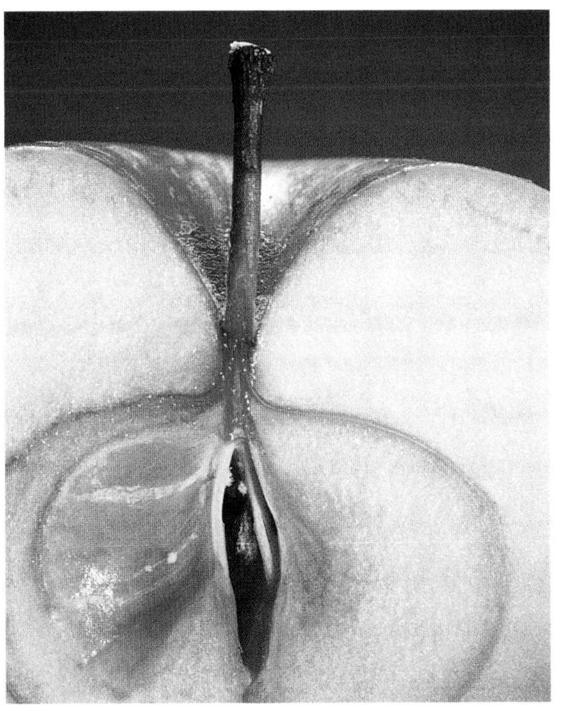

Table 8.1

The glycaemic index of selected carbohydrates

Food	GI
SUGARS	
Glucose	100
Sucrose	65
BREAD, RICE AND PASTA	
Bread – white	70
Bread – wholemeal	69
Pizza	60
Rice – brown	76
Rice – white	87
Rice – basmati	58
Macaroni	45
Instant noodles	46
BREAKFAST CEREALS	
Cornflakes	84
Weetabix	69
Muesli	56
Porridge with water	42
All-Bran	42
FRUIT AND VEGETABLES	
Pineapple	66
Raisins	66
Watermelon	72
Banana	55
Orange	44
Plum	39
Grapes	46
Apples	38
Baked potato	85
Chips	75
Boiled potato	56
Peas	48
Carrots	49
Broad beans	79
DAIRY PRODUCTS	
Ice cream	61
Custard	43
Full-fat milk	27
Skimmed milk	32
PULSES	
Red kidney beans	27
Butter beans	31
Soya beans	18
BISCUITS AND SNACKS	
Shortbread	64
Oatmeal	55
Ryvita	69
Rice cakes	85
Tortillas	72
Muesli bar	61
Mars bar	68
Muffin	44
Peanuts	14

Simple and complex carbohydrates

Carbohydrates can be divided into simple (sugars) and complex types (fibres and starches). Simple carbohydrates contain one or two sugar units in their molecules, while complex carbohydrates contain from 10 to thousands of sugar units. Many foods contain a mixture of simple and complex carbohydrates, so to measure their immediate energy release, foods are given a glycaemic index (GI) rating. This ranges from 1 to 100. Low-GI foods release their energy more slowly than high-GI foods.

Optimise your energy levels

Knowing the GI of foods will enable you to optimise your energy. If you need a quick boost, perhaps before a workout, then a high-GI food is a good choice, while low-GI foods eaten regularly throughout the day will provide you with a steady supply of energy. They will keep your metabolism revving nicely and will reduce cravings (see page 183 for a typical day's eating plan).

Despite its usefulness, GI also has its limitations: it measures the energy release from single foods rather than meals that usually combine different carbohydrates, fats and proteins. This 'mix' obviously affects energy release. On page 178, you'll find some factors to take into account when estimating the energy release of meals.

Factors to take into account when estimating the energy release of meals:

- Protein and fat reduce GI.
- For meals that combine two different GI-rated foods in roughly the same quantity, such as rice and kidney beans, you should total the GI of the two foods and divide by two. (Example: rice GI = 87, kidney beans GI = 27 total GI = 114; therefore the meal's average GI = 57 (114 divided by 2).)
- Sugar (sucrose): in the liver sucrose becomes one molecule of glucose and one molecule of fructose. The process of converting fructose into glucose in the liver takes time, and this results in a smaller increase in blood sugar.
- The smaller the size of the food particles the more quickly the food will be digested and therefore the quicker it will release its energy – hence the high GI of foods like bread and breakfast cereals.

Fat

Fat should constitute no more than 30 per cent of your daily calorific consumption for general fitness goals. If you are seeking specific fat burning for weight loss and body-shaping purposes then this figure may be reduced to 20 per cent, with a commensurate increase in protein.

The lazy fuel

As I mentioned in Chapter 7, *'Fat Burning; the real deal'*, fat is lazy. It's doesn't like to put in too much effort to fuel our daily or fitness lifestyle. It makes little contribution to the thermic effect of feeding (see page 157) and doesn't fill us up in the same way that carbohydrate does, which unfortunately encourages us to eat more and more of it. Combine all that with the facts that one gram of fat contains twice as many calories as protein and carbohydrate, and that our body can store it in almost unlimited quantities, and you'll more than understand why we must make this lazy food source work for us. We must control its consumption carefully and select the right fat for our diet.

DIETARY TIP

Not all fat is bad for you. You need some fat to survive, but you should stick to obtaining no more than 30 per cent of your daily calorific consumption from it and in the proportions described on page 179.

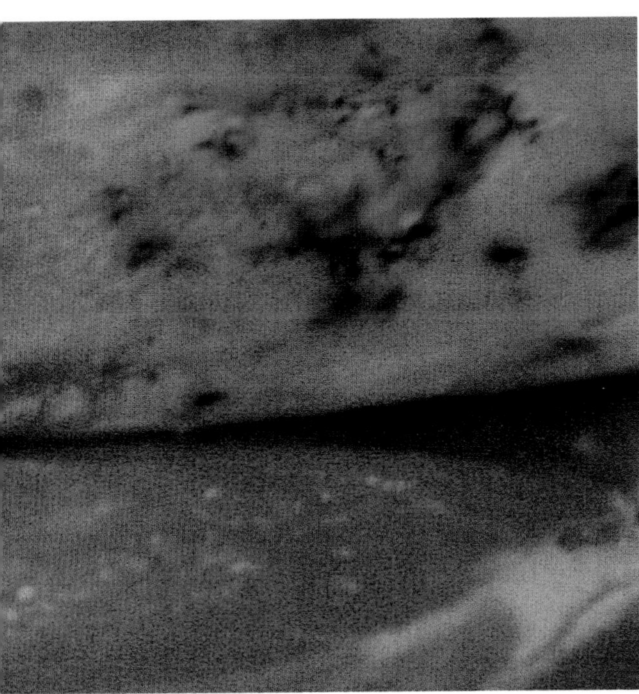

If your diet includes a healthy fat balance then your cholesterol levels will be kept in check.

Table 8.2
Just what does 'reduced fat' mean?

LABEL	FAT CONTENT
Fat free	Less than 0.15 g of fat per 100 g
Low fat	Less than 3 g of fat per 100 g
Reduced fat	Should contain 25% (or more) less fat than the full-fat alternative
Low-fat spread	40 g of fat per 100 g

Cholesterol and fats

Most of us are aware of cholesterol, and perhaps you think about it negatively. In reality, though, cholesterol performs a number of positive bodily functions. One of these is its assistance in the production of numerous hormones. Although 'LDL* cholesterol' is commonly referred to as 'bad', it's only actually bad when its levels in the body are pushed up by factors that include a lack of exercise, obesity and the consumption of too many saturated fats.

Knowing your fat facts

Saturated fat should constitute less than 10 per cent of your total fat consumption. This type of fat is found mainly, but not exclusively, in dairy and animal products, and is the most 'harmful' as in excess it can raise LDL cholesterol and, with it, the risk of heart disease.

Examples of saturated fats are butter, cheese and the fat on meat; all are hard at room temperature.

Monounsaturated fats are found in olive oil, nuts and seeds, and can reduce LDL cholesterol and its negative effects. These fats are normally liquid at room temperature. They should make up around 12 per cent of your daily food consumption.

Polyunsaturated fats are found in most vegetable oils, oily fish, nuts and seeds. They are liquid at room temperature and below. This type of fat can also reduce LDL cholesterol. It is recommended that around 10 per cent of your daily food consumption comes from polyunsaturated fats.

Essential fatty acids (Omega-3 and Omega-6 series) cannot be produced in the body and must be provided by food. Omega-3 essential fatty acids can prevent blood clotting, have anti-inflammatory properties and are beneficial to the immune system. Omega-3 fats are found in some nuts and seeds (such as flax seeds, walnuts, pumpkin seeds and soya beans) and oily fish (such as sardines, mackerel, salmon, trout and herring). Omega-6 fatty acids can reduce LDL cholesterol and are beneficial for healthy skin. They are found in nuts, seeds, some vegetable oils, such as sunflower, and the germ of whole grains.

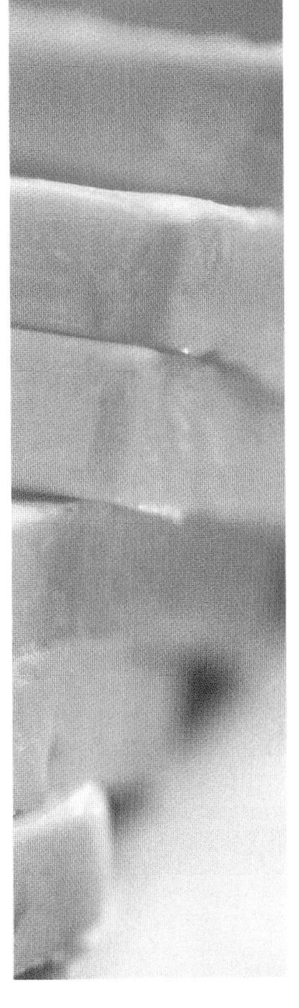

* Low density lipoprotein

FAT-BURNING DIETARY TIPS

- You could skip a pre-workout high-GI carbohydrate boost, as going without can encourage your body to use fat as its workout fuel source rather than carbohydrate.
- Throughout the day, go for low-GI foods as these will reduce your desire to snack, which will make you less prone to falling for high-calorie 'fatty temptations'.
- Don't yo-yo diet. Starving the body by going on a crash diet can lead to weight loss in the short term and weight gain in the long term. Your body is designed to cling on to calories in times of shortage. So it will attempt to eke out as much energy as it can from each gram it consumes – as when on a severely restricted calorie-controlled diet – if it knows the next one will be a long time coming. Yo-yo diets can slow your metabolic rate and inhibit your fat-burning efforts.

Protein

Protein should constitute 10–15 per cent of your daily food consumption.

With protein it's less a case of fuelling your fitness lifestyle and more a case of building it: about 25 per cent of your body is composed of protein. Protein is needed to repair and develop muscle tissue that has broken down through training – in short, it's a building block. When protein is digested it's converted into amino acids – some of these are known as 'essential' because they cannot be synthesised in the body. Non-essential amino acids, however, can be made in the body, provided enough of the essential amino acids are present.

DIETARY TIP

Here are some useful calculations.

- To convert Kcal to grams of carbohydrate, divide by four. (Example: if you need to consume 2000 Kcal of carbohydrate a day, then you would need to consume 500 g of it – remember that 60 per cent of your daily food consumption should derive from carbohydrate.)
- To work out your daily protein needs, multiply your weight by the number of grams of protein you need – this will vary with regard to your training goals (see page 181).

DIETARY TIP

Some 65 per cent of your body's total protein content is contained in your muscles, and this figure can be significantly increased by weight training. Weight training increases the rate of protein synthesis and breakdown in your muscles – hence the need for increased protein consumption if you want to sustain and increase muscle mass. Remember that the leaner you are the more effective fat burner you will be.

How much protein do you need?

If you mainly CV train, you should aim for at least 1.2–1.4 g protein/kg of body weight per day.

If you weight train, up this figure to 1.4–1.7g protein/kg of body weight per day.

Protein can supply some energy but this process only really becomes important during very prolonged and intense periods of exercise when your glycogen stores have been used up.

DIETARY TIP

Just because a food is high in protein does not mean it is the best thing to eat: meat is not only high in protein but also saturated fat.

Protein rating

Proteins are given a rating that indicates their level of inclusion of all the essential amino acids. For example, fish has a protein rating of 70–100, milk 67 and brown rice 57. Turkey, cottage cheese, egg whites, soya beans, semi-skimmed milk and pulses are great low-fat sources of protein.

DIETARY TIP

Soya, tofu and quinoa are rich protein sources for vegetarians and non-vegetarians, because they combine a high protein content with little fat and are also great carbohydrate sources. Quinoa can be obtained from health food shops and is a great rice substitute. Vegetarians should ensure that they get their protein from these and similar other great protein plant sources – but if you are a vegetarian, you should note that plant sources are generally not as effective at supplying your body with essential amino acids as are animal sources.

Go organic!

Organic foods are now a staple in our supermarkets. Why should you buy them? You might buy a food product, like cereal, that proudly promotes the fact that it is vitamin or mineral enriched or fortified — the sad thing is that this would not be the case if modern food processing and farming methods had not reduced the vital vitamin and mineral content of the product below an acceptable level in the first place. If you look at Table 8.3 you'll readily be able to see why going organic could optimise your mineral consumption without the need to supplement.

Table 8.3

Food processing and mineral loss: selected staple foods

	WHITE FLOUR	REFINED SUGAR	RICE
Chromium	98 per cent	95 per cent	92 per cent
Zinc	78 per cent	88 per cent	54 per cent
Manganese	86 per cent	89 per cent	75 per cent

Balance your eating for good health

The continuous consumption of the 'wrong' foods, like fatty products, fast food, processed foods and fizzy drinks, can lead to a number of illnesses, diseases and the inability of the body to detoxify itself. Maintaining the right equilibrium within our body by consuming the right balance of nutrients will go a long way to keeping us in good health.

EATING ON A TYPICAL FITNESS DAY

Breakfast

Breakfast really is the most important meal of the day. If you don't consume sufficient calories first thing, you'll run the risk of not having enough energy to get you through the day – or, more likely, through until mid-morning. A high-carbohydrate, low-fat start is what's required; this will enhance both your mental and physical mood.

Grab a bowl of muesli, it will provide 33 g of carbohydrate energy, and use low-fat semi-skimmed milk, which contains only 2.8 per cent fat per 100 g. Eat some fruit, it's a great energy source, and some (like plums and oranges with a low GI) will release their energy slowly over the next few hours. To maintain energy levels, bagels are another great breakfast option – high in carbohydrates and low in fat, you could combine them with honey or peanut butter.

Mid-morning

If you feel peckish around 11 am an energy bar makes a good choice. It will provide around 150 low-fat, high-carbohydrate calories. Raisin scones make another good choice.

Lunch

A pasta-based meal will set you up nicely for an early-evening workout. Pasta releases its energy slowly over a period of two to four hours; 100 g of (uncooked) pasta will provide 76 g of carbohydrate.

DIETARY TIP
500 ml of diluted fruit juice will provide 30 g of carbohydrate as will 500 ml of an isotonic sports drink.

Mid-afternoon

A similar mid-afternoon snack, to the one you had mid-morning should keep you going nicely. A banana, a handful of raisins or an energy bar will give you a further quick energy release if you need one before your workout.

Workout

If the workout lasts more than an hour, then consuming additional carbohydrate will also improve your performance. To derive maximum benefit it's crucial that this process is started within the first half an hour of the workout; you should aim for 30–60 g of carbohydrate, preferably from a sports drink or energy bar. This 'in-workout refuelling' should enable you to exercise for at least a further 45 minutes relatively comfortably.

Post-workout

The first hour or two after your workout is the ideal time to eat and rehydrate to maximise your body's recovery processes. Exercise burns glycogen and breaks down muscle protein – eating the right foods and in the right quantities post-workout will significantly kickstart your recovery and refuel you for your next workout. It will also have the added benefit of keeping your metabolism ticking over nicely.

After a workout, aim for at least 2 g of carbohydrate per kg of body weight and 40 g of protein. That's 130 g of carbohydrate for a 65 kg person.

Evening meal

You could go for a jacket potato filled with beans, fish, chicken or cheese. Lean beef, chicken and rice (preferably brown) are also great choices. They'll continue the refuelling and recovery process and will keep your energy levels elevated.

Personal reflections

I have to admit that I have never really paid enough attention to my diet. Now, in hindsight, I wish I had. Of course, I'm now doing my best to catch up and eat the right foods and in the right proportions – remember, it's never too late. I, like many of us who are active, thought that I could eat what I liked without having to worry too much about the consequences. Within certain boundaries that is the case, as we will of course burn more calories and be less likely to put on weight than the less active, but there are also, as I have been pointing out, other important fitness lifestyle and general health reasons for really paying attention to what we eat.

Drink water and boost your energy levels

Drinking two litres of water a day will prevent dehydration and keep your energy levels up. When you work out, you should increase your fluid consumption by an additional 0.5 to 1 litre for every hour of exercise.

FLUID FACTS

Dehydration can significantly affect workout performance. To prevent this, you shouldn't wait until you feel thirsty before drinking – it will be too late by then. You should drink plenty of water and use sports drinks, especially before and during training and immediately afterwards, to re-boost your energy levels and kickstart post-exercise glycogen refuelling. It's best to avoid tea and coffee as these are diuretics and can actually increase your level of thirst.

A 3–5 per cent loss in body weight caused by dehydration can significantly impair judgement, mental sharpness and reaction times, as well as aerobic performance. A runner could lose 1.2 litres of water running at six-minute-mile pace on a cool (10°c) day and a loss of just 2 per cent (that's 1.5 kg if you weigh 75 kg) in body weight caused by dehydration could impair performance by 10–20 per cent.

Drink alcohol moderately

Alcohol has no nutritional value and is high in calories. A glass of red wine contains 85 Kcal, and a shot of vodka, whisky or gin contains 55 Kcal.

DIETARY TIP

If you're well hydrated, your urine will be clear and odourless.

VITAMINS, MINERALS AND SUPPLEMENTS

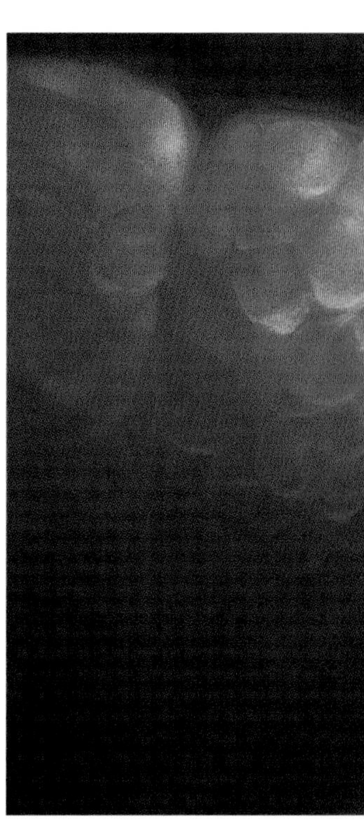

Minerals

A total of 22 mainly metallic minerals make up 4 per cent of your body mass; their main function is to balance and regulate your internal chemistry. For example, they play a crucial role in the maintenance of muscle contractions, regulation of heartbeat and nerve conduction.

Vitamins

Vitamins are crucial in facilitating energy release from food, but do not produce energy themselves. As with minerals, consuming excessive amounts (above the recommended Reference Nutrient Intake) does not enhance their metabolic contribution.

Table 8.6 contains a breakdown of what selected vitamins and minerals can do for your body fitness-wise; obviously they have many other positive health benefits too.

Table 8.6
Fitness-enhancing minerals and vitamins

VITAMINS/MINERAL	FUNCTION	REFERENCE NUTRIENT INTAKE (RNI)	SELECTED SOURCES
Biotin (vitamin)	Assists glycogen manufacture and protein metabolism for muscle building	No UK RNI: 10–200 ug/day is recommended	Egg yolk, nuts, oats and whole grain
Calcium (mineral)	Assists muscle contraction	Men 1000 mg/day Women 700 mg/day	Dairy products, seafood, vegetables, flour bread, pulses
Iron (mineral)	Can assist CV exercise	Men 8.7 mg/day Women 14.8 mg/day	Liver, red meat, pasta and cereals, green leafy vegetables
Zinc (mineral)	Important for metabolising proteins, carbohydrates and fats	Men 9.5 mg/day Women 7 mg/day.	Lean meat and fish, eggs, whole-grain cereals, dairy products
Magnesium (mineral)	Boosts energy production and assists muscle contraction, appears to play a role in blood sugar stabilisation	Men 300 mg/day Women 270 mg/day (current research indicates that these figures may need to be increased)	Green leafy vegetables, fruit, unrefined whole grains and cereals

Table 8.5

Antioxidant vitamins and minerals

ANTIOXIDANT VITAMINS AND MINERALS	REFERENCE NUTRIENT INTAKE (RNI) PER DAY	SELECTED SOURCES
A (vitamin)	Men 700 mcgs Women 600 mcgs	Dairy products, oily fish, liver, butter and margarine
Betacarotene (vitamin)	15–25 mgs (suggested intake, no official RNI)	Bright red, green, orange and yellow vegetables
C (vitamin)	Men and women 60 mgs	Citrus and other fresh fruits, vegetables, particularly dark green leafy ones, and berries
E (vitamin)	No official UK RNI, EU recommendation 10 mg	Pure vegetable oils, nuts, sunflower seeds, avocados, wholemeal bread
Selenium (mineral)	Men 75 mcgs Women 60 mcgs	Tuna, oysters, herrings, cottage cheese, seafood

Antioxidant vitamins and minerals

Don't know what mcgs are, or a mg? Don't worry, explanations are provided below.

Understanding units of measurement

Most people are familiar with the unit of weight called a gram, which is about the weight of a Smartie. Apart from calcium and potassium, the amounts of each nutrient required by the body each day are much less than a gram, so other (much smaller) units are used.

- The milligram is abbreviated mg and is one-thousandth of a gram. There are 1000 mgs in a gram.
- The microgram is abbreviated mcg and is one-millionth of a gram. There are 1000 mcgs in each milligram.
- The International Unit is abbreviated IU. It is sometimes used instead of mgs or mcgs for some of the vitamins, such as A, D and E, where there is more than one form available. International Units express the biological activity that different forms of a vitamin exhibit.
- The UK Reference Nutrient Intake is abbreviated RNI. It is the daily amount deemed adequate to prevent deficiencies in 97.5 per cent of the UK population.

ANTIOXIDANTS AND PHYTOCHEMICALS

Antioxidants

A diet rich in antioxidants (vitamins A, C, E, betacarotene and the mineral selenium) will prevent free radical damage to cells, reduce LDL cholesterol and defend your body against age-related illnesses such as heart disease and cancer.

These vitamins and minerals are especially important for those of us in hard training, particularly tough aerobic and/or anaerobic training. These workouts can increase free radical cellular damage. We need oxygen to survive – it fuels our heart and lungs and all our bodily processes, including energy release from food. Unfortunately, oxygen metabolism can create unstable molecular fragments, which can damage our cells if left unchecked. Antioxidant vitamins, minerals and phytochemicals (see page 188) will help combat this cellular damage.

Phytochemicals

Phytochemicals are not needed by our bodies to survive, so they are not regarded as nutrients, but they do play a vital role in maintaining our health. There are over 100 phytochemicals and, like essential amino acids, they cannot be stored in the body. Examples include bioflavonoids (the one you might have heard of because it's found in red wine, which has recently been advocated as being beneficial to health for this reason), phytoestogens, capasicin and allium compounds. Table 8.4 summaries selected phytochemical sources and their positive health benefits.

Are you getting enough?

To ensure a plentiful supply of antioxidants and phytochemicals in your diet you need to eat a variety of plant foods, rice, bread, pasta, and seven to eight daily servings of fruit and vegetables (this includes fruit juice and 'smoothies'). Many supermarkets now display what a daily serving of a particular fruit and vegetable source is. You'll soon see that you don't need to leave the supermarket with a wheelbarrow full of fruit and vegetables to consume the required amount.

Table 8.4

The positive health benefits of selected phytochemicals

PHYTOCHEMICAL	SOURCE	HEALTH BENEFIT
Allium compounds	Onions, garlic, chives, shallots	Can combat cancer and benefit the immune system
Bioflavonoids	Rosehips, citrus fruits, berries, grapes, tea, red wine	Antioxidant, they can act as an antibiotic and can benefit bleeding gums, bruises and soft tissue injuries
Ellagic acid	Strawberries, grapes, raspberries	Can combat cancer
Phytoestrogens	Soya, tofu, citrus fruits, pulses, wheat, celery	Significant effect on reducing the onset of breast and prostrate cancer, and can reduce the hormonal responses associated with the menopause

FITNESS-ENHANCING SUPPLEMENTS

Creatine

Creatine is one of the best-known training supplements on the market. It's naturally produced by the liver and kidneys and is found in muscles, where it is used to produce energy. Research indicates that loading muscles with additional creatine through supplementation will increase your exercise potential (i.e. you'll be able to perform more repetitions and sets when weight training or other short-term anaerobic and anaerobic energy-based activities, like interval training repetitions). Recent research also indicates that creatine can benefit aerobic training.

Any downsides to creatine use are more anecdotal than proven. Some people experience greater levels of muscular cramping when taking creatine, so to avoid this increase your fluid intake.

Creatine can be purchased in different forms, as pure creatine monohydrate, or mixed with other supplements to ease absorption and have other training and recovery enhancing effects.

Try sprinkling pure creatine monohydrate on to your food for ease of absorption.

Glucosamine sulphate

If you suffer from aching joints, or even if you don't, then taking glucosamine sulphate can be beneficial. This supplement gradually encourages soft tissue to repair and regenerate. Like creatine, the research that exists on the supplement is positive. It won't give you new knee joints, but it seems that it can prevent further deterioration and promote an active and long-lived fitness lifestyle.

Regular creatine supplementation can increase lean muscle by an average of 2.5 kg, which also makes it a great fat-burning supplement.

Obtaining nutritional advice

In the UK, a State Registered Nutritionist will have taken a four-year degree course in nutrition and dietetics. 'State Registered' is a protected title and ensures that the practitioner is a competent qualified nutritional adviser. It is possible for practitioners to gain qualifications from other sources. Numerous colleges and training bodies run sports nutrition courses; some of these are accredited by universities. Many State Registered Nutritionists will have also become qualified in sports nutrition.

Accredited Sports Dieticians will have taken a course accredited by the British Dietetics Society. A registration process for sports nutritionists (not dieticians) is also being developed to help ensure that those who offer advice on nutrition and sport are appropriately qualified, and a number of bodies have drawn up criteria on which competency can be assessed. It is also the intention for the Nutrition Society to accredit courses that offer appropriate training.

Just like when you're looking for a personal trainer it's in your best interest to find out as much as you can about a nutritional practitioner before booking yourself an appointment and parting with your money.

Your diet can significantly improve your fitness and everyday lifestyle; obtaining professional advice can therefore be very beneficial.

Useful contacts

THE BRITISH NUTRITION FOUNDATION (BNF)
High Holborn House
52–54 High Holborn, London
Tel 020 7404 6504
Website www.nutrition.org.uk
This is a charitable organisation, which 'influences all in the food chain from the government, [and] the professions to media'.

BRITISH DIETETIC SOCIETY
5th Floor, Charles House
148/9 Great Charles Street
Queensway, Birmingham B3 HT
Tel 0121 643 5487
Website www.bda.uk.com

NUTRITION SOCIETY
10 Cambridge Court
210 Shepherds Bush Road
London W6 7NJ
Tel 020 7602 0228
Website www.nutsoc.org.uk
'Formed in 1941 to advance the scientific study of nutrition and its maintenance of human and animal health.'

9 Fitness Classes

Go to any gym and pick up the fitness studio timetable and you'll be bombarded with a multitude of fitness class options. This is great for choice, but not so great if you don't know what a particular class is or does. In this chapter I'll identify the key fitness elements of the most popular classes and will also show you how to construct a training programme based around fitness classes. Note that, literally every week, a new fitness class hits the gyms. Many are fusions of two or more fitness formats, such as Yogalates — surprise, surprise an amalgamation of yoga and Pilates. It is beyond the scope of this chapter to consider these newer 'fusion classes' in detail.

FITNESS CLASSES

Fitness classes obviously develop different aspects of fitness. To help you understand these differences, I have identified the key fitness features of the most popular classes usually available. At a glance you'll be able to see the extent to which a class develops CV fitness, strength, co-ordination, flexibility and agility, and how much effort you will be expected to put into it.

Suggested target heart rate ranges and rates of perceived exertion (RPE) have also been provided for each option. Information is also provided on the calorie-burning potential of each class.

Note that the suggested heart rate ranges should only be viewed as estimates. The fitter you are, the closer you will be able to work towards the upper end of the range. Calorie-burning figures are also estimated and should not be regarded as exact. They are based on a 45-minute workout unless indicated otherwise.

Class structure

All classes will follow a broadly similar pattern whether CV, resistance, agility or flexibility based. You'll begin with a warm-up, and then the intensity will gradually increase, either in terms of physical exertion and/or the complexity of the movements required. Finally, as the class nears its end, a cool-down will take place.

Fitness classes are a great way to get fit in a sociable, fun and safe way.

TRAINING TIP

Chopping and changing between fitness classes will not produce systematic fitness gains. As with individually orientated training, you need to perform the same type of (in this case) class regularly to optimise your fitness.

What makes a good instructor?

Your instructor should be courteous, professional and knowledgeable. They should be able to address both the needs of the class and its individual members – this is no easy task. Before you start, they should ask whether any participants have any medical issues that might prevent them from taking part safely. This can be a difficult time for both instructor and class participant. It's very unusual for someone to pipe up if they do have a concern. I'd recommend that if you are in any way unsure about your suitability for taking part in a particular fitness class that you get to the gym early and speak to the instructor, or another suitably qualified member of staff, or you could of course phone first.

TRAINING TIP

Although fitness classes are a great way to exercise they can sometimes create circumstances where you can try that bit too hard. No one likes to be left behind, but with the adrenaline flowing and peer pressure all around, you could find yourself pushing a bit too hard. To avoid this, you should always work within yourself. You don't have to keep up with the fittest class members straight away – you will catch them up.

Personal reflections

I was never a great one for fitness classes, I'd rather lift weights or train for a sport. But since writing on health and fitness I've had to do numerous classes; these have ranged from Pilates to yoga, exercise bike to rowing classes, salsacise to martial arts. As I've got two left feet, I didn't find some quite as easy as others. But what I did derive from all of them was fun, irrespective of their intended fitness purpose. So if you are like I was – a bit of a fitness class sceptic – don't be. Select the right class or classes for you and enjoy yourself while you get fit.

UNDERSTANDING FITNESS CLASSES

Class ratings

Ratings have been provided out of 10 (where relevant) for the various types of fitness a class can develop. Use these to inform your selection and to gain an appreciation of what a particular class is designed to do.

Class rate of perceived exertion (RPE)

In the CV chapter (Chapter 4), RPE was used as a self-rating tool for CV workouts, based largely on heart rate, breathing and level of sweating. For fitness classes I have adapted this as a means of indicating the amount of effort that is normally associated with that fitness class. Scores are given out of 10.

An exercise bike-based class will require substantially more effort than a core stability class. The former will tax your CV system to a very high level, whereas the latter will have a much more localised and potentially less fatiguing effect. Hence I have given the former a rating of 9 out of 10 and the latter one of 6 out of 10.

Table 9.1

Estimated calorie-burning potential of fitness classes*

RATING	ESTIMATED CALORIE BURNING RANGE (KCAL)
Low	Less than 200
Medium	200–300
High	300–450
Very high	More than 450

* Figures are based on a 45-minute class.

Aerobics

Jane Fonda brought aerobics to the fitness mainstream and enthused about 'going for the burn' many years ago. Her early exercise videos have even become collector's items. Aerobics classes, or variations of them, still form the mainstay of most gym's studio timetables. They involve a series of choreographed dance and fitness moves, designed to increase and maintain heart rate. Classes are graded in terms of their energy requirement: low impact, medium and high impact are commonly used terms.

Rating and comments

CV this is the main class component	**8/10**
Strength very little direct contribution to strength development	**4/10**
Co-ordination good level required; don't give up, with repetition you will improve	**8/10**
Agility medium, but could be far greater, depends on the level of class	**7/10**
Flexibility little direct emphasis	**3/10**
Fat-burning potential	**high**
Suggested heart rate range	**60–80%**
RPE	**6–8**
Not suited to Anyone can enjoy and benefit from aerobics	

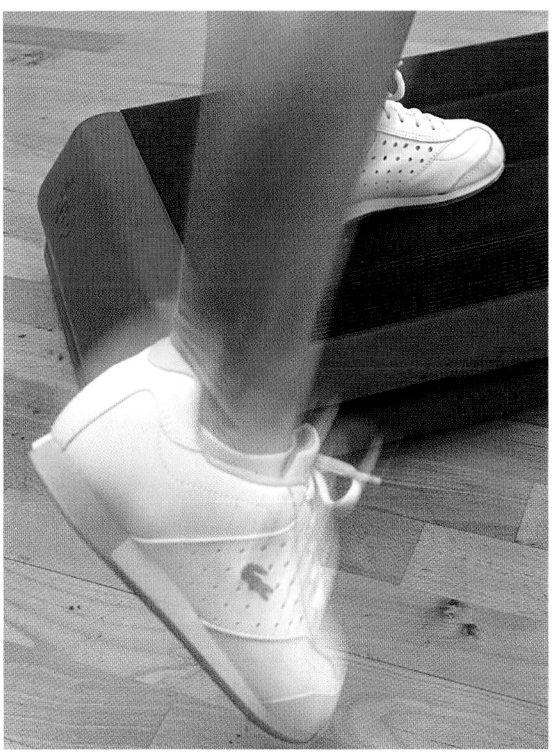

Step aerobics

Reebok® brought step aerobics to the fitness mainstream. Its multi-coloured plastic steps can be found in most gyms up and down the country. Aerobic dance moves and other exercises are performed on and around the step.

Rating and comments

CV like aerobics, the main class aim **8/10**
Strength due to the need to jump and step on to the step (and its potential for upper body exercises) you can expect a slightly greater improvement in strength from step **5/10**
Co-ordination step classes, in particular low-impact ones, require less co-ordination than aerobics classes, due to the more limited range of exercise options available **6/10**
Agility as aerobics **7/10**
Flexibility not emphasised **5/10**
Fat-burning potential **high**
Suggested heart rate range **60–80%**
RPE **6–8**
Not suited to Advanced classes involve repeated dynamic jumps that can place your knees, ankles and back under strain – so if you have weaknesses in these areas then these classes are best avoided.

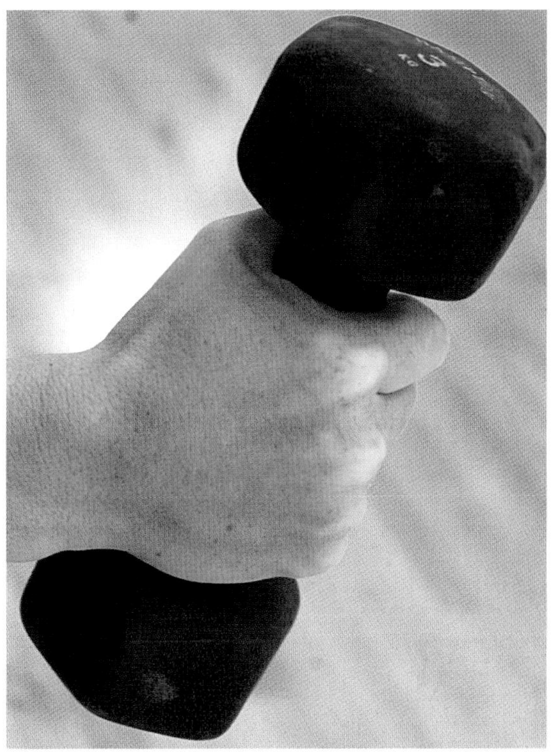

Body conditioning (sculpting)

Body sculpting classes combine light weights exercises, aerobics moves and circuit training exercises like press-ups and sit-ups in a mix designed to shape and tone the body.

Rating and comments

CV as you'll be moving around the studio with aerobic moves, your heart rate will maintain an elevated level, but this will not be as great as during aerobics and step classes. **7/10**
Strength with light weights (normally dumbbells) the class will have a primarily strength endurance and toning effect **6/10**
Co-ordination depends on the aerobics component **6/10**
Agility again, depends on the aerobics component **7/10**
Flexibility no real specific attention paid to improving flexibility **5/10**
Fat-burning potential **medium/high**
(this results from the class's CV aspect and its ability to increase everyday fat-burning potential by increasing lean muscle)
Suggested heart rate range **60–80%**
RPE **6–8**
Not suited to Those looking for significant gains in muscular strength.

Weights-based classes (BodyMax®, BodyPump®)

These classes take weight training moves out of the gym and into the fitness studio. With pre-choreographed routines and motivational music, the class aims to get women into using weights and men into the female focused world of the aerobics studio. To these ends, these classes have been very successful.

After a warm-up the class works its way up and down the body in terms of exercise selection. Large muscle group exercises, like squats and bench presses, are worked in together with smaller moves, like biceps curls. The instructor will vary the speed of movement of the lifts, and additional variation will be provided by use of part and full repetitions. You decide for yourself what weight to load on to your bar.

Rating and comments

CV this class will increase your CV fitness, but as you'll mainly be focused around your weight bench, you'll not move around sufficiently to develop it to a high level **6/10**

Strength you'll develop strength and local muscular endurance from the class, although the former aspect will be compromised by the high-repetition nature of the workout; expect very good muscular endurance and much more tone than a body-sculpting class **8/10**

Co-ordination not high, as most weights moves are straightforward to perform **4/10**

Agility low **3/10**

Flexibility could decrease, so stretch away from the class **3/10**

Fat-burning potential **high**

As a result of calories burned during the workout and in response to increased lean muscle mass

Suggested heart rate range **60–70%**

Classes that include an element of circuit resistance training (see page 109) will generate higher heart rates and an increased calorie burn

RPE **6–8**

Not suited to Those with back problems.

Army-style boot camp workouts

These often take place in parks during the warmer months as well as in gyms. If you fancy yourself as a bit of a commando or GI Jane and like getting barked at by a fatigue-clad sergeant major type then these classes are a great way to get fit. Don't expect much sympathy from your instructor though!

Circuit training

Circuit training combines mainly body-weight exercises with high repetitions and relatively short recoveries, the permutations of which are endless. If you are new to a class, you should always work within your own level of fitness and set yourself your own personal targets. By holding back, you will complete the session and when you return to your next class you'll be able to work that bit harder.

Whatever the circuit training (or fitness) class you take, being pushed is fine, but your instructor should always be aware of the acceptable limits for class members. Circuit training is considered in detail in Chapter 5.

Rating and comments

CV circuit training can significantly boost aerobic performance **7/10**

Strength a weights (CRT)-based class will develop more strength than a body-weight-orientated one; either way, you should expect increased muscle tone and more strength **8/10**

Co-ordination most exercises are straightforward **5/10**

Agility could be high if plyometric (jumping) and sports moves are incorporated **5/10**

Flexibility should be emphasised away from the class **3/10**

Fat-burning potential **high**

Like CV training, circuits can create the right conditions for benefiting from an everyday increase in metabolic rate

Suggested heart rate range **70–90%**

RPE **7–9**

Not suited to Those with joint problems, especially if the class involves jumping exercises.

Pilates

Pilates is a unique floor- and machine-based method of exercise, developed by Joseph Hubertus Pilates. Born in 1880, Pilates used his own approach to the body's mechanics, posture and breathing, and based his techniques on his own background in martial arts and gymnastics, and his observations of animals. Classes and sessions last between 45 and 90 minutes.

You can get involved in Pilates at your local gym or at a specialist Pilates centre. Mat-work classes are very popular in gyms. These focus on developing core stability and require (as do all Pilates forms) a distinctive breathing pattern. This can take some getting used to. A number of high-street gyms have also introduced machine-based Pilates workouts into their programmes – these items look like no other pieces of gym equipment and have names like 'Reformer' and 'Cadillac'.

Women can benefit from improved pelvic floor strength through Pilates.

Rating and comments

CV little CV effect **4/10**

Strength core stability will be improved significantly; with machine-based Pilates, greater overall body strength will also be developed **7/10**

Co-ordination some moves are quite difficult to co-ordinate, and it might take some time to be able to breathe in the required Pilates fashion in harmony with the exercises **7/10**

Agility more advanced exercises will require good agility and body awareness **7/10**

Flexibility a good level of flexibility is required to perform some exercises – this quality will be enhanced with regular Pilates training **8/10**

Fat-burning potential **low**
Because of the pace of the class

Suggested heart rate range not provided as most Pilates exercises are performed slowly and with control, precluding a significantly elevated heart rate level

RPE **6/7**

Not suited to Those who want increased muscle, significant improvements in lean muscle or increased CV fitness.

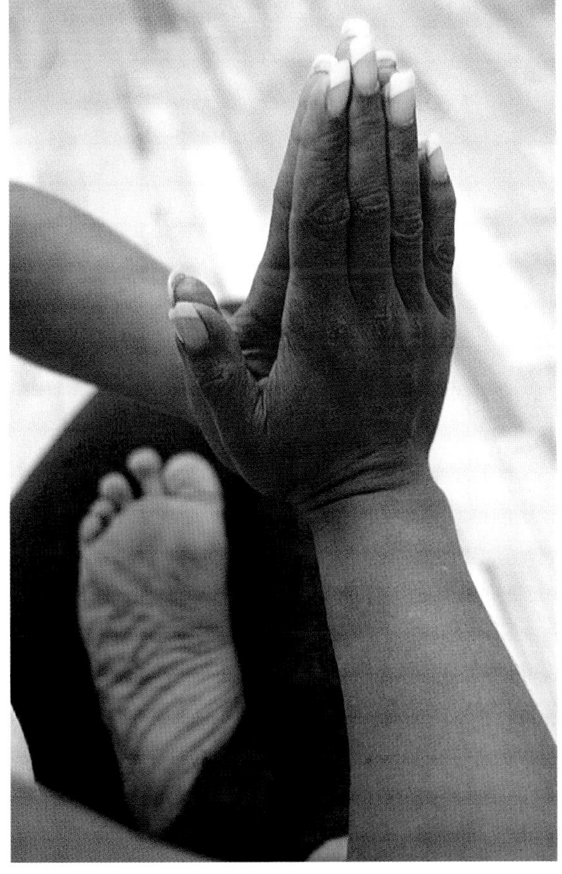

Yoga

Yoga's popularity has been boosted by the numerous celebrities that practise it, although it has been around for thousands of years. The most widely practised form of yoga is Hatha yoga, the physical discipline, however, there are different braches of yoga, characterised by a specific balance of exercise, meditation and spiritual aspects. Classes last 60 to 90 minutes. Yoga can be a great stress buster.

BodyBalance®

This is a mix of yoga, Pilates and the martial arts. Classes are standardised by the company that runs them (Les Mills International) in terms of specific content and progression. This is great for those of us that travel frequently and/or train at different gyms; basically you get the same workout wherever you go. Other classes that follow the same format wherever you may find them include BodyPump, RPM and BodyCombat.

Rating and comments

CV 'power' yoga classes can significantly elevate heart rate; other forms will have less of a CV effect **6–8/10**

Strength yoga can develop all-over body strength, because of the way positions are attained and held; regular class attendance can create a lean and honed physique **7/10**

Co-ordination most moves are relatively straightforward (if you have the flexibility and strength to attain them!) **8/10**

Agility similar to Pilates, a good level of body awareness is beneficial **7/10**

Flexibility many yoga moves are designed to elongate and relax muscles; numerous passive and active stretches will be involved and you should expect significant improvements in your range of movement **8/10**

Fat-burning potential **medium/high***

Suggested heart rate range **65–85%**

RPE **6–9***

* Depending on level and style of yoga.

Not suited to Certain positions should be avoided if you have back problems. Always inform your instructor if you have any concerns about a particular move. If you are carrying a little too much weight then you should combine yoga with CV work; this also applies to core stability and Pilates classes.

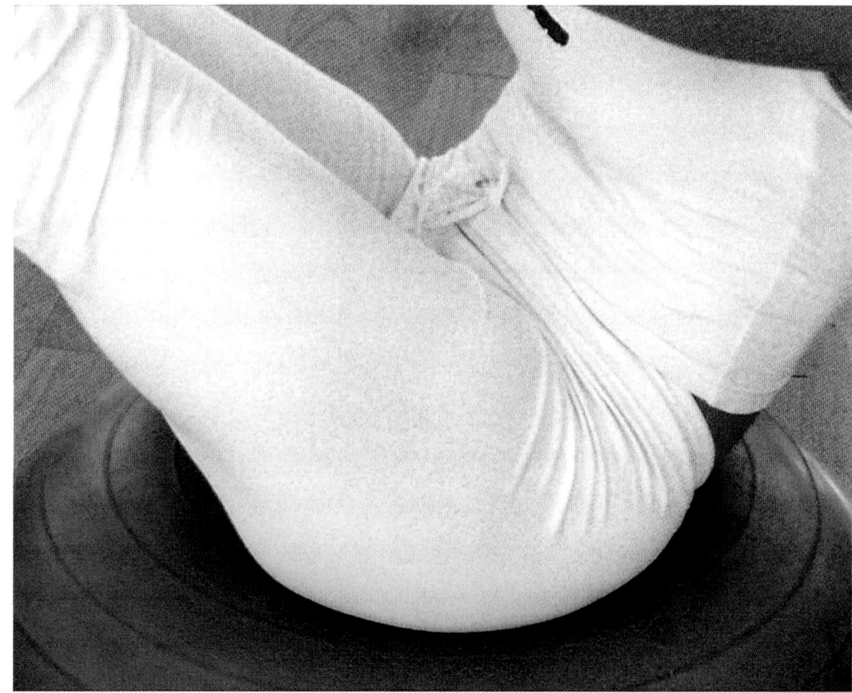

Core training

Core training is one of a new breed of very focused and targeted fitness classes. Wobble boards and BOSU board workouts (see page 132) are two typical examples. They build power, balance and functional strength, primarily, although not exclusively in the abdominals and back, through the use of specialist items of kit.

Rating and comments

CV these classes can elevate heart rate to relatively significant levels **6/10**

Strength will obviously emphasise core strength, but will also develop overall strength endurance **7/10**

Co-ordination due to the balance required, co-ordination requirements can be high **7/10**

Agility the agility required can also be high, a response again to the balance aspects of the class **7/10**

Flexibility good level of attention to flexibility **6/10**

Fat-burning potential **low/medium**

Suggested heart rate range **60–80%**

RPE **6–7**

Not suited to Those looking for significant fat loss.

Water- and pool-based classes

Numerous fitness class formats have transferred successfully from the fitness studio to the pool – aqua-aerobics is perhaps the most obvious example. These classes use the resistance provided by the water to exercise the heart and muscles effectively.

Rating and comments

The level of effort required will usually be lower than that required by the land-based equivalents; this is due to the restrictions placed on movement by the water, plus its cooling and buoyancy properties. Use the lower end of the RPE guides provided for land-based classes that have a water-based equivalent to gain an indication of the effort levels required.

Fighting-based classes (Tae-Bo, Khai-Bo, KO-BO, Boxercise, Kick Aerobics, BodyCombat)

These classes combine, to varying degrees, martial arts, boxing, circuit moves and aerobic exercise to make a demanding and exciting workout. Your instructor should spend some time teaching the correct techniques for the various punching and kicking moves, like the upper cut, jab, side, back and front kick. As the class progresses the speed and complexity of combinations will increase.

Rating and comments

CV high, be aware of this if you are new to exercise or to this type of class **8/10**

Strength high particularly strength endurance **7/10**

Co-ordination high, to master complex combinations **8/10**

Agility you'll be moving rapidly around the gym, so being light on your feet with quick reactions will be all-important **8/10**

Flexibility moderate to high requirement. Many of the moves performed require dynamic flexibility; these should be approached with care and with the mastery of correct technique **7/10**

Fat-burning potential **high**

Suggested heart rate range **70–90%**

RPE **7–9**

Not suited to Those seeking an easy workout or an increase in muscle size.

UNDERSTANDING FITNESS CLASSES

continued

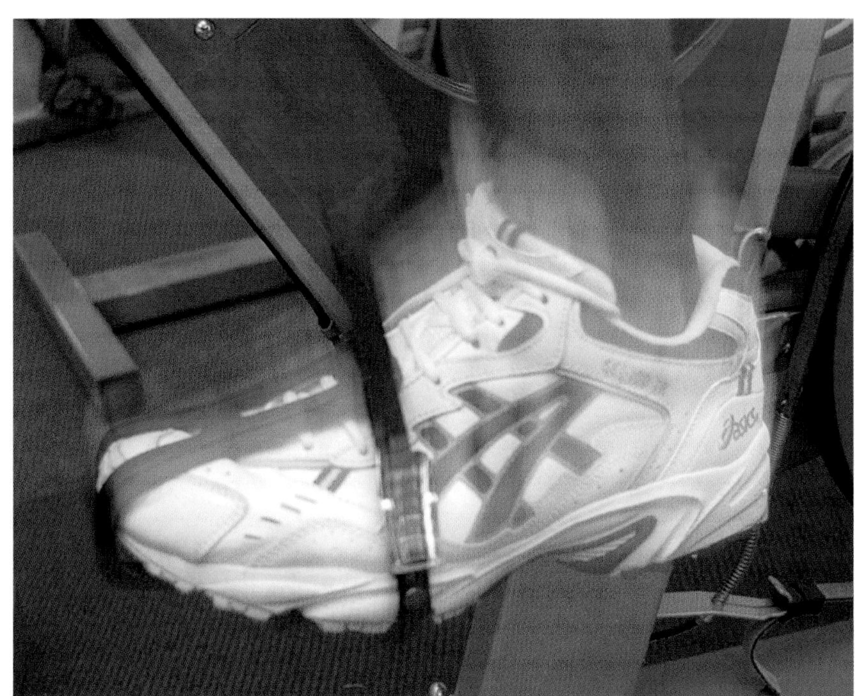

Exercise bike-based classes (Spinning®, Studio Cycling, RPM®)

These classes use exercise bikes that owe a great deal to road racing bike design. These 45–60-minute classes take you on a virtual race. After being shown how to set the bike up into a your personalised riding position, the class will begin with a gentle warm-up; this will be followed by some long sustained efforts, some short sprints, some out-of-the-saddle cruising and some hill climbs. These are achieved by adjusting the bike's resistance. You'll then go through a very welcome cool-down.

Rating and comments

CV very high; of all the exercise class formats mentioned so far, exercise bike classes can develop real 'competitive' high-end CV fitness; many amateur cyclists take these classes to break up their road work **9/10**

Strength upper and lower leg specific to the cycling action; no effect on arms **6/10**

Co-ordination minimal **3/10**

Agility minimal **3/10**

Flexibility no real contributory function, stretch away from the class **2/10**

Fat-burning potential **very high**

Suggested heart rate range **60–95%**

RPE **8–10**

Not suited to Those with little previous CV fitness experience, even entry-level classes can be tough. I'd recommend that you build up a background of CV fitness before saddling up for one of these classes.

Kids' classes

With ever increasing concerns over childhood obesity and lack of exercise, it's good to see that some high-street gyms are introducing kid's fitness classes. These are designed to introduce children to fitness in a fun and exciting way.

Indoor rowing

Rowing is a superb physical activity. It involves virtually all of the major muscles. It's a great way to develop CV fitness and muscular strength. Rowing classes enable everyone to row in time, at their own pace and level of effort. The instructor will ensure that sound rowing technique is mastered and will, as with exercise bike classes, construct a virtual race for you.

Rating and comments

CV high to very high **8/10**

Strength primarily strength endurance but rowing, unlike most other CV activities, can develop significant upper and lower body strength, power and muscle size **7/10**

Co-ordination required initially to master the rowing stroke **5/10**

Agility low **2/10**

Flexibility not specifically developed, stretch away from the class, paying particular attention to your back and hamstrings **2/10**

Fat-burning potential **very high**

Suggested heart rate range **60–95%**

RPE **7–10**

Not suited to: Those looking for a light workout or those with lower back problems. I'd also recommend that you have had a couple of workouts on a rowing machine before you take part in a class.

Fitness classes: training combinations

I've grouped together certain fitness classes that complement each other. These packages target specific fitness goals. So if you specifically want to get fit with fitness classes, here's how …

Weekly fitness class workouts for those seeking all-round fitness and tone (suitable for those new to exercise and intermediates)

Monday	Aerobics (low impact)
Wednesday	Yoga
Friday	Step aerobics (low impact)

Weekly fitness class workouts for intermediate exercisers after weight loss and body shaping

Monday	Cycle class
Wednesday	Weights-based class
Thursday	Pilates
Saturday	Fighting based class

Weekly fitness class workouts for intermediates and advanced trainers seeking high-quality CV fitness

Monday	Aerobics
Wednesday	Rowing class
Friday	Exercise bike-based class
Saturday	Fighting based class

Weekly fitness class workouts for intermediate and advanced trainers looking for significant increases in lean muscle

Monday	Weights-based class
Wednesday	Circuit training
Thursday	Yoga or Pilates
Saturday	Weights-based class

How to get the most out of your exercise class

1. Know your class! With all the information offered in this chapter, you should be able to choose the most suitable fitness class options for you.

2. Turn up in good time. Few instructors will let you join in a class once it has started.

3. Bring a bottle of water or sports drink with you to remain hydrated, and take sips throughout the class. Many instructors and class formats schedule in water breaks for this purpose.

4. Inform the instructor if you are new to a class or if you have any injury concerns. Better still, find out in advance if it's ok for you to take part.

5. Take a towel with you and follow the advice of notices often put up in gyms and exercises studios that proclaim 'Don't be a Drip!'

6. Wear good-quality cushioned and stabilising training shoes, particularly for step, aerobics, martial arts-based and circuit-training classes.

7. Wear clothing that will enable you to both move and sweat. It's also a good idea to bring a tracksuit with you to keep yourself warm immediately after the workout, to stop you getting a chill.

8. Use a heart rate monitor if you want to work to your own designated fitness levels.

9. Perform the same class for at least six weeks, once or twice a week, if you want to really benefit from it.

10. Try packaging your fitness classes into a weekly training plan, designed to meet a specific set of training goals. You'll find some suggestions on this page.

Fitness classes – useful contacts

Specialist class providers

BOSU Balance Training
Sportesse
Tel 01458 832210
Website www.bosu.uk.com
e-mail Alison@sportesse.com

Pilates
Body Control Pilates Association
Tel 020 7379 3734
Website www.bodycontrol.co.uk

RPM, BodyBalance, BodyCombat, BodyPump, BodyJam
FitPro/Les Mills Body Training Systems
Tel 08705 133434
Website www.fitpro.com

Yoga
British Wheel of Yoga
Tel 01529 306 851

Core training and step
Reebok
Tel 01908 512 244
Website www.reebokfitness.co.uk

Rowing classes
Concept2
Tel 0115 945 5522
Website www.concept2.co.uk

Rowing
Delta Fitness
Tel 01242 582739
Website www.deltafit.com
e-mail delta@dltafit.com

Watercrew (WaterRower)
Tel 020 8749 8400
Website www.waterrower.co.uk

Boxercise
Tel 01604 846658 to become an instructor
Website www.boxercise.co.uk

Kick aerobics
Tel 0800 389 6032 to become an instructor

Tae-Bo
Website www.taebo.co.uk

Spinning® (studio cycling)
Tel 01494 688260
Website www.spinning.com

Kids' fitness
Virgin Active
Tel 01908 546 616

Fancy becoming a fitness instructor or personal trainer yourself?

In addition to some of the contacts listed above you could contact the following organisations.

Focus Training
Tel 0800 731 9781
Website www.focus-training.com

Premier Global
Tel 01225 353535
Website www.premierglobal.co.uk

YMCA Fit
Tel 020 7343 1850 for London, the south-east and Birmingham
Website www.ymcafit.org.uk

10

Training through and beyond Pregnancy

I have shied away from providing a whole chapter on women's fitness in this book, as all the training principles provided apply equally to men and women. There is no such a thing as woman's muscle or a man's heart – they will respond to training in the same way whether male or female. However, men don't get pregnant! That's why in this brief chapter I will specifically consider how to train and plan your training during this beautiful period of life.

HOW HARD SHOULD YOU TRAIN DURING PREGNANCY?

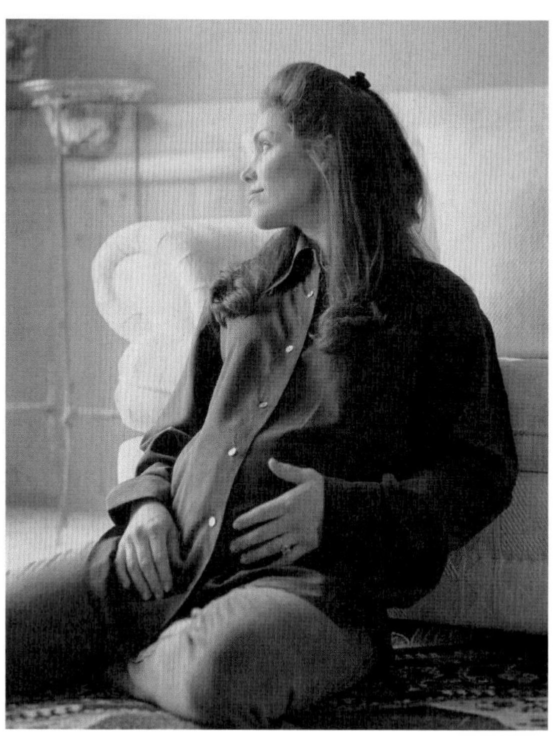

'Put your feet up on the sofa, I'll get you a cup of tea. Don't you move.' How many times have we heard or seen this sentiment when it comes to a husband or boyfriend 'protecting' their partner on hearing the news that they're going to become a father? Obviously this is no bad thing, as partners should nurture each other, but they could also do this by saying, 'I'll come with you to the gym: we'll do 20 to 30 minutes on the treadmill today, at an RPE of 5–6.'

Women can train throughout their pregnancy. This contrasts dramatically with what our mothers and grandmothers may have been told when they were expecting.

TRAINING THROUGH PREGNANCY – WHAT TO DO

Frequency

You can train most days of the week, if you want.

Intensity

This should be at a moderate level for CV exercise, to an RPE of 5–6, possibly 7 if you were very fit prior to your pregnancy. For resistance training, light to medium weights should be performed (40–60 per cent of 1RM). Your emphasis should be on smooth technique and rhythm: 12–20 reps, 2–4 sets.

Duration

This depends on your previous level of fitness. As a guide you should aim for 15–30 minutes of CV exercise per workout.

Should you avoid running?

Many female athletes continue to run well into their pregnancies without complications. You'll 'know' when it becomes uncomfortable to run. You should in any case vary your mode of exercise, just as you would if you were not pregnant, to prevent boredom, stagnation and potential injury. Switch between load-bearing activities like running and non-load-bearing ones, like rowing, cycling and pool-based fitness classes.

Many women successfully keep fit during their pregnancy and find that 'they get their body back' much more quickly after their baby is born. They may also find that the process of giving birth is made easier because of their fitness.

What about baby?

Women, not surprisingly, worry that exercising during pregnancy could harm their baby. But if they use common sense, and listen to their body and any professional advice that they are receiving, all will be OK.

It's good for baby too

Babies born to fit mothers are leaner, larger and healthier. In terms of miscarriages, research shows that levels are within the norm for the wider population (i.e. between 15 and 20 per cent).

What not to do

Don't over-stretch

As your body prepares for birth your levels of flexibility will increase due to the presence of the hormone relaxin. With this in mind, you should not attempt to stretch beyond your pre-pregnancy levels as this could lead to damage to joints and soft tissue. After your baby is born, your flexibility levels will return to normal.

Avoid dynamic and contact activities

Changes in your body shape and hormonal changes increase the risk of injury or falls if you take part in dynamic activity and, obviously, you should not take part in contact sports.

Listen to your body. If you are feeling tired, rest. Don't overdo it.
You will quickly be able to get back to pre-pregnancy levels of fitness.

Diet

Calorie control should not be adhered to when pregnant. You'll need to eat more because you are 'eating for two'. It is recommended that from the middle of the second trimester onwards, you should consume an additional 200–300 calories a day.

It is key that you and your developing baby receive the best nutrients. To this end carbohydrates are very important; not only will they provide you with energy, they'll also supply your growing baby with placental and foetal glucose. Your protein consumption should be 75 g to 100 g per day. Most women's weight will increase by 10–15 kg during pregnancy.

Remaining hydrated is equally important, so aim to drink two to three litres of water or fruit juice a day.

Table 10.1
Selected recommended vitamin and mineral consumption during pregnancy

VITAMIN /MINERAL	RECOMMENDED DAILY INTAKE
Calcium	1000–1200 mg
Iron	30 mg
Folic acid	800 micrograms (mcg)

You should also ensure that you are getting enough B vitamins. If you supplement, you should be aiming for 20 mcg of vitamin B12, 200 mg of vitamin B6 and 250 mg of magnesium.

Returning to your fitness regime

After the birth of your baby, good diet and great nutrition should be the goal for you and your child. When it comes to returning to your fitness regime use common sense. The presence of a newborn baby is a great source of joy and occasional stress. There will be sleepless nights and your lifestyle will have to adapt, but this does not mean that you should not train. Moderate your workouts and ensure that they add to your energy levels and don't deplete them. Gradually build up to your pre-pregnancy levels. Due to the hormonal changes that take place, many women find that they are able to achieve greater levels of fitness after the birth of their baby than before.

Finding the time and the facilities

Nearly all gyms have crèches that will enable you to continue working out. You could also set up your own support group with a couple of other mums and dads whose families have just been extended.

Walking while pushing your baby is a great form of exercise when the weather is good. Once, when I was in Los Angeles, I remember having to dodge numerous running mums and dads with specially designed pushchairs as I also ran along the beachfront. Baby joggers are available from some specialist baby and children shops, or contact babyrunner.com (Tel 01844 278314).

11 Sports Training

tips and drills

I have always kept fit by training for sport – normally track and field, and in particular the long jump. Whatever your sporting passion, the challenge to get fit so that you can perform at your best offers a great source of motivation. OK, so you might never lift the FA Cup or win an Olympic medal but there's still the satisfaction of knowing that on a certain day or at a certain time during a sports contest you achieved your best or performed a skill to an extent that you had only previously dreamed about. I know what it's like to experience occasions like these – the resultant high is hard to surpass. These peak-performance moments rely not only on your specific sports skills but also on the right physical conditioning. In this chapter I'll provide an introduction to sports training. You'll find information on specific warm-ups and a section on how to make you more dynamic, by improving your speed, power and agility.

SPECIFICITY: TRAIN YOUR MUSCLES THE RIGHT WAY FOR SPORT

The general principles of fitness training planning also apply to sports training: each training phase should build on the fitness achieved in the previous one as you develop and progress towards optimum playing condition.

Use the SMARTER planning principles to establish your sports training goals (see page 228).

Sport performance and core stability

Core stability is crucial for optimum sports performance. The abdominal and back muscles act as a shock absorber between the lower and upper limbs. If this region is specifically conditioned it will increase your power-generation capability, whatever your sport. For example, a runner or anyone involved in a running-based sport would not lose vital propulsive force through unwanted twisting movements with well-conditioned core strength.

Core stability will also reduce your potential for injury, caused either directly by your sport or through its specific preparation.

Fit ball exercises are great for developing sports-specific core stability as are powerbag and medicine ball exercises. (Powerbags are tubular padded sacks made with rip-stop vinyl with webbing handles at shoulder width; this means they are easily carried, lifted and thrown. You can perform a myriad of sports-specific exercises with them.)

The key to any successful sports training programme is specificity. Your training must dovetail into your sport and it must reflect its requirements. Never lose sight of this.

All body dynamic power can be developed by throwing Powerbags or weighted balls

Selecting and adapting training methods for sport

To get the most out of your sports-specific training you need to 'condition' yourself for your sport.

Table 11.1

Understanding the fitness conditioning requirements of selected sports

SPORT	FITNESS CONDITIONING REQUIREMENTS
Football, rugby, hockey, basketball, netball volleyball and racquet sports	A good base of aerobic fitness to enable quick recovery between efforts in training and matches. However, this is not as important as anaerobic fitness. Anaerobic training will specifically address the stop-start nature of these sports. You'll need to train the short-term and the anaerobic energy systems. Speed – straight line and multi-directional. Medium to high levels of power – to push past an opponent or jump and reach a ball. This can be developed by weight training and plyometrics. Agility – to move quickly and deftly in complex situations. This can be developed by specific drills (see page 223). Strength endurance – to perform powerful and specific skills – a tennis volley or basketball block – time after time. Circuit training and CRT are great options.
Sprinting, jumping and throwing athletic field events	Reasonable aerobic base for general fitness purposes. Excellent mid-region anaerobic fitness (achieved mainly via interval training of less than one minute's duration). High short-term anaerobic ability (less than 10 seconds), to enable multiple training and competition high-powered efforts. High power levels – to jump, throw, or propel oneself or an object as far as possible. Power weight training and plyometric drills.
Skiing/snow boarding	Medium to good CV ability; this should be built on a combination of aerobic and anaerobic training. Powerful thighs – complemented by good all-body strength endurance. Power and strength endurance weight training and CRT are great options. High level of core stability for injury avoidance and power transference. Agility.
Golf	Reasonable aerobic base. Core stability – selected fit ball exercises would be very beneficial. Upper-body power and flexibility – developed through weights and medicine ball throws.

For a description of energy systems, see page 47.

The sports-specific warm up

As was indicated in Chapter 3, certain types of stretching have a limited relevance to sports performance. The drills that follow are relevant, and offer a great way to warm up for the majority of sports. Always raise your body temperature by jogging for 5–10 minutes before completing them. Start slowly and perform them with control before increasing their speed. Perform them over 15 metres, four to six times each on a flat surface.

LUNGE WALK

Great for loosening up the hips, improving your running, and strengthening the buttocks and hamstrings. From a lunge position, step forwards into another lunge. Keep your chest up and look straight ahead.

To increase the specific strength-developing aspect perform some of the exercises using a powerbag or holding a weighted ball.

HIGH KNEE LIFT

Great for hip flexor, ankle strength and improved knee lift when running. Extend up on to the toes and lift each thigh to a position parallel to the ground as you move forwards.

ELBOW TO INSIDE OF ANKLE LUNGE

Great for hip flexibility and hamstring strength. The forward lean also stretches out the lower back. Similar to the lunge walk, but extend your trunk forwards over your front leg. If your left leg was in front of you, you would take the left elbow down towards the inside of the left ankle as in the picture opposite. Watch your balance.

CALF EXTENSION WALK

Great for lower limb strength and achilles tendon flexibility. Extending the ankle on each step will warm up the calf muscles and achilles tendons.

SIDEWAYS AND BACKWARD SKIPPING AND RUNNING

Great for lower limb strength, agility and flexibility. Performing these drills can reduce the incidence of common running-related injuries such as shin splints and achilles tendon problems, and can also 'protect' the knee and ankle joints against injury. Always concentrate on being light on your feet.

Adapting fitness options for sports-specific purposes

Table 11.2 displays how fitness options can be adapted to the specific demands of various sports. Look at the adaptations and use them to develop similar training ideas for your own sport. You should also refer to the suggested positions for them in a sports training pyramid (see Chapter 6 for a detailed account of how to construct a training pyramid).

Table 11.2

Adapting fitness options for sports-specific purposes

FITNESS OPTION AND LOCATION IN TRAINING PYRAMID	SPORT	ADAPTATION	WHY?
Circuit training **Location** Phases 1, 2, 3	**Football**	In between stations or at certain points during the circuit, juggle with a football, or repeatedly pass the ball to a partner or against a wall.	Football, like many field sports, is played under conditions of fatigue. This adapted circuit will enhance your ability to perform specific football skills under these conditions and will also provide a base of CV ability and strength endurance.
Circuit training **Location** Phases 1, 2, 3	**Basketball**	Construct a largely plyometric circuit, with tuck jumps, squat jumps and actual jump shots at a target or to a partner, plus core stability and upper-body moves.	Similar to the above example, this circuit will develop the repeated explosive capacity that basketball and volleyball players need.
Location Phase 1	**Track and field, sprinters jumpers and throwers**		A similar circuit (minus the jump shots) would also provide a great base of specific fitness for these athletes.
Interval training **Location** Phases 1, 2	**Rugby** **Football** **Hockey**	Perform an interval session with no set distances or recovery periods, or set recovery method. You could do this on your own, by running relevant distances and taking as much recovery as you like by walking, standing still or jogging, or by getting a partner to shout the distance to run, when to go again and the way to recover. To make it more specific, occasionally dribble a football or run with a rugby ball, depending on your sport.	This session reflects the sporadic nature of these games. Unlike a controlled interval training session, like a runner would do, a rugby, football or hockey match doesn't allow you to take two minutes between every 20 m run, tackle and pass you make. You have to go as the game and your fitness dictates. Note: controlled interval training will provide a great base for this more specific workout.

SPEED, AGILITY AND POWER

All other things being equal, the player who is the most powerful, the fastest and the most agile will be the best player. He or she will be able to get to the ball first, hit a harder serve or tackle an opponent more forcefully. Develop your speed, agility and power with the following exercises

Plyometric exercises

Plyometric muscular action was considered in detail on page 8. It's a great way to develop the type of power required for sprinting, quick changes of direction, kicking and jumping.

Plyometric exercises: safety tips

- Warm up specifically as indicated on pages 218-219.
- Progress gradually and stop if you feel any pain.
- Wear well-cushioned training shoes.
- Perform the exercises on a firm, flat, non-slippery, giving surface like a synthetic running track, flat dry grass area or sports hall floor.
- Don't perform intense plyometric workouts prior to important sports competitions; allow at least seven days to recover from them.
- Emphasise quality: take long recoveries and don't perform them when you are tired.
- Don't perform these exercises if you have a bad back or knee problems.

DEPTH OR REBOUND JUMPS

Starting position

Stand on top of a step or box (50–100 cm high). Maintain a neutral spine position and look straight ahead.

Action

Step off the box, land on both feet and immediately spring back up into the air. Swing your arms back as you step off the box and forwards and upwards, just prior to rebounding into the air.

Points to note

The higher the step or box within the confines mentioned above, the greater the strength component of the exercise; the lower the height, the greater the speed component.

TRAINING TIP

When gaining familiarity with this exercise you should bend your knees to absorb some of the impact. After this, you should try to react as quickly as possible to the ground without undue yielding. Perform four sets of six repetitions. Take 30 seconds' recovery between jumps and two minutes' recovery between sets.

HOPPING AND BOUNDING

Hops are performed on the same leg. Bounds are performed from one leg to the other in an accentuated-running-stride manner.

HOPPING

Starting position

Stand facing the direction of hopping. Keep your chest up.

Action

Bend your hopping leg slightly and push back up to generate the force to propel you off the ground and forwards. Land flat-footed and, without 'giving' too much at the knee, spring immediately into another hop. Cycle your hopping leg in the air underneath you as you progress from hop to hop. Try to co-ordinate your arms with your legs.

Points to note

See bounding (below).

BOUNDING

Starting position

As above.

Action

Leap forwards on to one leg, land flat-footed and immediately leap forwards on to the other leg. Try to stay in the air for as long as you can. Maintain balance and don't look down. Co-ordinate your arms with your legs.

Points to note

Hopping is more intense than bounding, so start with the former until you feel confident enough to incorporate hops into your routines.

TRAINING TIPS

Perform hops and bounds from a standing start when you first introduce them into your training. When you have gained strength and confidence you can use a run-up of 7–10 strides before launching into them. This additional speed will develop more power. Perform no more than 15–20 repetitions of hops and bounds over 10–20 m. Use a long recovery between repetitions and sets (30 seconds and two minutes respectively).

Agility

There are numerous agility drills you can do to make you a winning player. You'll have probably seen images of top sports teams in training running through floor ladders or round cones, or jumping over low hurdles. It's very easy to develop drills like these for your sport.

COMPASS RUN

Suitable for field and racquet sports. This drill will develop short-duration speed and turning ability.

Equipment needed

Five cones or suitable markers.

How to set up the drill

Place one cone in a central position. The others should be placed 4 m apart from the central one at the points of the compass.

How to perform the drill

From the central cone, sprint 'east', touch the cone, sprint back to the central point, touch the cone and then sprint 'north'. Repeat until you have covered all the points of the compass. You should finish back in the centre.

> **TRAINING TIP**
> **Keep your body low and practise turning in both directions. Time your performance and record how you improve.**

FAST-FEET DRILLS

Developing the ability to move your feet fast will improve both your agility and your speed.

Equipment needed

Tape/chalk/cord or floor ladder (these can be purchased from specialist sports and fitness retailers).

How to set up the drill

Rather like hopscotch, mark out a series of lines (10 to 15) on the ground 0.6 to 1 m apart, to form a grid, or rest the floor ladder on the ground.

How to perform the drill

There are many permutations but here are some examples.

- **Variation 1** – step once in each grid, co-ordinate your arms with your legs as when running.
- **Variation 2** – step twice in each grid.
- **Variation 3** – side step through each grid; keep your body low and hold your arms up in line with your shoulders.
- **Variation 4** – step backwards one grid at a time.

Perform three to five repetitions of each drill.

Vary your recovery for all fast feet drills depending on whether you want to develop endurance or speed.

> **TRAINING TIPS**
> **1. Generate speed by moving your arms faster, where appropriate.**
> **2. Don't lift your feet too high off the ground as you step through the grid.**
> **3. A rugby player could perform the drill holding a ball, while a tennis player could hold a racquet; these options add more specificity.**

DEVELOPING POWER: SPORTS-SPECIFIC WEIGHT TRAINING

Choose relevant exercises

Look at the basic movements of your sport and utilise exercises that work your muscles in a similar way. For example, the leg extension (page 102) is a good exercise for all sports that involve kicking, because the lower leg is moved by the quadriceps muscles in much the same way as the actual kicking action. The squat and split squat are, likewise, great strength and power builders for running and jumping sports (see pages 100–103).

Train with weights to develop sports power and endurance

Sports power

Use a medium to heavy weight (70–85 per cent of your 1RM) and perform the exercise as dynamically but as safely as possible. Do two to three sets of six to eight repetitions.

Sports endurance

Use light weights and high numbers of repetitions combined with a short recovery.

All sports require power, whether it be sustained (rowing), interrupted (football) or short-lived (sprinting). Weight training alone will not make you a better player, but it can make you a more powerful player if the strength developed through it is channelled specifically into your sport.

Build sports power with complex training

Complex training combines a weight-training exercise with a related plyometric one, and is a great way to develop power for dynamic sports. The system generates a heightened response from your fast-twitch muscle fibres, which can boost your sports performance if included in your training regularly. (See page 87 for a more detailed consideration.)

Example

Squats	4 x 6 @75 per cent 1RM
Squat jumps	4 x 8

Take one minute's rest between the weights exercise set and the plyometric one, and 30 seconds between each plyometric exercise, then take two to three minutes between each pair of exercises.

SQUAT JUMP

The squat jump is a great sports power exercise. To perform it, jump up off the ground from a two-footed position. Swing your arms back and up to assist your take-off. Keep your chest and head up, and land with your knees slightly flexed.

Useful contacts

Speed Agility and Quickness (SAQ International)
Runs training courses for anyone interested in developing sports-specific power and speed knowledge
Tel 01644 810101
www.saqinternational.com

Powerbag
For further information on powerbags, contact Performance Technology
Tel 01432 870 818
e-mail mail@performt.com

Sportdimensions
Offer a specialist speed development and injury rehabilitation service using specialist equipment and drills
Tel 020 8563 0007
www.sportdimensions.com

12 Motivating

your fitness lifestyle

Most of us at some time in our workout lives will have decided that we can't be bothered to go to the gym or train. I know I have. After a hard day at work the reality of putting your feet up on the sofa and relaxing can seem a much more appealing option than going for a workout. In this chapter I'll show you how to make these days rare occasions. Mental strategies and practical advice will be provided that will motivate you to stay the fitness lifestyle course. This chapter also considers body image and takes a detailed look at how to make the right gym and personal trainer choices for you. This chapter should be specifically read in conjunction with Chapter 6, 'Planning your training'.

GOALS AND GOAL SETTING

Deciding on and directing your goals

It's no good deciding that you want to lose 10 kg in weight a week before you go on holiday, this training goal is obviously unachievable. The training planning process towards this (or any other fitness goal) should have started many months earlier. But even before you (or your personal trainer) put together the most relevant training plan for you, you need to have established an attainable goal or set of goals. To help guide you to put these together I recommend that you use the 'SMARTER' principles.

If you don't set yourself any goals you are likely to drop out of your fitness programme.

How to train SMARTER

Your goals should be:

Specific focused on a real target: wanting to gain 4 kg of lean fat-burning muscle in six months, while training three times a week is specific, just aiming to 'put on a bit of muscle' is not

Measurable you've got to be able to measure how you're doing; speak to your personal trainer and find out what kinds of tests you could use, or construct your own (see Chapter 2)

Achievable don't establish an unattainable goal; look at your body type and your lifestyle, and what training options you have available to you, and pull together your goals accordingly

Responsible your goals must be responsible, that's to yourself and to any others that might be affected by your pursuit of them; your training should complement your everyday life and not affect it negatively

Targeted it may seem obvious that your goals need to be targeted, but many people don't line up their training efforts; the best way to do this is by constructing a relevant and progressive training plan – if you can't do this yourself, then consult with an expert, it will be well worth it when you achieve the results you desire

Empowering going for it and achieving that fitness goal, whatever it is, will make you feel great

Revisable this is perhaps the most important SMARTER principle; your goals should not be set in stone, they need to be adaptable and revisable, in response to both positive and negative factors; if you become ill, for example, you'll need to revise your goals, perhaps by extending their attainment date

TRAINING TIP

When you sit down to plan your training goals make sure that they are defined and have a viable time span. Don't set your long-term goal too far into the future as you could lose your focus. Six months is a good achievable time frame for most general fitness goals.

Establishing short-term and long-term goals

The SMARTER principles should be applied to both your short- and long-term goals.

Long-term goals

Long-term goals reflect your ultimate fitness destination. Here are some examples:

- to drop a dress size in six months and attain a body fat percentage of 21 per cent
- to tone up your bottom, legs and arms in three months
- to develop your CV fitness so that, in three months, you can run effortlessly for 30 minutes
- to improve your speed and CV ability so that you become a better football player by the start of the playing season in eight weeks.

> **TRAINING TIP**
> **Whether they are short or long term, you need to make sure that your goals are linked to your training plan.**

Short-term goals

Short-term goals: your short-term goals should be established in terms of monthly, weekly or even daily targets; you should see them as the staging posts on the way to the attainment of your long-term goal. Here are some examples that reference potential long-term goals:

- to run for 20 minutes three times a week – allied to a long-term goal of running for an hour in six months' time
- to move from simple sets to pyramids after two months of using the former weights system – allied to a long-term goal of increasing upper body strength by 10 per cent in six months
- to increase the speed of medium-intensity rowing interval sessions by one second per 500 m each week in a six-week training phase – allied to a long-term goal of rowing a 2 km best in six months' time
- to burn 3500 calories (0.45 kg of fat) every three weeks – allied to a long-term goal of losing 6 kg of fat in four months.

Putting the SMARTER principles into practice: establishing realistic goals

Let's use one of the long-term training goal examples provided earlier – 'dropping a dress size and achieving 21 per cent body fat' – to show how the SMARTER principles work in practice.

This long-term goal is specific, is obviously measurable and targeted, but is it achievable, responsible, empowering and revisable? If our female with this goal in mind had been training for a long time, was a size 10 and already had a low healthy body fat level, such as 23 per cent, then this goal might not be achievable, responsible or empowering. Instead, it might actually be irresponsible, unrealistic and frustrating. In this situation the goal is not a smart one at all, and should not have been established in the first place.

TRAINING TIP

The revising aspect of the SMARTER principles is perhaps the key to staying the fitness lifestyle course. You should not be afraid to give your goals a new slant or new focus to keep you motivated and feeling empowered.

Body image

Many of us would like to change something about the way we look. The pressure is on us all to be leaner, fat-free and sexier. This can, of course, be a great source of motivation to embark on a workout programme, but it can also be a great source of frustration and anxiety.

Perhaps you've brought this book because you want to 'improve' the way you look. The training information and plans provided will certainly give you every opportunity to achieve the body you desire, but you have to be realistic. You should never become dissatisfied with the way you look and start to devalue your training efforts and more importantly yourself. In Chapter 2, I made reference to specific body types and the best ways to train them. I indicated that there are certain limits to what you can achieve through a fitness and healthy eating regime, and indicated that you should always focus on what you can achieve (hence the importance of realistic goal setting). If you do this, you'll always have a positive appreciation of yourself and your training efforts. Other people will see this reflected in you and, in consequence, you'll project a positive attitude that will make you more attractive, whatever your body shape.

But if our individual, after careful reconsideration and use of the SMARTER principles, still wanted to improve her appearance, she could revise her long-term goal and work to a fitness programme designed to increase muscle tone and/or CV fitness. Sometimes a new slant or interpretation of an existing goal is all that is needed to make it smart. The new long-term goal could now be, 'to improve all-over muscle tone (as measured by improvements in strength and appearance) and CV fitness (as measured by the ability to train at high exercise intensities) in six months'. The previous long-term cosmetically orientated goal has now been replaced with a fitness-performance-orientated one, which will provide motivation and will have every chance of being achievable. It may even bring about the desired reduction in body fat and dress-size drop.

TRAINING TIP

Reward your training! Getting fitter will be reward enough for many, but it's all right to give yourself some rewards along the way to keep you on your training course and your motivation levels high.

Personal reflections

I have worked out at least three or four times a week for the last 25 years. My prime motivation has been derived through sport. Athletics gave me a reason to, run, lift weights and circuit train. I know I would find it hard to be as 'dedicated' without a reason to exercise. You, like me, need a reason to work out, but unlike mine, your reason need not be sports-related. Giving yourself a different reason to train, by varying your long-term fitness goals can be very motivational. Why not get fit with fitness classes for six months and then develop your CV fitness through rowing, before moving on to a weight-training period? Variety will not only keep you motivated but will also keep your fitness adaptations coming.

10 tips for achieving and maintaining a fitness lifestyle

1. Construct a training routine that you will stick to

If you work long hours and have a family, and still aim to be in the gym six days a week, then you could be asking too much of yourself. You must construct a responsible training programme.

2. Don't set yourself up to fail

Make sure you establish realistic training goals and follow the SMARTER principles.

3. Add to your fitness lifestyle without realising it

Add to your fitness lifestyle by burning some extra calories and exercising as you go about your everyday activities. You could do this by taking the stairs at work or by getting off the bus one stop earlier on your way home. This additional non-gym-based activity could be all that is needed to achieve further fat loss and enhanced general fitness.

4. Enjoy your training

You mustn't see your training as a chore. Yes, there will be days when you don't feel up to it, but there will be many more when you do if you find your exercise fun and have established the right motivational goals.

Your life partner could make a good training partner choice. You'll have a common goal and will be able to work together to do something that will really benefit both of you.

5.Get into a routine

As we tend to be creatures of habit, the longer we maintain an exercise routine the greater the likelihood there is of maintaining it. On the other hand, it's not good to become too fanatical about training. Missing the odd workout is not a crime. Over-training syndrome (see page 146) is often the consequence of not knowing when to take it easy. This is something that can particularly affect advanced trainers.

6. Think 'fit for life'

Don't pressure yourself with attaining an unrealistic body image or striving for equally unrealistic fitness goals. Instead, you should find motivation in congratulating yourself on the steps you're taking to make your life as active and healthy as possible by adopting a fitness lifestyle.

7. Enter a fitness competition or take up a sport

At Ultra-FIT we are only too well aware that maintaining a workout programme can be difficult. That's why we introduced the Ultra-FIT X-Training Challenge and the Ultra-FIT Club Sport Challenge (see page 122) to motivate and provide a specific training focus. Look out for other similar motivational fitness challenges and competitions at your local gym, or those run by equipment manufacturers.

TRAINING TIP

Fitness classes are a great way to motivate your fitness lifestyle. They'll take away the worry of workout planning as well as providing a very social way to get fit.

8. Get a training partner

Going to the gym on your own can be a soul-destroying activity, but having someone to go with can make all the difference to staying the fitness lifestyle course.

9. Use a personal trainer

A personal trainer offers a great way to motivate your fitness lifestyle.

10. Join the right gym

Joining the right gym is equally crucial if you want to remain motivated to keep fit.

The latter two motivating factors are covered in detail on pages 234 and 236.

Don't think you've got the time to train? Got a family? Here's a suggestion …

Suggested week's training:

- two gym-based workouts, perhaps at lunchtime, so you've got your evenings free
- one home workout (perhaps by way of an exercise video or piece of home CV or resistance kit)
- one 'lifestyle workout' – where you exercise 'almost without knowing it'; you could run around with the kids in the park at the weekend, do the gardening or go for a family cycle ride.

A fitness lifestyle is not just about what you do in the formal setting of the gym, but is as much about what you can do to keep in shape in the more informal setting of everyday life.

JOINING THE RIGHT GYM

There are now over nine million gym users in the UK, and lifestyle surveys indicate that working out is one of the nation's favourite pastimes. The fitness industry is enjoying something of a boom. We gym consumers have an incredible amount of choice: we can become members of one of the major high-street fitness chains like Fitness First, Holmes Place, Virgin Active or David Lloyd, or one of the numerous local authority-run facilities, or one of the smaller one-off-type private clubs. Whatever your fitness goals or level of fitness, there is a club out there for you, but if you make the wrong decision you could easily find yourself giving up on your fitness quest. To prevent this, here are some tips to assist you in making the right choice.

Membership fees can burn a considerable hole in your pocket, but this won't matter if you enjoy going to the gym regularly enough to burn plenty of calories too!

TRAINING TIP

Research indicates that if you visit your gym at least once a week after joining then you will be 30–40 per cent less likely to leave by the end of the year.

Try before you buy

Visit a couple of gyms at peak time (or at the time when you will be training) and see how many people are using the equipment and how well presented it is. The reception area of a gym is very important and can tell you a great deal about the facility – take a look to see if publicity material is readily available and clearly displayed. Consider how the staff greet you and whether they are knowledgeable about what's on offer, like fitness classes, opening times and personal training. As a leisure centre manager I believed that the most important members of staff were the receptionists; they would be the first people a prospective member would come into contact with, and if they were not helpful or courteous then the customer could easily be lost to the centre or, more importantly, to the fitness lifestyle.

Whatever the size of the facility, ask for a tour and with your fitness goals in mind look out to see whether there are the right CV and weights kit or fitness class options for you. Some gyms have numerous ancillary facilities designed to make your visit all the more attractive and convenient. These include crèches, nurseries, hairdressers, beauty salons, physiotherapists, video clubs, saunas, steam rooms, social and business clubs, cafés and bars. Although you'll invariably have to pay more for these in your membership fee, if they keep you going back to the club week in week out and you can afford it, then they're well worth the additional expense. On the other hand, it's no use joining a gym with facilities you are not going to use. Some clubs don't provide swimming pools or are not as lavishly equipped as others, so this means they charge a lower membership fee. Decide on what you want and what you can afford, and make your choice accordingly.

Location, location, location

Location and opening hours are equally important considerations when determining your gym choice. You might choose a club close to where you work for ease of morning or lunchtime training, or you might choose one closer to home so that you can train there at weekends.

How to find a gym

Take a look in your local paper or Yellow Pages or check out the Internet. Some websites are very sophisticated and will permit you to take a virtual tour of a facility. All the major chains, like Holmes Place, Fitness First and David Lloyd have extensive websites and list all their clubs.

For more varied gym searches try:

- www.thehealthfinder.co.uk
- www.gymuser.co.uk
- www.gym-directory.co.uk.

Study what a gym offers before making your choice

Gym membership policies

Club membership policies can be complicated. Here are some tips.

- Find out if you can use other clubs in the same chain (if it is part of one) and whether your membership is refundable or can be frozen if you have to go away on business or are not around for any reason.
- See if you can try the club out for a day or longer period on a trial basis; you might also be able to 'pay as you go' for a while rather than immediately signing up for a longer, normally yearly, period. By doing this, you'll be able to take your time to see if you 'get along' with the facility.
- If you work shifts or odd hours, you could save yourself money by joining on an off-peak membership basis.
- Find out about guest membership and whether you can bring along friends on an occasional basis to work out with you; this is a great way to keep yourself motivated, by providing you with the opportunity to show off your new-found fitness!
- Ascertain whether your membership fee includes personal training and gym instruction or fitness testing, as these can be costly add-ons.

There's a great deal to keep in mind when you eventually do sign on the dotted line of the gym membership form, but by spending some time making your decision you could save yourself a lot of money and, crucially, keep your fitness journey constantly motivated.

HOW TO CHOOSE A PERSONAL TRAINER (PT)

A personal trainer (PT) will be a great source of motivation for your fitness training exploits. Perhaps their most important contribution is the fact that they'll save you time. They'll very quickly get you on a progressive training programme that is safe and specifically tailored to your needs, and will then be able to monitor, progress and revise your training as you progress.

The majority of gyms will have onsite PTs, but you can also source them in Yellow Pages or the local press, and increasingly on the Internet, if you want to work out at home. Irrespective of their location, you need to check out the following things.

Qualifications

Don't be afraid to ask what qualifications your potential PT has. A PT can become qualified in many ways. Some may have sports science degrees, while others may have done intensive training courses run by market-leading fitness training companies like Premier Global, the American College of Sports Medicine or the YMCA, others still will have gained NVQs. You should also make sure that, whatever their level and route of qualification, they are insured and are preferably first aid qualified.

A good personal trainer will not be afraid to let you go, or to recommend less frequent visits when the time is right. Their aim should be to empower you with the skills and motivation to enable you to get on with your own training systematically and safely under your own supervision.

Does your personal trainer have the right fitness knowledge for you?

Although qualifications count for a lot, you should not neglect experience. Fitness knowledge is complicated, but so is putting it into practice. Ask about the type of clients your prospective PT has worked with and the places he or she has worked. You may find out that they have a particular specialisation, like CV training or weight training. You should also find out about what type of training your PT does themselves; they may have a particular talent that could be of use to you. Perhaps they are a martial artist or have reached a high level in a competitive sport, or maybe they run 10 km races for fun. The knowledge that they will have gained through their own training is highly valuable and should not be ignored.

Ask to see your PT's references. Many personal trainers will include in their résumé letters from satisfied clients, or testimonies from other fitness professionals. Don't be afraid to check these out.

A good PT will know when to listen, when to encourage and when to shut up. To do this they'll need to get to know your personality and this cannot be achieved overnight.

Are they are professional?

You will be paying good money for a PT, anything from £20 to £70-plus an hour; for this you should expect them to be punctual, prepared and professional. You don't have to go for the first one you meet. Consider a couple and see who you gel with, and whether their knowledge and experience suits your needs. If things aren't working out don't be afraid to say so. But don't sack your PT because you've not become ultra-fit in a couple of weeks – allow time for their programme to work.

The team approach

Some PTs work as a part of a team, which can include nutritionists, sports masseurs, psychologists, aerobics instructors, sports coaches and other specialists. You shouldn't feel pressured to buy into these additional services unless you feel that they will really benefit you. Other PTs offer phone and Internet coaching as well as face-to-face visits. These can be very useful options for intermediate and advanced trainers who possess the skills and motivation to train without supervision, but want to discuss their training and receive new ideas and training plans from a 'professional' in much the same way as an athlete is set training schedules by his or her coach.

How to find a personal trainer

As well as looking in your local press or Yellow Pages or working with a PT at (or provided by) your gym, you can also contact a PT via the following methods.

The National Register of Personal Trainers

Tel 0870 200 6010. Website www.nrpt.co.uk

The NRPT recognises industry-based qualifications and practical competency, and requires its members to work within a code of ethical practice.

Premier Global Qualified Personal Trainers

Tel 01225 717 200. Website www.Premierglobal.co.uk

***Ultra-FIT* magazine**

References

Bean, A. (2002) *Complete Guide to Sports Nutrition* (third edition), A & C Black.

Dick, F.W. (2002) *Sports Training Principles* (fourth edition), A & C Black.

O'Donovan, G. (2002) 'Why athletes, fitness enthusiasts and slimmers should steer clear of the fat burning zone.' *Peak Performance* (newsletter produced monthly by Peak Performance Publishing, 67–71 Goswell Road, London EC1V 7EP). Issue 142, December.

Further reading

Barder, O. (2002) Running for Fitness, A&C Black.

Bean, A. (2004) Fitness on a Plate, A&C Black.

Bean, A. (2002) Food for Fitness (second edition), A&C Black.

Bean, A. (2002) Kids Food for Fitness, A&C Black.

Bean, A. (2003) The Complete Guide to Sports Nutrition (fourth edition), A&C Black.

Brooks, D. (2001) Effective Strength Training, Human Kinetics.

Burney, L. (1999) Optimum Nutrition for Babies and Young Children; Over 150 Quick and Tempting Recipes for the Best Start in Life, Piaktus Books.

Donald, A. (1998) Jumping into Plyometrics, Human Kinetics.

Goldenberg, L. G. et al. (2000) Strength Ball Training, Human Kinetics.

Juba, K. (2001) Swimming for Fitness, A& C Black.

Lawrence, M. (2003) The Complete Guide to Core Stability, A&C Black.

Nitti, J. et al. (2002) Interval Training for Fitness, A&C Black.

Norris, C. (2002) Bodytoning, A&C Black.

Smith, D. (2001) Cycling for Fitness, A&C Black.

Willett, W. et al. (2004) Eat, Drink and Be Healthy; The Harvard Medical School Guide to Eating, Simon and Schuster.

Index

Index continued

Notes